Guided Practice Activities

Needham, Massachusetts
Upper Saddle River, New Jersey

2 3 4 5 6 7 8 9 10 08 07 06 05

ISBN 0-13-116475-9

Table of Contents

Tema 6: La televisión y el cine

Tema 7: Buen provecho

Tema 8: Cómo ser un buen turista

Tema 9: ¿Cómo será el futuro?

Dear Parents and Guardians:

Learning a second language can be both exciting and fun. As your child studies Spanish, he or she will not only learn to communicate with Spanish speakers, but will also learn about their cultures and daily lives. Language learning is a building process that requires considerable time and practice, but it is one of the most rewarding things your child can learn in school.

Language learning calls on all of the senses and on many skills that are not necessarily used in other kinds of learning. Students will find their Spanish class different from other classes in a variety of ways. For instance, lectures generally play only a small role in the language classroom. Because the goal is to learn to communicate, students interact with each other and with their teacher as they learn to express themselves about things they like to do (and things they don't), their personalities, the world around them, foods, celebrations, pastimes, technology, and much more. Rather than primarily listening to the teacher, reading the text, and memorizing information as they might in a social studies class, language learners will share ideas; discuss similarities and differences between cultures; ask and answer questions; and work with others to practice new words, sounds, and sentence structures. Your child will be given a variety of tasks to do in preparation for such an interactive class. He or she will complete written activities, perform listening tasks, watch and listen to videos, and go on the Internet. In addition, to help solidify command of words and structures, time will need to be spent on learning vocabulary and practicing the language until it starts to become second nature. Many students will find that using flash cards and doing written practice will help them become confident using the building blocks of language.

To help you help your child in this endeavor, we offer the following insights into the textbook your child will be using, along with suggestions for ways that you can help build your child's motivation and confidence—and as a result, their success with learning Spanish.

Textbook Organization

Your child will be learning Spanish using ***REALIDADES***, which means "realities." The emphasis throughout the text is on learning to use the language in authentic, real ways. Chapters are organized by themes such as school life, food and health, family and celebrations, etc. Each chapter begins with a section called **A primera vista** (*At First Glance*), which gives an initial presentation of new grammar and vocabulary in the form of pictures, short dialogues, audio recordings, and video. Once students have been exposed to the new language, the **Manos a la obra** (*Let's Get to Work*) section offers lots of practice with the language as well as explanations of how the language works. The third section, **¡Adelante!** (*Moving Ahead!*), provides activities for your child to use the language by understanding readings, giving oral or written presentations, and learning more about the cultural perspectives of Spanish speakers. Finally, all chapters conclude with an at-a-glance review of the chapter material called **Repaso del capítulo** *(Chapter Review)*, with summary lists and charts, and practice activities like those on the chapter test. If students have trouble with a given task, the **Repaso del capítulo** tells them where in the chapter they can go to review.

Here are some suggestions that will help your child become a successful language learner.

Routine:

Provide a special, quiet place for study, equipped with a Spanish-English dictionary, pens or pencils, paper, computer, and any other items your child's teacher suggests.

- Encourage your child to study Spanish at a regular time every day. A study routine will greatly facilitate the learning process.

Strategy:

- Remind your child that class participation and memorization are very important in a foreign language course.
- Tell your child that in reading or listening activities, as well as in the classroom, it is not necessary to understand every word. Suggest that they listen or look for key words to get the gist of what's being communicated.
- Encourage your child to ask questions in class if he or she is confused. Remind the child that other students may have the same question. This will minimize frustration and help your child succeed.

Real-life connection:

- Outside of the regular study time, encourage your child to review words in their proper context as they relate to the chapter themes. For example, when studying the chapter about community places, Capítulo 3B, have your child bring flash cards for place names on a trip into town and review words for the places you pass along the way. Similarly, while studying Capítulo 4A vocabulary, bring out family photos and remind your child of the toys he or she used to have and the activities that he or she liked. Ask your child to name the toys and activities in Spanish. If your child can include multiple senses while studying (see the school and say *escuela*, or taste ice cream and say *helado*), it will help reinforce study and will aid in vocabulary retention.
- Motivate your child with praise for small jobs well done, not just for big exams and final grades. A memorized vocabulary list is something to be proud of!

Review:

- Encourage your child to review previously learned material frequently, and not just before a test. Remember, learning a language is a building process, and it is important to keep using what you've already learned.
- To aid vocabulary memorization, suggest that your child try several different methods, such as saying words aloud while looking at a picture of the items, writing the words, acting them out while saying them, and so on.
- Suggest that your child organize new material using charts, graphs, pictures with labels, or other visuals that can be posted in the study area. A daily review of those visuals will help keep the material fresh.
- Help your child drill new vocabulary and grammar by using the charts and lists in the **Manos a la obra** and **Repaso del capítulo** sections.

Resources:

- Offer to help frequently! Your child may have great ideas for how you can facilitate his or her learning experience.
- Ask your child's teacher, or encourage your child to ask, about how to best prepare for and what to expect on tests and quizzes.
- Ask your child's teacher about the availability of audio recordings and videos that support the text. The more your child sees and hears the language, the greater the retention. There are also on-line and CD-ROM based versions of the textbook that may be useful for your child.
- Visit www.PHSchool.com with your child for more helpful tips and practice opportunities, including downloadable audio files that your child can play at home to practice Spanish. Enter the appropriate Web Code from the list on the next page for the section of the chapter that the class is working on and you will see a menu that lists the available audio files. They can be listened to on a computer or on a personal audio player.

Capítulo	A primera vista	Manos a la obra	Repaso
Para empezar			jdd-0099
Capítulo 1A	jdd-0187	jdd-0188	jdd-0189
Capítulo 1B	jdd-0197	jdd-0198	jdd-0199
Capítulo 2A	jdd-0287	jdd-0288	jdd-0289
Capítulo 2B	jdd-0297	jdd-0298	jdd-0299
Capítulo 3A	jdd-0387	jdd-0388	jdd-0389
Capítulo 3B	jdd-0397	jdd-0398	jdd-0399
Capítulo 4A	jdd-0487	jdd-0488	jdd-0489
Capítulo 4B	jdd-0497	jdd-0498	jdd-0499
Capítulo 5A	jdd-0587	jdd-0588	jdd-0589
Capítulo 5B	jdd-0597	jdd-0598	jdd-0599
Capítulo 6A	jdd-0687	jdd-0688	jdd-0689
Capítulo 6B	jdd-0697	jdd-0698	jdd-0699
Capítulo 7A	jdd-0787	jdd-0788	jdd-0789
Capítulo 7B	jdd-0797	jdd-0798	jdd-0799
Capítulo 8A	jdd-0887	jdd-0888	jdd-0889
Capítulo 8B	jdd-0897	jdd-0898	jdd-0899
Capítulo 9A	jdd-0987	jdd-0988	jdd-0989
Capítulo 9B	jdd-0997	jdd-0998	jdd-0999

Above all, help your child understand that a language is not acquired overnight. Just as for a first language, there is a gradual process for learning a second one. It takes time and patience, and it is important to know that mistakes are a completely natural part of the process. Remind your child that it took years to become proficient in his or her first language, and that the second one will also take time. Praise your child for even small progress in the ability to communicate in Spanish, and provide opportunities for your child to hear and use the language.

Don't hesitate to ask your child's teacher for ideas. You will find the teacher eager to help you. You may also be able to help the teacher understand special needs that your child may have, and work together with him or her to find the best techniques for helping your child learn.

Learning to speak another language is one of the most gratifying experiences a person can have. We know that your child will benefit from the effort, and will acquire a skill that will serve to enrich his or her life.

Realidades 2

Nombre _______ Hora _______

Para empezar

Fecha _______

Vocabulary Flash Cards, Sheet 1

Write the Spanish vocabulary word below each picture. If there is a word or phrase, copy it in the space provided. Be sure to include the article for each noun.

¿Quién(es)? ________	**¿Cómo?** ________	**¿De dónde?** ________ ________
viejo, vieja ________, ________	**atrevido, atrevida** ________, ________	**desordenado, desordenada** ________, ________
reservado, reservada ________, ________	**gracioso, graciosa** ________, ________	**sociable** ________

Nombre ______ Hora ______

Para empezar

Fecha ______

Vocabulary Check, Sheet 1

Tear out this page. Write the English words on the lines. Fold the paper along the dotted line to see the correct answers so you can check your work.

¿Cómo eres tú? ______

alto, alta ______

atrevido, atrevida ______

bajo, baja ______

desordenado, desordenada ______

estudioso, estudiosa ______

gracioso, graciosa ______

guapo, guapa ______

impaciente ______

inteligente ______

ordenado, ordenada ______

reservado, reservada ______

sociable ______

trabajador, trabajadora ______

Fold In ←

Realidades 2 | Nombre ______ | Hora ______

Para empezar | Fecha ______ | **Vocabulary Check, Sheet 2**

Tear out this page. Write the Spanish words on the lines. Fold the paper along the dotted line to see the correct answers so you can check your work.

What are you like? ______

tall ______

daring ______

short ______

messy ______

studious ______

funny ______

good-looking ______

impatient ______

intelligent ______

neat ______

reserved, shy ______

sociable ______

hard-working ______

Fold In ←

Adjectives (p. 3)

- Remember that adjectives describe nouns: people, places, and things. The following is a list of some common adjectives in Spanish.

Masculine		Feminine	
Singular	**Plural**	**Singular**	**Plural**
serio	serio**s**	seri**a**	seri**as**
deportista	deportista**s**	deportista	deportista**s**
trabajado**r**	trabajado**res**	trabajado**ra**	trabajado**ras**
paciente	paciente**s**	paciente	paciente**s**
joven	jóven**es**	joven	jóven**es**

A. Read each sentence and circle the adjective. Follow the model.

Modelo Enrique es un joven (serio.)

1. Mi primo es joven.
2. Mis hermanas son chicas jóvenes.
3. Carlos y Pedro son chicos deportistas.
4. Tú eres una persona paciente.
5. Yo soy una chica trabajadora.
6. Nosotras somos estudiantes serias.

- In Spanish, if a person, place, or thing is masculine, the adjective that describes it must be masculine: **El chico es muy serio.**
- If it's feminine, then the adjective must be feminine: **María es muy alta.**

B. Fill in the missing letter in each adjective: **-o** for masculine nouns and **-a** for feminine nouns. Follow the model.

Modelo Ricardo es muy seri_o_.

1. Mi amiga Karla es alt___.
2. Mi tía es una mujer ordenad___.
3. Mi abuelo es un hombre desordenad___.
4. Ese chico es muy gracios___.

Go Online WEB CODE jdd-0001 PHSchool.com

Adjectives (*continued*)

- In Spanish, if the person, place, or thing is singular, the adjective that describes it must be singular.
  Mi hermano es paciente. *My brother is patient.*
- If the person, place, or thing is plural, then the adjective is also plural.
  Mis abuelos son pacientes. *My grandparents are patient.*

C. Circle the adjective that best completes the sentence. Use the underlined word to help you. Follow the model.

Modelo	Mi abuela es	(**a.**) graciosa.	**b.** graciosas.
1.	Mis hermanas son	**a.** joven.	**b.** jóvenes.
2.	Pedro es	**a.** guapo.	**b.** guapos.
3.	Los niños son	**a.** serios.	**b.** serio.
4.	Marta es	**a.** trabajadoras.	**b.** trabajadora.
5.	Eduardo es	**a.** altos.	**b.** alto.
6.	Nosotras somos	**a.** desordenadas.	**b.** desordenada.

D. Circle the correct adjective in parentheses to complete the sentences.

1. Mis primos son chicos (**sociable** / **sociables**).
2. Mi padre es un hombre (**bajo** / **bajos**).
3. Tú no eres una chica (**ordenada** / **ordenadas**).
4. Tú y Pancho son estudiantes (**reservados** / **reservado**).
5. Mis hermanos no son niños (**atrevidos** / **atrevido**).

The verb *ser* (p. 5)

- **Ser** is an irregular verb and it means "to be." These are its present-tense forms:

yo	**soy**	nosotros/nosotras	**somos**
tú	**eres**	vosotros/vosotras	**sois**
usted/él/ella	**es**	ustedes/ellos/ellas	**son**

- Remember that you can use **ser** with adjectives to tell what someone is like:
  Esas chicas son altas. *Those girls are tall.*

A. Choose the correct form of the verb **ser** in the word bank to complete the sentences. Follow the model.

eres	somos	soy	son	es

Modelo Tú *eres* reservado.

1. Yo ____________ sociable.
2. Nosotros ____________ deportistas.
3. Elena ____________ alta.
4. Tú ____________ inteligente.
5. Ustedes ____________ trabajadores.

- To tell where someone is from, use **ser + de** + place:
  Ricardo es de México. *Ricardo is from Mexico.*

B. Help Mariana say where her friends are from by writing **de** on the short line and the name of a country on the long line. You can choose countries from the word bank below.

Panamá	Argentina	México	Brasil

Modelo Alejandra es *de* *México*.

1. Fernanda y Maruca son ______ ____________.
2. Gustavo es ______ ____________.
3. Rosa es ______ ____________.

 Nombre ____________ Hora ____________

 Fecha ____________ **Vocabulary Flash Cards, Sheet 2**

Write the Spanish vocabulary word below each picture. If there is a word or phrase, copy it in the space provided. Be sure to include the article for each noun.

bailar ____________	**cantar** ____________	**caminar** ____________
comer ____________	**correr** ____________	**dibujar** ____________
escuchar música ____________ ____________	**usar la computadora** ____________ ____________ ____________	**practicar deportes** ____________ ____________

Realidades 2 Nombre ____________ Hora ____________

Para empezar Fecha ____________ **Vocabulary Check, Sheet 3**

Tear out this page. Write the English words on the lines. Fold the paper along the dotted line to see the correct answers so you can check your work.

practicar deportes ____________

bailar ____________

caminar ____________

cantar ____________

comer ____________

dibujar ____________

nadar ____________

usar la computadora ____________

música ____________

a menudo ____________

a veces ____________

nunca ____________

siempre ____________

después (de) ____________

Fold In ←

Nombre ______ Hora ______

Fecha ______

Vocabulary Check, Sheet 4

Tear out this page. Write the Spanish words on the lines. Fold the paper along the dotted line to see the correct answers so you can check your work.

to play sports ______

to dance ______

to walk ______

to sing ______

to eat ______

to draw ______

to swim ______

to use the computer ______

music ______

often ______

sometimes ______

never ______

always ______

afterwards, after ______

Fold In ←

To hear a complete list of the vocabulary for this chapter, go to www.phschool.com and type in the Web Code jdd-0099. Then click on **Repaso del capítulo.**

Present tense of regular verbs (p. 9)

- **Hablar** (to talk), **comer** (to eat), and **vivir** (to live) are regular verbs. To form the present tense, drop the **-ar, -er,** or **-ir** endings and add the present-tense endings.

	hablar	*comer*	*vivir*
yo	**hablo**	**como**	**vivo**
tú	**hablas**	**comes**	**vives**
usted/él/ella	**habla**	**come**	**vive**
nosotros/nosotras	**hablamos**	**comemos**	**vivimos**
vosotros/vosotras	**habláis**	**coméis**	**vivís**
ustedes/ellos/ellas	**hablan**	**comen**	**viven**

A. Circle the present-tense verb form in each sentence.

1. Mis amigas viven en Nueva York.
2. Carlos come en casa a las seis.
3. Yo escribo mi tarea en el cuaderno.
4. Ustedes hablan inglés y español.

B. Look at the drawings below and complete each sentence with a phrase from the word bank.

comemos	toca la guitarra	cantan muy bien	usas la computadora

1. Tú ________________________.

2. Nosotras ________________________.

3. Marta ________________________.

4. Ustedes ________________________.

Presentación escrita (p. 13)

Task: Write a poem in the shape of a diamond. The poem is going to describe you.

A. Look at the poem about Linda in your textbook. Then, copy the missing words from the poem in the lines below. The first one has been done for you.

Me *llamo* Linda.

No soy ni **1.** ____ ni vieja.

Soy **2.** ____, sociable, estudiosa.

Todos los días yo **3.** ____ música, leo, corro, uso la computadora.

En el verano mis amigos y yo **4.** ____, cantamos, bailamos.

Nunca **5.** ____ ni monto en bicicleta.

¡Así soy yo!

B. Look at the word list below and complete the sentence with two words from the list that do *not* describe you. Remember to use the **-o** ending if you are a boy and **-a** if you are a girl. And remember that **sociable** and **impaciente** don't change gender. Follow the model.

alto, -a	**atrevido, -a**	**desordenado, -a**	**estudioso, -a**	**gracioso, -a**
ordenado, -a	**reservado, -a**	**sociable**	**impaciente**	

Modelo No soy ni *ordenada* ni *sociable*.

No soy ni ____ ni ____.

C. Now, choose three words from the list in **part A** that describe you. Complete the sentence with those words.

Soy ____, ____ y ____.

Presentación escrita (*continued*)

D. Circle the activities that you like to do and complete the sentence with those activities.

bailo	**canto**	**camino**	**dibujo**
leo revistas	**monto en bicicleta**	**uso la computadora**	**escucho música**

Todos los días yo ____________, ____________, ____________ y ____________.

E. Which of the activities in **part D** do you like to do with friends? Complete the sentence using three of those activities.

En el verano, mis amigos y yo ____________, ____________ y ____________.

F. Complete the sentence with two activities you never do.

Nunca ____________ ni ____________.

G. Finally, use your answers from **parts B** through **F** to complete this poem in the shape of a diamond.

Me llamo ____________.

No soy ni ____________ ni ____________.

Soy ____________, ____________ y ____________.

Todos los días yo ____________, ____________,

____________ y ____________.

Mis amigos y yo ____________, ____________ y ____________.

Nunca ____________ ni ____________.

¡Así soy yo!

Notes

Realidades 2 Nombre ______ Hora ______

Capítulo 1A Fecha ______

Vocabulary Flash Cards, Sheet 1

Write the Spanish vocabulary word below each picture. If there is a word or phrase, copy it in the space provided. Be sure to include the article for each noun.

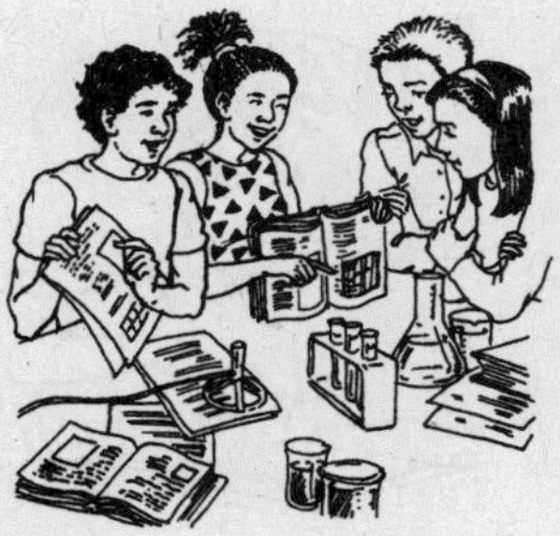

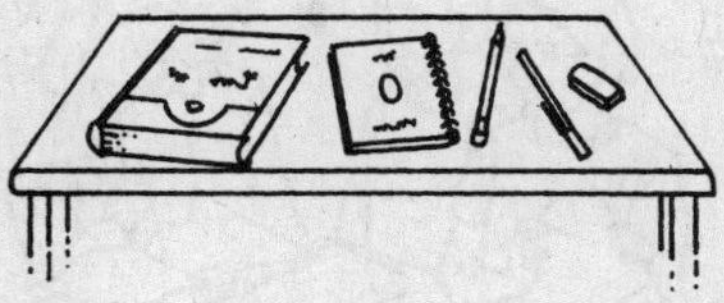

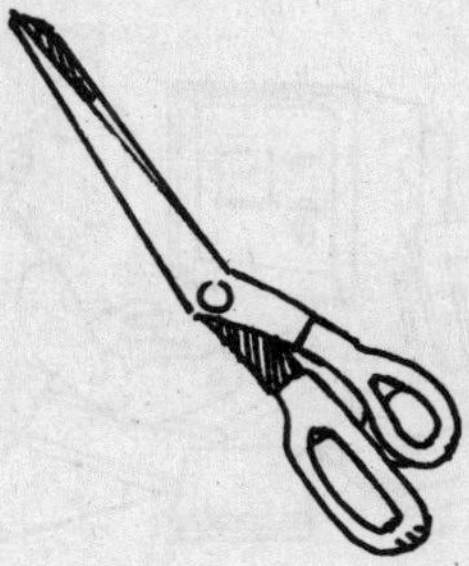

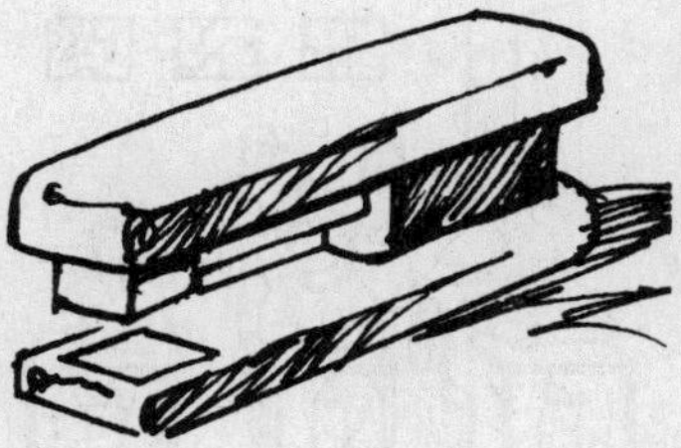

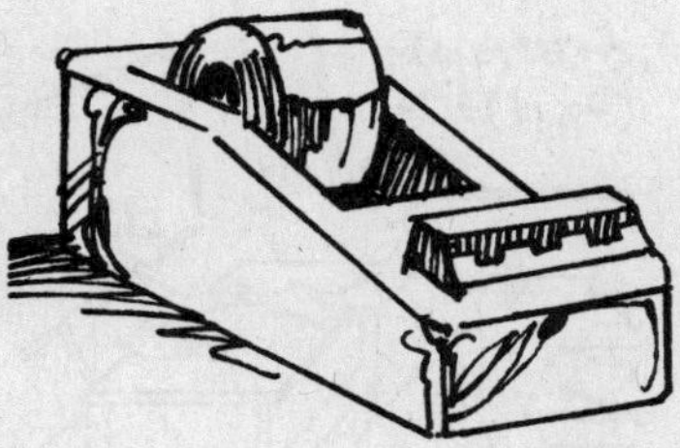

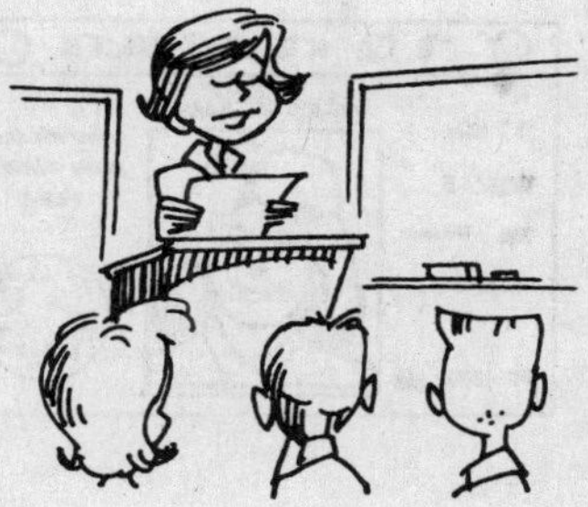

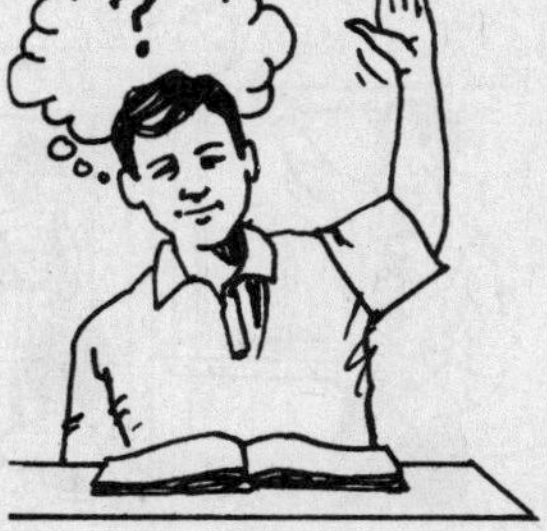

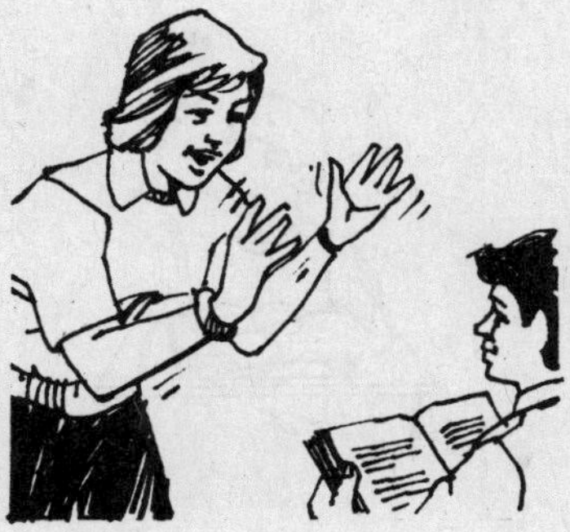

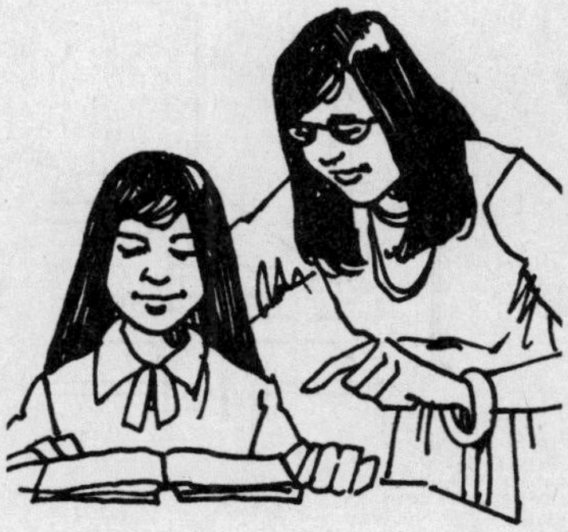

Nombre ______ Hora ______

Fecha ______

Vocabulary Flash Cards, Sheet 2

Write the Spanish vocabulary word below each picture. If there is a word or phrase, copy it in the space provided. Be sure to include the article for each noun.

Write the Spanish vocabulary word below each picture. If there is a word or phrase, copy it in the space provided. Be sure to include the article for each noun.

el proyecto	**conocer**	**lo que**
la palabra	**la regla**	**respetar**

Write the Spanish vocabulary word below each picture. If there is a word or phrase, copy it in the space provided. Be sure to include the article for each noun.

se prohíbe...	**alguien**	**algún, alguna, algunos, algunas**
nadie	**ningún, ninguno, ninguna**	**almorzar**
empezar	**entender**	**repetir**

Write the Spanish vocabulary word below each picture. If there is a word or phrase, copy it in the space provided. Be sure to include the article for each noun.

sobre ______	______ ______	______ ______
______ ______	______ ______	______ ______
______ ______	______ ______	______ ______

Realidades 2 Nombre ______________________ Hora __________

Capítulo 1A Fecha ______________________ **Vocabulary Check, Sheet 1**

Tear out this page. Write the English words on the lines. Fold the paper along the dotted line to see the correct answers so you can check your work.

prestar atención ______________________

se prohíbe... ______________________

la regla ______________________

respetar ______________________

entregar ______________________

explicar ______________________

pedir ayuda ______________________

el informe ______________________

el proyecto ______________________

alguien ______________________

nadie ______________________

contestar ______________________

discutir ______________________

hacer una pregunta ______________________

llegar tarde ______________________

Fold In ←

Tear out this page. Write the Spanish words on the lines. Fold the paper along the dotted line to see the correct answers so you can check your work.

to pay attention ______

it's forbidden... ______

rule ______

to respect ______

to turn in ______

to explain ______

to ask for help ______

report ______

project ______

someone, anyone ______

no one, nobody ______

to answer ______

to discuss ______

to ask a question ______

to arrive late ______

Fold In ←

Tear out this page. Write the English words on the lines. Fold the paper along the dotted line to see the correct answers so you can check your work.

aprender de memoria ______

el laboratorio ______

la palabra ______

sacar una buena nota ______

a tiempo ______

el armario ______

el asiento ______

el carnet de identidad ______

la cinta adhesiva ______

la grapadora ______

los materiales ______

las tijeras ______

Fold In ←

Nombre ______________________ Hora ______________

Fecha ______________________

Vocabulary Check, Sheet 4

Tear out this page. Write the Spanish words on the lines. Fold the paper along the dotted line to see the correct answers so you can check your work.

to memorize	______________
laboratory	______________
word	______________
to get a good grade	______________
on time	______________
locker	______________
seat	______________
I.D. card	______________
transparent tape	______________
stapler	______________
supplies, materials	______________
scissors	______________

Fold In ←

To hear a complete list of the vocabulary for this chapter, go to Disc 1, Track 1 on the Guided Practice Audio CD or go to www.phschool.com and type in the Web Code jdd-0189. Then click on **Repaso del capítulo.**

The verb *tener* (p. 15)

- Remember that **tener** means "to have." It is also used to tell how old you are **(tener años)**, or to say that you're hungry **(tener hambre)**, sleepy **(tener sueño)**, or thirsty **(tener sed)**.
- Here are the present-tense forms of **tener**:

yo	**tengo**	nosotros/nosotras	**tenemos**
tú	**tienes**	vosotros/vosotras	**tenéis**
usted/él/ella	**tiene**	ustedes/ellos/ellas	**tienen**

A. Circle the correct form of **tener** to complete each sentence.

1. Yo no (**tienes** / **tengo**) los carteles.
2. Paco y Lulú (**tenemos** / **tienen**) el sacapuntas.
3. Nosotros (**tenemos** / **tienen**) los bolígrafos.
4. Marco (**tiene** / **tienes**) la carpeta.
5. ¿Cuántos diccionarios (**tiene** / **tienes**) tú?
6. Alicia y tú no (**tienen** / **tienes**) calculadoras, ¿verdad?

- The **yo** form of **tener** in the present tense is irregular. It ends in **-go (Yo ten*go*)**.
- Other verbs that are irregular in the **yo** form are:

hacer *(to do, to make)*	**poner** *(to put)*	**traer** *(to bring)*
hago	**pongo**	**traigo**

B. Write the **yo** form of each verb in parentheses.

1. Yo **(tener)** ______________ un asiento.
2. Yo **(poner)** ______________ los cuadernos en la mesa.
3. Yo **(hacer)** ______________ la tarea.
4. Yo **(traer)** ______________ la papelera.

Stem-changing verbs (p. 27)

- Stem-changing verbs have one spelling change in their stem in the present tense: **almorzar → Yo almuerzo en la escuela.**
- Look at the **yo** form of the verbs in the chart below.

e → ie	o → ue	e → i	u → ue
empezar → empiezo	poder → puedo	pedir → pido	jugar → juego
entender → entiendo	almorzar → almuerzo	repetir → repito	

A. Write the **yo** form of each verb and circle the stem change in each form. Follow the model.

Modelo empezar *empiezo*

1. poder ____________
2. pedir ____________
3. entender ____________
4. almorzar ____________
5. jugar ____________

B. Look at the underlined verb in each sentence. Then, write the stem of this verb in its original form. Follow the model.

Modelo Claudia empieza a hablar. *empez-*

1. Tú juegas al fútbol. ____________

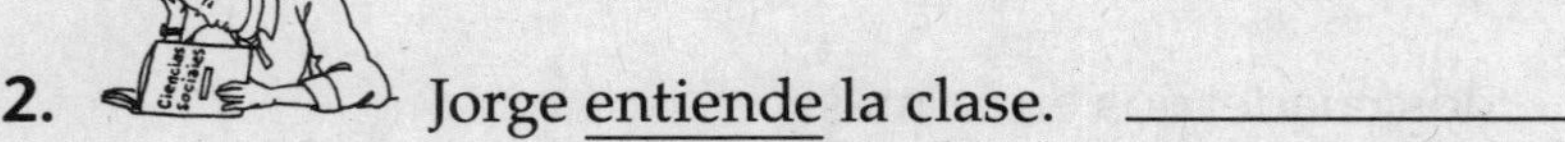

2. Jorge entiende la clase. ____________

3. Yo almuerzo con Juan y Rebeca. ____________

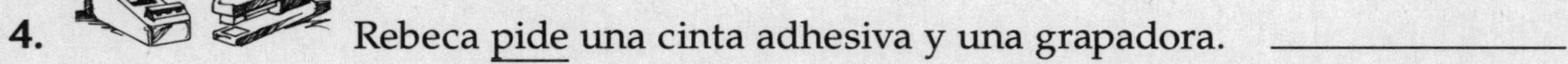

4. Rebeca pide una cinta adhesiva y una grapadora. ____________

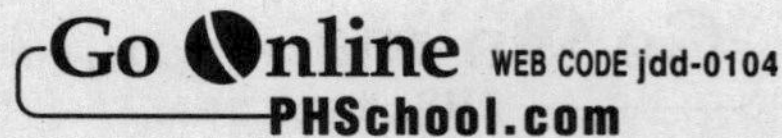

Go Online WEB CODE jdd-0104 PHSchool.com

Affirmative and negative words (p. 31)

- Affirmative words are used to say that something does exist, or that it does happen. Negative words are used to say that something doesn't exist, or that it doesn't happen.
- **Yo siempre hago preguntas** is an affirmative sentence. It means "I always ask questions."
- **Yo nunca hago preguntas** is a negative sentence. It means "I never ask questions."

Affirmative	Negative
alguien *someone, anyone*	**nadie** *no one, nobody*
algo *something*	**nada** *nothing*
algún *some, any* **alguno(s)** **alguna(s)**	**ningún** *no, none, not any* **ninguno** **ninguna**
siempre *always*	**nunca** *never*
también *also, too*	**tampoco** *neither, either*

A. Each sentence below has an affirmative or negative word from the above chart. Find the word and circle it. Follow the model.

Modelo Yo (siempre) respeto las reglas.

1. Alguien contesta la pregunta.
2. Lucía siempre llega tarde.
3. Mis padres nunca dan un discurso.
4. Tú también haces tu proyecto.
5. Marta y María tampoco piden ayuda.
6. Yo no tengo ninguna clase aburrida.

- When you want to say "some," change the ending of **alguno** so it matches what you're describing in gender (masculine or feminine) and number (singular or plural): **alguna chica, algunos libros, algunas chicas.** The same is true for **ninguno: ninguna clase, ningunos materiales, ningunas tijeras.**
- Before a masculine singular noun, **alguno** and **ninguno** change to **algún** and **ningún**.

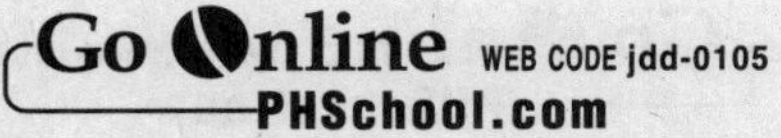

Affirmative and negative words (*continued*)

B. Look at the list of school supplies below. Is the word (or words) masculine or feminine, singular or plural? Circle the correct form of **alguno** or **ninguno** in parentheses.

1. (**ningunas** / **ningunos**) asientos
2. (**alguna** / **algunos**) cinta adhesiva
3. (**algunos** / **algún**) armario
4. (**ningún** / **ningunas**) tijeras
5. (**algunos** / **alguna**) materiales
6. (**ninguna** / **ningunas**) grapadora

- **Alguien** is an affirmative word and means "someone." The word **nadie** is a negative word and means "no one:"
  Alguien llega tarde. *Someone arrives late.*
  Nadie llega tarde. *No one arrives late.*

C. Circle the letter of the answer that best completes each sentence.

1. —¿Conoces a alguien en el laboratorio?
   —No, yo no conozco a
   a. alguien. b. nadie.
2. —¿Conoce Sandra a alguien en el laboratorio?
   —Sí, ella conoce a
   a. alguien. b. nadie.
3. —¿Conoce el maestro a alguien en el laboratorio?
   —No, el maestro no conoce a
   a. alguien. b. nadie.

D. Rubén and Nora are talking about a class. Look at the underlined affirmative or negative words in each sentence. Then, write + next to the sentence if the word is affirmative and – if the word is negative. The first one is done for you.

1. RUBÉN: ¿Por qué tú siempre haces preguntas en esa clase? ___+___
   NORA: Porque yo nunca entiendo y me gusta entender. _______
2. RUBÉN: ¿Conoces a Marina? A ella también le gusta hacer preguntas. _______
   NORA: ¡Sí! Ella tampoco entiende la clase. _______
3. RUBÉN: Yo siempre te quiero ayudar. _______
   NORA: Yo también quiero ayudar a Marina. _______

Go Online WEB CODE jcd-0105 PHSchool.com

Lectura: Para estudiar mejor... (pp. 34–35)

A. The reading in your textbook is an article about good study habits. First, look at the heads and subheads in the article. They can help you understand what the material will be about before you begin reading. Then, based on the information you read in the heads and subheads, list three things you would expect to find in this article.

1. ______________________________

2. ______________________________

3. ______________________________

B. The following words are cognates from the reading. Remember that cognates are words that have similar spellings and meanings in English and Spanish. Write the letter of the English word that matches the Spanish word.

1. ____ comprender a. comprehend b. communicate
2. ____ clases a. cases b. classes
3. ____ atención a. attitude b. attention
4. ____ hábitos a. habits b. abilities

C. Read the following excerpt from the first section of the article in your textbook. Then, complete the chart below based on the excerpt. Write the answers in the space provided.

> *¿Qué debes hacer a la hora de estudiar?*
>
> *Para estudiar mejor necesitas una buena organización del trabajo y unos hábitos saludables. Siempre debes ser positivo. Repite frases como "yo puedo hacerlo" o "soy capaz (capable)". Cuida (Take care of) tus libros y otros materiales.*

Para estudiar mejor, necesitas...	Debes ser positivo(a) y usar frases como...	Debes cuidar...

Presentación oral (p. 37)

Task: You have been invited to be a school principal for a day. As principal, you will make new school rules and display them on a poster. Then you will present your poster to a partner.

A. Think about what students will and will not be allowed to do in your school. Then list some verbs to describe these rules. A few verbs have been provided to get you started.

llegar, hacer, conocer, ______, ______, ______, ______

B. Using the verbs from **part A,** complete the columns. In the **Hay que...** column, write three verbs to describe what students should do at your school. In the **Se prohíbe...** column, write three verbs to describe what should not be done at your school. One has been done for you.

Hay que...	*Se prohíbe...*
1. hacer	1. ______
2. ______	2. ______
3. ______	3. ______

C. On a piece of posterboard, write out *complete* sentences using the verbs from **part B.** Follow the models.

Modelos Hay que *hacer la tarea*.
Se prohíbe *llegar tarde a la clase*.

D. Illustrate each of your school rules on the poster.

E. Tell a partner about your school rules. Refer to the illustrations on your poster as you speak. Be sure to:

- include three things that students must do and three things that are not allowed
- use complete sentences
- speak clearly

Write the Spanish vocabulary word below each picture. If there is a word or phrase, copy it in the space provided. Be sure to include the article for each noun.

Realidades 2 Nombre ______ Hora ______

Capítulo 1B Fecha ______ **Vocabulary Flash Cards, Sheet 2**

Write the Spanish vocabulary word below each picture. If there is a word or phrase, copy it in the space provided. Be sure to include the article for each noun.

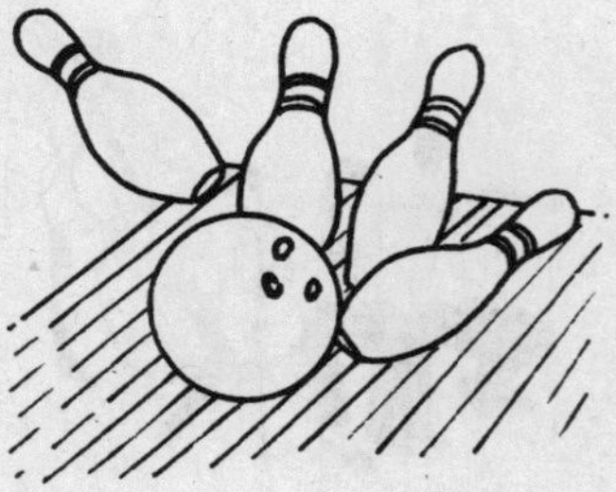

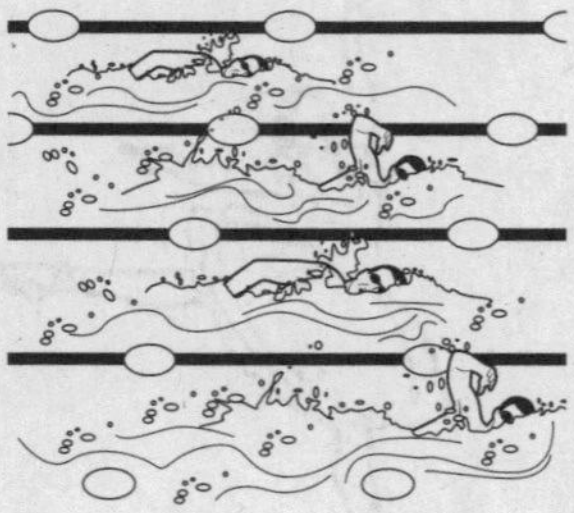

Realidades 2 Nombre ____________________ Hora ____________

Capítulo 1B Fecha ____________________ **Vocabulary Flash Cards, Sheet 3**

Write the Spanish vocabulary word below each picture. If there is a word or phrase, copy it in the space provided. Be sure to include the article for each noun.

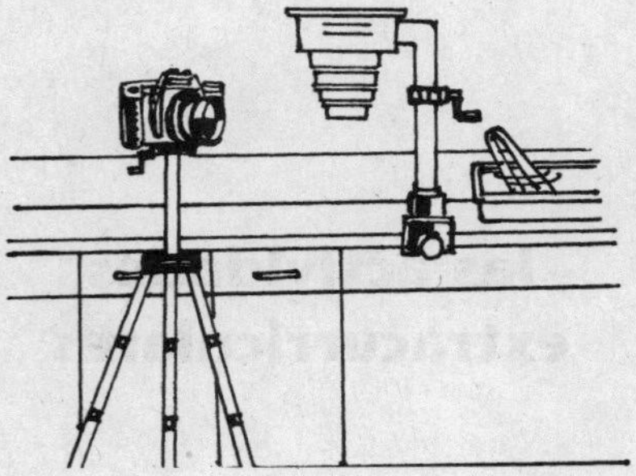

Write the Spanish vocabulary word below each picture. If there is a word or phrase, copy it in the space provided. Be sure to include the article for each noun.

la canción	**las actividades extracurriculares**	**navegar en la Red**
el club	**el club atlético**	**el equipo**
ser miembro	**el pasatiempo**	**la reunión**

Realidades 2 | Nombre | Hora

Capítulo 1B | Fecha | **Vocabulary Flash Cards, Sheet 5**

Write the Spanish vocabulary word below each picture. If there is a word or phrase, copy it in the space provided. Be sure to include the article for each noun.

el coro	**ensayar**	**el ensayo**
asistir a	**ganar**	**participar (en)**
tomar lecciones	**volver**	**entre**

Write the Spanish vocabulary word below each picture. If there is a word or phrase, copy it in the space provided. Be sure to include the article for each noun.

el interés	**la oportunidad**	**¿Cuánto tiempo hace que...?**
saber	**conocer**	**el miembro**
Hace + *time* + que...	**tantos, tantas + *noun* + como**	**tan + *adj.* + como**

Vocabulary Check, Sheet 1

Tear out this page. Write the English words on the lines. Fold the paper along the dotted line to see the correct answers so you can check your work.

el músico, la música ______

la orquesta ______

el equipo ______

la natación ______

el ajedrez ______

la fotografía ______

hacer una búsqueda ______

ser miembro ______

ganar ______

el pasatiempo ______

participar (en) ______

la reunión ______

volver ______

asistir a ______

Fold In ←

Realidades 2 | Nombre ______________________ | Hora ______

Capítulo 1B | Fecha ______________________ | **Vocabulary Check, Sheet 2**

Tear out this page. Write the Spanish words on the lines. Fold the paper along the dotted line to see the correct answers so you can check your work.

musician ______________________

orchestra ______________________

team ______________________

swimming ______________________

chess ______________________

photography ______________________

to do a search ______________________

to be a member ______________________

to win, to earn ______________________

pastime ______________________

to participate (in) ______________________

meeting ______________________

to return ______________________

to attend ______________________

Fold In ←

Tear out this page. Write the English words on the lines. Fold the paper along the dotted line to see the correct answers so you can check your work.

el hockey ______

jugar a los bolos ______

hacer gimnasia ______

las artes marciales ______

el animador,
la animadora ______

la práctica ______

los jóvenes ______

el club ______

la banda ______

el bailarín,
la bailarina ______

el coro ______

ensayar ______

tomar lecciones ______

entre ______

el interés ______

Fold In ←

Tear out this page. Write the Spanish words on the lines. Fold the paper along the dotted line to see the correct answers so you can check your work.

hockey ____________

to bowl ____________

to do gymnastics ____________

martial arts ____________

cheerleader ____________

practice ____________

young people ____________

club ____________

band ____________

dancer ____________

chorus, choir ____________

to rehearse ____________

to take lessons ____________

among, between ____________

interest ____________

Fold In ←

To hear a complete list of the vocabulary for this chapter, go to Disc 1, Track 2 on the Guided Practice Audio CD or go to www.phschool.com and type in the Web Code jdd-0199. Then click on **Repaso del capítulo.**

Making comparisons (p. 53)

- To say that people or things are equal to each other, use **tan** + *adjective* + **como.**

  El hockey es tan popular como la natación. *Hockey is as popular as swimming.*
- To say that people or things are not equal, use the negative.

  El hockey no es tan popular como la natación. *Hockey is not as popular as swimming.*

A. Look at the pictures and the sentences comparing two sports or activities. Then, fill in the blank with **tan** or **como** to correctly complete the sentences. Follow the model.

Modelo   El hockey es tan popular *como* la fotografía.

1.   La banda es ________ popular como la orquesta.

2.   Jugar a los bolos no es tan popular ________ el ajedrez.

3.   Hacer gimnasia es ________ popular como las artes marciales.

4.   Las animadoras no son ________ populares como los miembros del equipo.

5.   El bailarín no es tan popular ________ el cantante.

Making comparisons (*continued*)

B. Some friends are comparing school activities. Use the expression **tan** + *adjective* + **como** with the word in parentheses to complete the sentences. Follow the model.

Modelo ¿La natación es *tan popular como* (**popular**) el hockey?

1. Creo que el ajedrez es ______________ (**interesante**) jugar a los bolos.
2. Yo creo que las dos actividades son ______________ (**aburridas**) la fotografía.
3. ¡Ay! Para mí, las actividades son ______________ (**difíciles**) las clases de la escuela.

- Use **tanto, -a** + *noun* + **como** to say "as much as:"
  tanto interés como, *as much interest as*
- Use **tantos, -as** + *noun* + **como** to say "as many as:"
  tantos jóvenes como, *as many young people as*
- Note that **tanto** agrees in gender and number with what is being compared.
  Elena no hace tantas actividades extracurriculares como Juan.
  Elena doesn't do as many extracurricular activities as Juan.

C. Look at the following sentences and decide if the underlined word is masculine or feminine, singular or plural. Then, circle the correct form of **tanto** in parentheses. Follow the model.

Modelo Yo asisto a (**tantas** / **tantos**) reuniones como Elena.

1. Yo tengo (**tantos** / **tantas**) prácticas como mi hermano.
2. Juan toma (**tantas** / **tantos**) lecciones de artes marciales como Carlos.
3. Elena tiene (**tantas** / **tantos**) pasatiempos como Angélica.
4. Camilo tiene (**tanto** / **tanta**) interés en el hockey como Juan.
5. Hay (**tantas** / **tantos**) bailarinas como bailarines.

Go Online WEB CODE jdd-0114 PHSchool.com

The verbs *saber* and *conocer* (p. 56)

- **Saber** means to know information and facts.
  ¿Sabes si tenemos una reunión mañana? *Do you know if we have a meeting tomorrow?*
- **Conocer** means to know a person or to be familiar with a place or thing. Use the **a** *personal* with **conocer** to say you know a person:
  ¿Conoces a María? *Do you know María?*

A. Read the following sentences and choose the verb from the list that best completes each sentence.

saben	conocemos	conozco	conoces	sabe

1. Mi amiga ________________ mucho del hockey.
2. Yo no ________________ al cantante nuevo.
3. ¿Tú ________________ a Juan?
4. ¿________________ ustedes cuándo son las reuniones del club?
5. Mi madre y yo ________________ a un músico.

- Use the verb **saber** + *infinitive of another verb* to say that you know how to do something:
  Sabemos hacer gimnasia. *We know how to do gymnastics.*
  Sabes crear una página Web. *You know how to create a Web page.*

B. Read the following questions. Complete the answers with the verb form of **saber** and the infinitive. The first one is done for you.

1. ¿Sabes jugar a los bolos? Sí, yo *sé* *jugar* a los bolos.
2. ¿Saben ellos hacer gimnasia? No, ellos no ____________ ____________ gimnasia.
3. ¿Sabe Luis visitar salones de chat? No, él no ____________ ____________ salones de chat.
4. ¿Sabe Mario crear una página Web? Sí, él ____________ ____________una página Web.
5. ¿Saben ustedes jugar al ajedrez? No, nosotros no ____________ ____________ al ajedrez.

Hace + time expressions (p. 58)

- When you want to ask how long something has been going on, use **¿Cuánto tiempo + hace que +** *present-tense verb*?

  ¿Cuánto tiempo hace que ***eres*** **miembro del coro?**
  How long have you been a member of the choir?

A. Complete the following sentences with the present tense of the verb in parentheses. Follow the model.

Modelo ¿Cuánto tiempo hace que ustedes ___ensayan___ (ensayar) con el club de música?

1. ¿Cuánto tiempo hace que nosotros no __________ (volver) al club atlético?
2. ¿Cuánto tiempo hace que Juana __________ (tomar) lecciones de fotografía?
3. ¿Cuánto tiempo hace que tú no __________ (asistir) a las reuniónes del club?

- To tell how long something has been going on, use **hace +** *period of time* **+ que +** *present-tense verb.*

  Hace cuatro meses que ***soy*** **miembro del club atlético.**
  I have been a member of the athletic team for four months.

B. Read the following questions and answer with the information provided in parentheses and the present tense of the verb. Remember to use the word **no** for negative sentences. Follow the model.

Modelo ¿Cuánto tiempo hace que tú no participas en la natación? (2 meses)
Hace ___2___ ___meses___ que yo ___no___ ___participo___ en la natación.

1. ¿Cuánto tiempo hace que Carlos juega en el equipo? (1 año)
   Hace ________ ____________ que Carlos ____________ en el equipo.
2. ¿Cuánto tiempo hace que ustedes no navegan en la Red? (5 años)
   Hace ________ ____________ que nosotros ________ ____________ en la Red.
3. ¿Cuánto tiempo hace que tú no grabas música? (2 días)
   Hace ________ ____________ que yo ________ ____________ música.
4. ¿Cuánto tiempo hace que tu hermana no visita salones de chat? (3 semanas)
   Hace ________ ____________ que mi hermana ________ ____________ salones de chat.

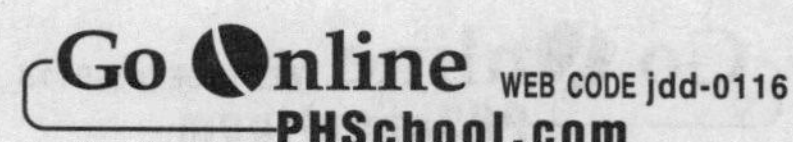

Realidades 2 | Nombre ______ | Hora ______

Capítulo 1B | Fecha ______ | **Guided Practice Activities 1B-5**

Lectura: ¡A bailar! (pp. 62–63)

A. The reading in your textbook is about a dance school. Here you will find information about the many dance classes at this school. What kind of information do you expect to find about each class? Some information has already been provided.

1. ______ 4. ______

2. ______ 5. ______

3. ______

B. Read the following schedule from the reading in your textbook. Then answer the questions that follow.

Cursos	Día y hora
Tango	*lunes* *17.30h a 18.30h*
Merengue	*martes* *17.00h a 18.00h*

1. ¿Qué curso enseña la escuela los martes? ______

2. ¿A qué hora empieza el curso de tango? ______

C. Read the following class descriptions from the schedule in the reading. Then, look at the sentences that follow and write **L** (for **Lectura**) if the sentence tells about something you read. Write **N** (for **No**) if the sentence tells something you didn't read.

Swing
Baila toda la noche con tu pareja este baile muy popular de los Estados Unidos.

Tango
Ven a aprender este baile romántico de Argentina que se hizo famoso por las composiciones musicales de Gardel y de Piazzolla.

1. El tango es el baile tradicional de Argentina. ____

2. El swing es un baile popular en los Estados Unidos. ____

3. El tango es un baile romántico de Andalucía. ____

4. El swing se baila con una pareja. ____

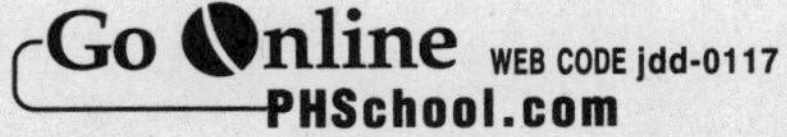

Presentación escrita (p. 65)

Task: Your school offers many extracurricular activities. Your teacher wants you to write about the activities you like and why you like them.

❶ Prewrite. Look at the following activities and circle the ones that you like to do.

jugar al béisbol	**usar una computadora**	**jugar al ajedrez**
sacar fotos	**jugar a los bolos**	**tocar la guitarra**
leer libros	**hacer gimnasia**	**cantar en el coro**

❷ Draft. Complete the sentences below using the answers from **part 1**. Tell why you like those activities, and how long you have been doing them.

1. Me llamo ____ y tengo ____ años.
2. Me gustaría ____ y ____.
3. Me gustan estas actividades porque ____
____.
4. Hace ____ que ____.

❸ Revise. Use your answers from **part 2** to help you write a paragraph. Then read and check your paragraph. You may use the following questions:

- Does my paragraph list two activities?
- Does my paragraph describe the activities?
- Does my paragraph explain why I like these activities?

❹ Evaluation. Your teacher may give you a rubric for how the paragraph will be graded. You will probably be graded on:

- how much information you provide about yourself
- use of vocabulary
- accuracy and use of the writing process

Nombre ______ Hora ______

Fecha ______

Vocabulary Flash Cards, Sheet 1

Write the Spanish vocabulary word below each picture. If there is a word or phrase, copy it in the space provided. Be sure to include the article for each noun.

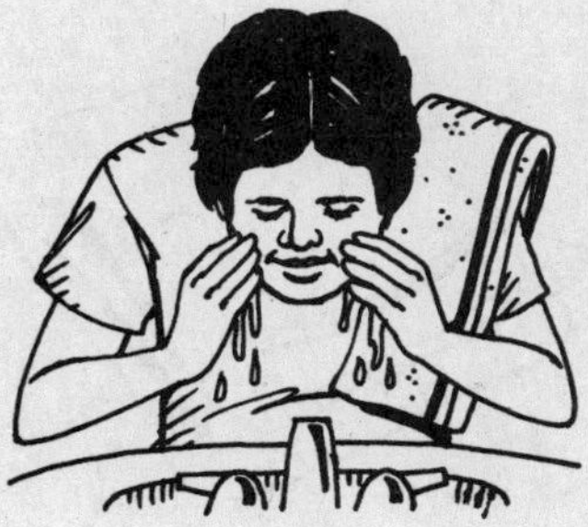

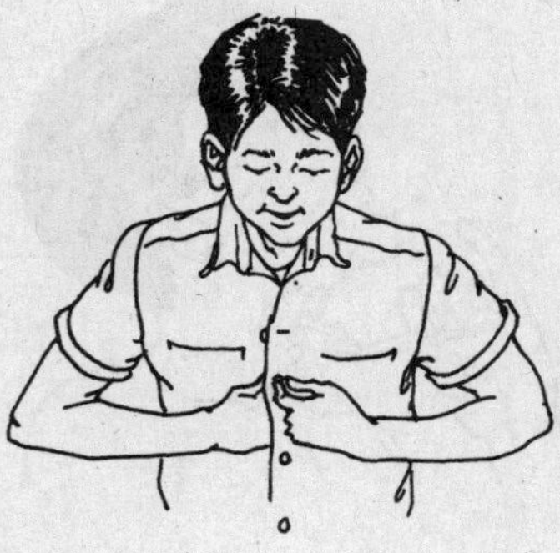

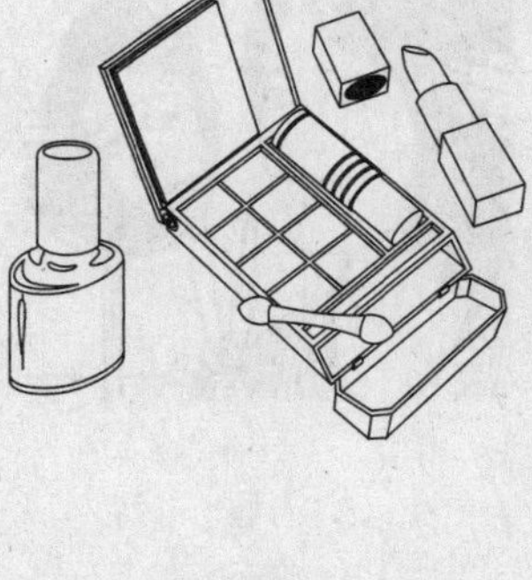

Realidades 2 Nombre ______ Hora ______

Capítulo 2A Fecha ______ **Vocabulary Flash Cards, Sheet 2**

Write the Spanish vocabulary word below each picture. If there is a word or phrase, copy it in the space provided. Be sure to include the article for each noun.

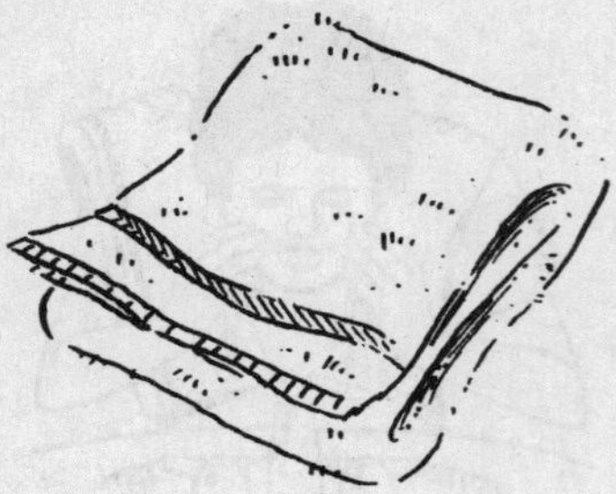

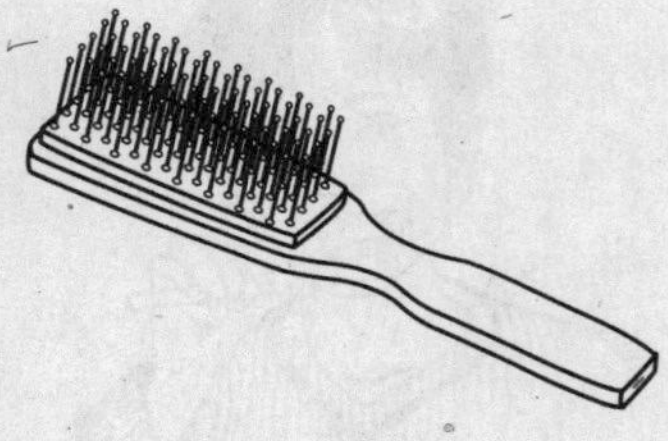

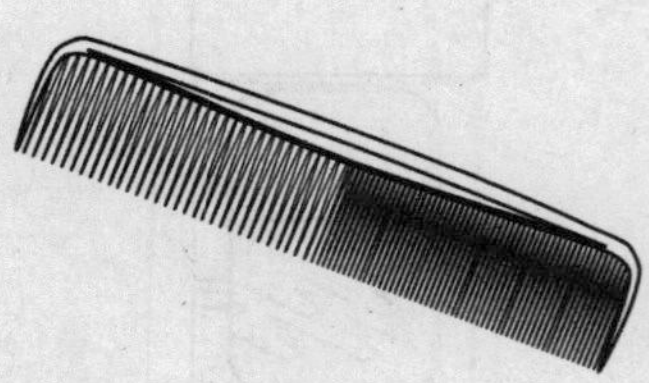

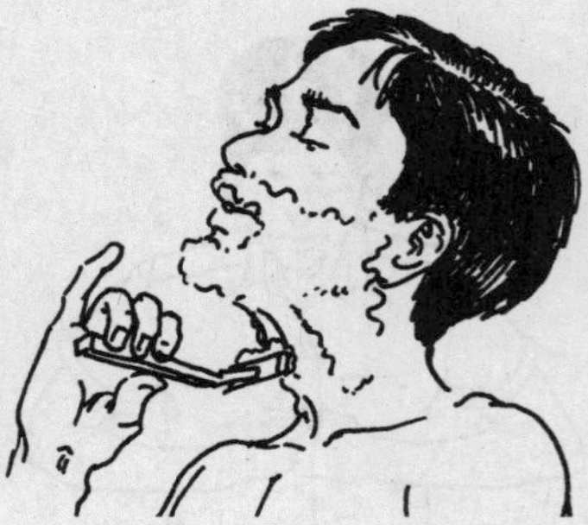

Write the Spanish vocabulary word below each picture. If there is a word or phrase, copy it in the space provided. Be sure to include the article for each noun.

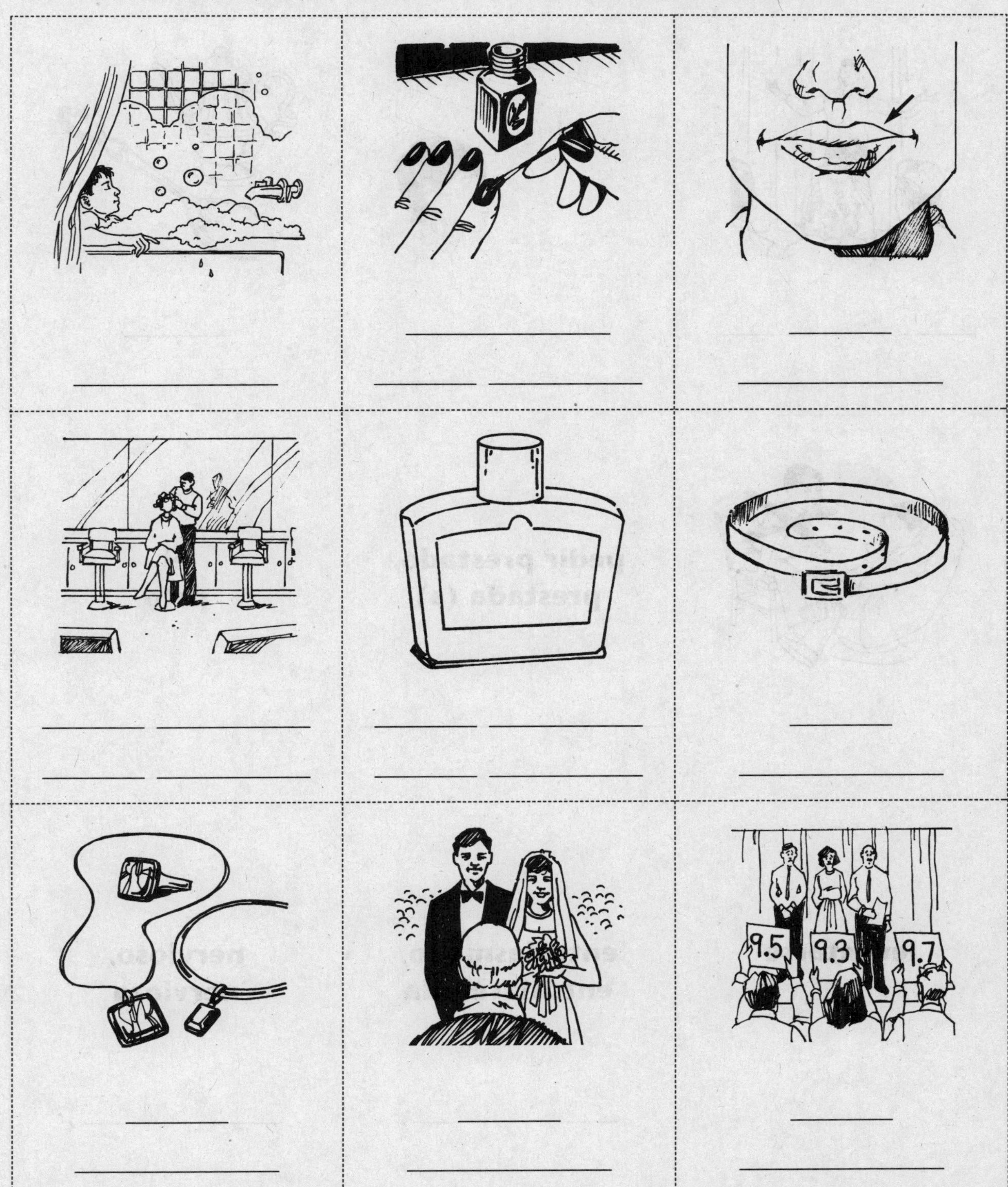

Write the Spanish vocabulary word below each picture. If there is a word or phrase, copy it in the space provided. Be sure to include the article for each noun.

 ______ ________ ____________	 ______ ____________	 ______ ____________
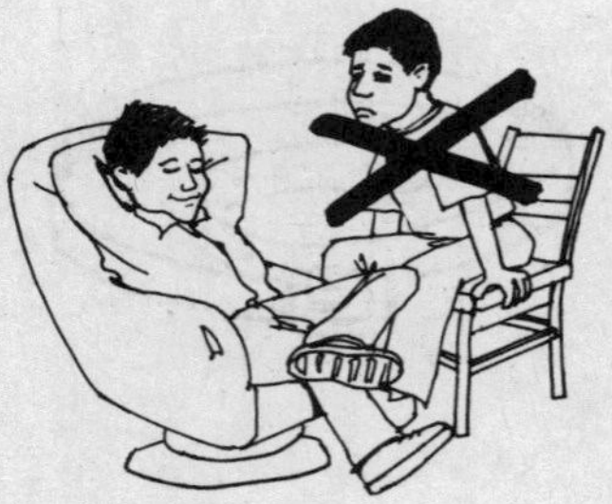 ____________	**pedir prestado, prestada (a)** ________ ________, ________ ______	**el pelo** ______ ____________
levantarse ____________	**entusiasmado, entusiasmada** ____________, ____________	**nervioso, nerviosa** ____________, ____________

Nombre _______________ Hora _______

Fecha _______________

Vocabulary Flash Cards, Sheet 5

Write the Spanish vocabulary word below each picture. If there is a word or phrase, copy it in the space provided. Be sure to include the article for each noun.

tranquilo, tranquila _______________, _______________	**las uñas** _______ _______________	**la cita** _______ _______________
ponerse _______________	**prepararse** _______________	**antes de** _______________ _______
depende _______________	**elegante** _______________	**lentamente** _______________

Write the Spanish vocabulary word below each picture. If there is a word or phrase, copy it in the space provided. Be sure to include the article for each noun.

luego	**por ejemplo**	**rápidamente**
te ves (bien)	**la audición**	

Realidades 2

Capítulo 2A

Nombre ______ Hora ______

Fecha ______

Vocabulary Check, Sheet 1

Tear out this page. Write the English words on the lines. Fold the paper along the dotted line to see the correct answers so you can check your work.

acostarse ______

afeitarse ______

arreglarse (el pelo) ______

bañarse ______

cepillarse (los dientes) ______

cortarse el pelo ______

despertarse ______

ducharse ______

levantarse ______

lavarse (la cara) ______

pintarse (las uñas) ______

ponerse ______

prepararse ______

secarse ______

Fold In ←

Realidades 2 | Nombre ____________ | Hora ________

Capítulo 2A | Fecha ____________ | **Vocabulary Check, Sheet 2**

Tear out this page. Write the Spanish words on the lines. Fold the paper along the dotted line to see the correct answers so you can check your work.

to go to bed ____________

to shave ____________

to fix (one's hair) ____________

to take a bath ____________

to brush (one's teeth) ____________

to cut one's hair ____________

to wake up ____________

to take a shower ____________

to get up ____________

to wash (one's face) ____________

to paint, to polish (one's nails) ____________

to put on ____________

to get ready ____________

to dry ____________

Fold In ←

Realidades 2 | Nombre ______ | Hora ______

Capítulo 2A | Fecha ______ | **Vocabulary Check, Sheet 3**

Tear out this page. Write the English words on the lines. Fold the paper along the dotted line to see the correct answers so you can check your work.

el agua de colonia ______

el cepillo ______

el cinturón ______

el desodorante ______

la ducha ______

el gel ______

las joyas (de oro, de plata) ______

el maquillaje ______

el peine ______

el pelo ______

el salón de belleza ______

el secador ______

la toalla ______

las uñas ______

Fold In ←

Tear out this page. Write the Spanish words on the lines. Fold the paper along the dotted line to see the correct answers so you can check your work.

cologne ____________________

brush ____________________

belt ____________________

deodorant ____________________

shower ____________________

gel ____________________

(gold, silver) jewelry ____________________

make-up ____________________

comb ____________________

hair ____________________

beauty salon ____________________

blow dryer ____________________

towel ____________________

nails ____________________

Fold In ←

To hear a complete list of the vocabulary for this chapter, go to Disc 1, Track 3 on the Guided Practice Audio CD or go to www.phschool.com and type in the Web Code jdd-0289. Then click on **Repaso del capítulo.**

Reflexive verbs (p. 80)

- You use reflexive verbs to say that people do something to or for themselves. All reflexive verbs in the infinitive form end with **-se**. For example, **secarse el pelo** means *to dry one's hair.*
- The reflexive pronouns are **me, te, se, os,** and **nos.** Here is the present-tense form of **secarse:**

yo	**me seco**	nosotros/nosotras	**nos secamos**
tú	**te secas**	vosotros/vosotras	**os secáis**
usted/él/ella	**se seca**	ustedes/ellos/ellas	**se secan**

- Some verbs can be used in reflexive and non-reflexive forms.

  Me lavo el pelo todos los días. *I wash my hair every day.*
  Lavo el coche. *I wash the car.*

A. Look at the underlined word(s) and circle the correct reflexive pronoun for each sentence.

1. Ellos (**nos** / **se**) lavan el pelo todos los días.
2. Tú (**te** / **se**) pintas las uñas.
3. Javier y yo (**nos** / **se**) lavamos la cara antes de acostarnos.
4. Roberto (**nos** / **se**) cepilla los dientes antes de vestirse.

B. Write the correct reflexive pronoun and form of the verb to complete each answer. Follow the model.

Modelo —¿A qué hora te despiertas en la mañana?

—Yo siempre (despertarse) *me* *despierto* a las 6:30.

1. —¿A qué hora se duchan ustedes?

   —Nosotras (ducharse) ____ __________ a las 7:00 de la mañana.

2. —¿A qué hora te arreglas el pelo?

   —Yo (arreglarse) ____ __________ el pelo a las 7:30 de la mañana.

3. —¿Se cepillan ustedes los dientes todos los días?

   —Sí, nosotros (cepillarse) ____ __________ los dientes todos los días.

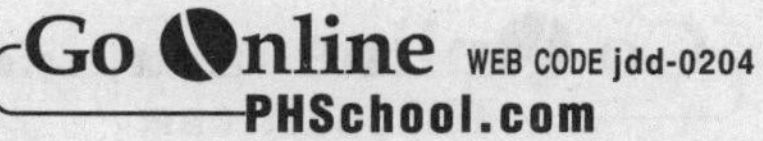

Reflexive verbs (*continued*)

- Reflexive pronouns can be placed before the conjugated verb or attached to the infinitive. These two sentences have the same meaning:

  Me voy a duchar. *or* **Voy a ducharme.** *I am going to take a shower.*

C. Complete the following sentences with the correct reflexive pronoun **me, te, se,** or **nos.** The first one is done for you.

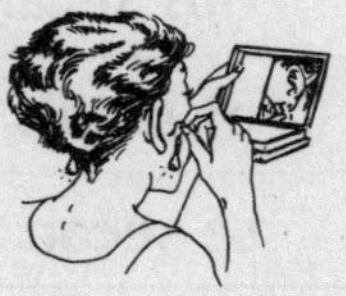

1. Elena __se__ tiene que maquillar. *or* Elena tiene que maquillar__se__.
2. José ______ va a duchar. *or* José va a duchar______. 
3. Yo ______ voy a arreglar el pelo. *or* Yo voy a arreglar______ el pelo.  
4. Elena e Isabel siempre ______ tienen que preparar lentamente. *or* Elena e Isabel siempre tienen que preparar______ lentamente.

D. Read Héctor's description of his morning routine. Complete the sentences with the appropriate words from the list.

arreglo	cepillo	despierto	ducho	levanto	seco	visto

1. Primero, me ____________ a las 6:30 de la mañana y despierto a mi hermano.
2. Luego, me ____________ de la cama y voy al baño.
3. Entonces, me ____________ los dientes y me ____________.
4. Después, me ____________ con la toalla y me ____________ el pelo.
5. Finalmente, me ____________ con la ropa que preparé anoche y ¡tengo que despertar a mi hermano otra vez!

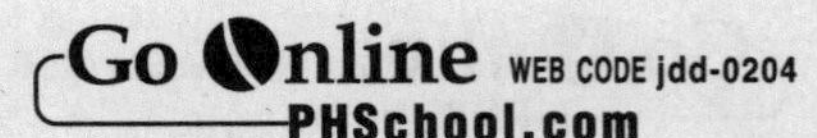

The verbs *ser* and *estar* (p. 86)

- The verb **ser** means "to be." Use **ser** to describe what a person or thing is like or where they are from, or what a thing is made of.
  María es simpática. *María is nice.*
  Tú eres de Argentina. *You are from Argentina.*
  El anillo es de plata. *The ring is made of silver.*

A. Complete the following sentences with the correct form of **ser**.

1. Las joyas ______________ de oro.
2. Yo ______________ Mateo.
3. Tú ______________ elegante.

- The verb **estar** also means "to be." Use **estar** to tell how a person is or feels at the moment or where a person or thing is located.
  Elena está entusiasmada hoy. *Elena is excited today.*
  Alonso está en el baño. *Alonso is in the bathroom.*

B. Complete the following sentences with the correct form of **estar**.

1. Yo ______________ muy nervioso.
2. Ramón y yo ______________ tranquilos.
3. Tú ______________ en el salón de belleza.

C. Complete the conversation using the verbs from the word bank. Use each verb only once.

soy	eres	estoy	estás	es

1. CARMEN: Yo soy de México. ¿De dónde ________ tú?

   ELENA: Yo ________ de Honduras.

2. CARMEN: Yo estoy nerviosa hoy porque tengo una audición. Y tú, ¿cómo ________ hoy?

   ELENA: Yo ________ muy contenta porque tengo una cita con Rafael.

3. CARMEN: ¿Sí? Yo conozco a Rafael. Él ________ muy simpático.

   ELENA: Sí, Rafael es mi amigo de Honduras.

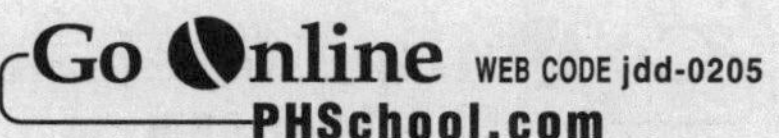

WEB CODE jdd-0205

Possessive adjectives (p. 88)

- Spanish possessive adjectives have a long form that comes after the noun:
  ¿Tienes un peine mío? *Do you have a comb of mine?*
  El secador es nuestro. *The dryer is ours.*
- After the verb **ser**, you can use the possessive adjective by itself:
  Esta toalla es tuya. *This towel is yours.*
- Possessive adjectives agree in gender and number with the noun they describe:
  El peine es mío. *The comb is mine.*
- These forms are often used for emphasis:

mío/mía	**míos/mías**	**nuestro/nuestra**	**nuestros/nuestras**
tuyo/tuya	**tuyos/tuyas**	**vuestro/vuestra**	**vuestros/vuestras**
suyo/suya	**suyos/suyas**	**suyo/suya**	**suyos/suyas**

A. Look at the drawings and the sentences. Then, circle the possessive adjective in each sentence. You can look at the above chart to help you. Follow the model.

Modelo El  es (mío).

1. Este  no es mío.

2. Las son nuestras.

3. El  es mío.

4. El 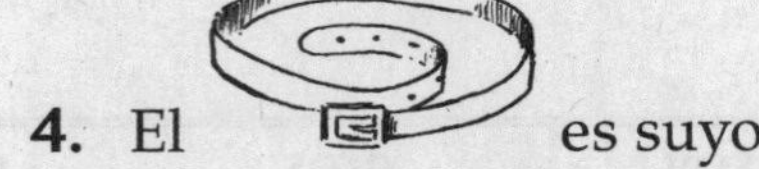 es suyo.

B. Read the conversations about who owns various objects. Then, complete each answer with the correct possessive adjective. Follow the model.

Modelo —¿Es tu secador?
—Sí, el secador es *mío*.

1. —¿Es tu toalla?
—Sí, la toalla es __________.

2. —¿Son estas joyas de tu madre?
—Sí, las joyas son __________.

3. —¿Son nuestros salones de belleza?
—No, los salones de belleza no son __________.

Realidades 2

Capítulo 2A

Nombre ______________________ Hora __________

Fecha ______________________ **Guided Practice Activities 2A-5**

Lectura: El Teatro Colón: Entre bambalinas (pp. 90–91)

A. The reading in your textbook is about a theater in Argentina called **El Teatro Colón.** How do you think the author feels about singing or acting in a theater? Look at the following section from the reading and underline the words that tell how the author feels.

> *Pasar una noche en el Teatro Colón de Buenos Aires siempre es un evento especial y hoy es muy especial para mí. Vamos a presentar la ópera "La traviata" y voy a cantar en el coro por primera vez. ¡Estoy muy nervioso! ... "La traviata" fue la ópera que se presentó en la inauguración del teatro el 27 de abril de 1857. Por eso estamos muy entusiasmados.*

B. Look at the following words and circle the ones that describe how you would feel before giving a performance in a theater. Then write three more descriptive words.

nervioso(a), contento(a), ______________, ______________, ______________

C. Read the following advertisement about student auditions from your textbook reading. Then, use the information to decide if the following students are qualified to audition. Circle **Sí** if they are qualified or **No** if they are not qualified.

> *AUDICIONES*
> *para jóvenes de 15 a 25 años de edad.*
> *Si quieres ser músico, cantante o bailarín, tienes talento, eres joven y vives en Buenos Aires, tienes la oportunidad de hacer tus sueños realidad.*

1. José Luis es músico y tiene mucho talento. Él tiene 15 años.
   (Sí / No)

2. A Isabel no le gusta bailar ni cantar, pero le interesa la tecnología y el arte. Ella tiene 18 años.
   (Sí / No)

3. Elena quiere ser bailarina. Ella tiene 13 años.
   (Sí / No)

4. Enrique toca la guitarra. Él tiene 30 años y vive en Los Ángeles.
   (Sí / No)

5. A Juan le gusta cantar. También sabe tocar el piano. Tiene 25 años.
   (Sí / No)

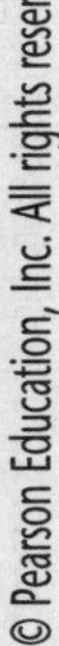

Presentación oral (p. 93)

Task: Pretend you are an exchange student in Mexico. Your host family wants to know how you celebrate special events in the United States. Bring in a photo from home or from a magazine that shows a special event.

A. Look at your photo and use it to answer the following questions.

1. What is the special event? ______________________________
2. What clothing are people wearing? ______________________________
3. How do you think the people feel? ______________________________

B. Look again at your photo and your answers from **part A.** Imagine you are going to attend the special event in the photo. How do you get ready? How do you feel before, during, and after the special event? Complete the sentences below.

Me gusta prepararme antes de un evento especial. Primero, yo ________________.

Después, yo ________________. Antes de salir, yo ________________.

Antes de un evento especial yo estoy ________________. En un evento especial,

me gusta estar ________________. Después de un evento, yo estoy

________________.

C. Use the information from **parts A** and **B** to write some ideas about the special event. Write your ideas on index cards. Make sure you describe the event, how you prepare for the event, and how you feel before, during, and after the event.

D. Then, practice giving an oral presentation using your index cards and photo. Go through your presentation several times. Try to:

- provide as much information as you can about each point
- use complete sentences
- speak clearly

Realidades 2 Nombre ______ Hora ______

Capítulo 2B Fecha ______ **Vocabulary Flash Cards, Sheet 1**

Write the Spanish vocabulary word below each picture. If there is a word or phrase, copy it in the space provided. Be sure to include the article for each noun.

FRUTAS

Liquidación

20%

40%

50%

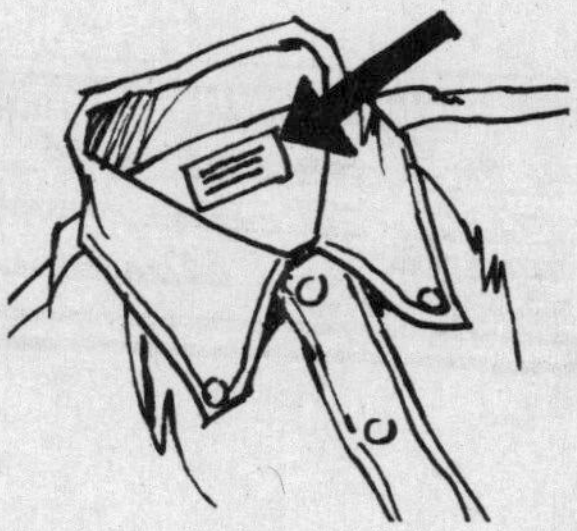

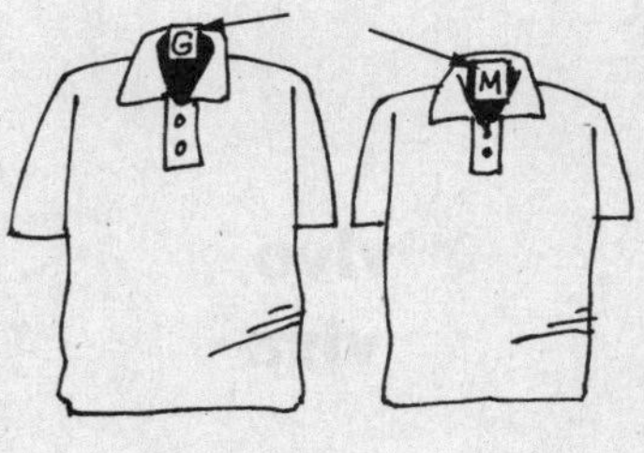

G

M

12

9½

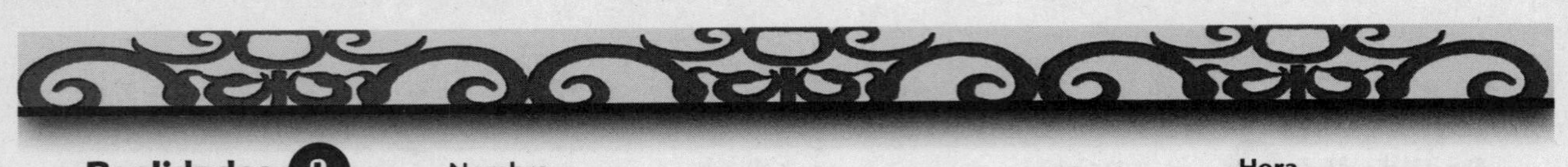

Write the Spanish vocabulary word below each picture. If there is a word or phrase, copy it in the space provided. Be sure to include the article for each noun.

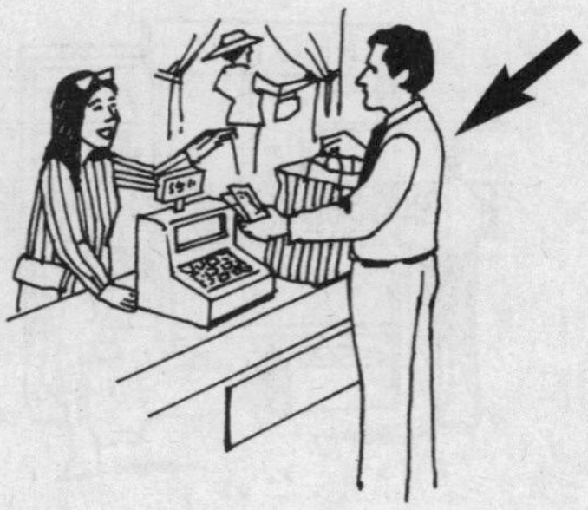

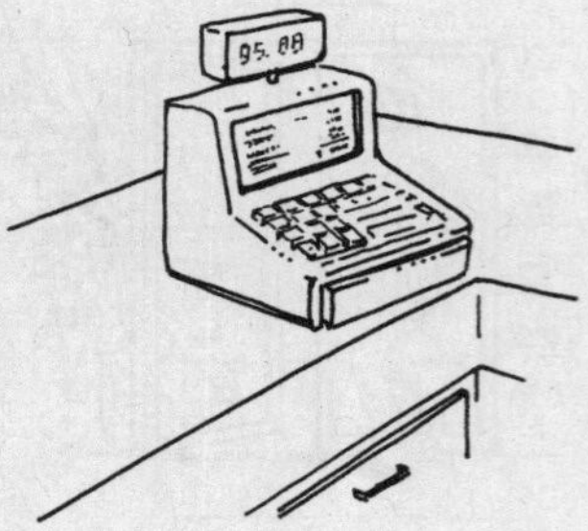

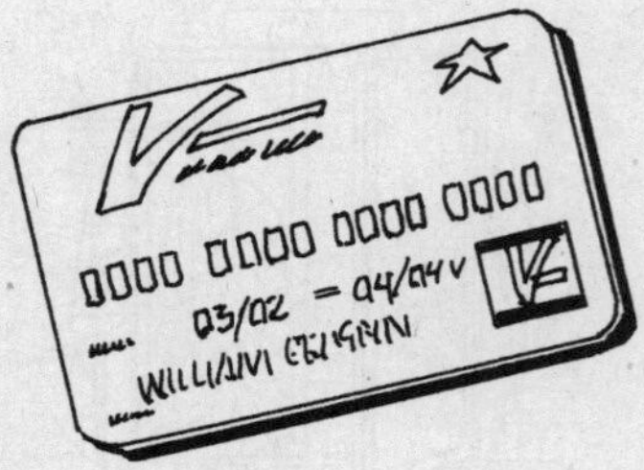

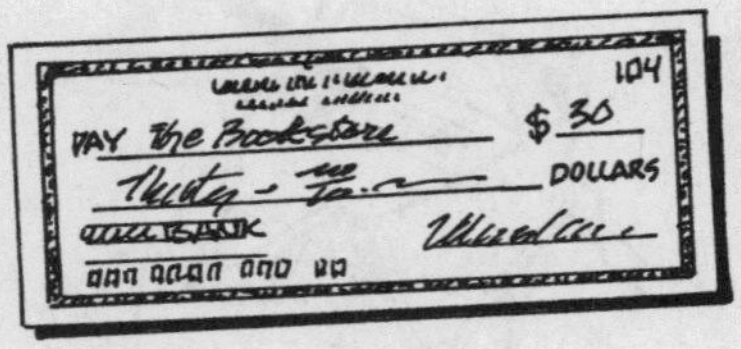
PAY The Bookstore
$ 30
DOLLARS

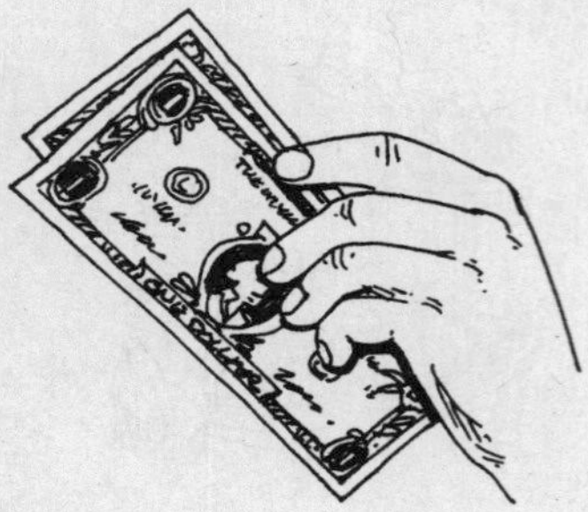

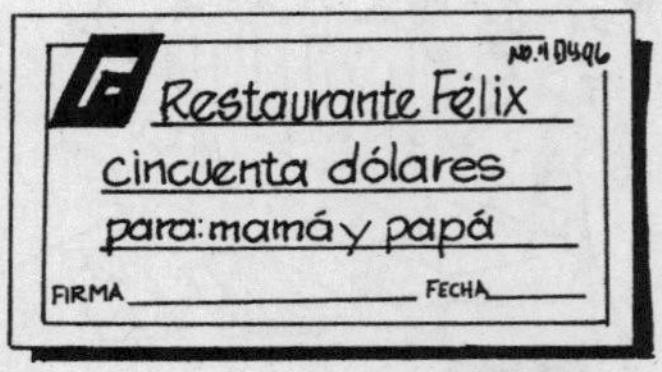
Restaurante Félix
cincuenta dólares
para: mamá y papá
FIRMA
FECHA

flojo, floja

apretado, apretada

vivo, viva

Write the Spanish vocabulary word below each picture. If there is a word or phrase, copy it in the space provided. Be sure to include the article for each noun.

la liquidación ________ ________________	**tan + *adjective*** ________ ________ ________________	**me/te importa(n)** ____________ ________________
claro, clara ________________, ________________	**de sólo un color** ________ ____________ ________ ____________	**oscuro, oscura** ________________, ________________
pastel ________________	**¿De qué está hecho, hecha?** ________ ________ __________ __________, ________________	**Está hecho, hecha de...** __________ __________, __________ ________

Realidades 2 | Nombre ______ | Hora ______

Capítulo 2B | Fecha ______ | **Vocabulary Flash Cards, Sheet 4**

Write the Spanish vocabulary word below each picture. If there is a word or phrase, copy it in the space provided. Be sure to include the article for each noun.

algodón ______	**cuero** ______	**lana** ______
seda ______	**tela sintética** ______ ______	**alto, alta** ______, ______
bajo, baja ______, ______	**gastar** ______	**el precio** ______ ______

Realidades 2 | Nombre ________ | Hora ________

Capítulo 2B | Fecha ________ | **Vocabulary Flash Cards, Sheet 5**

Write the Spanish vocabulary word below each picture. If there is a word or phrase, copy it in the space provided. Be sure to include the article for each noun.

escoger	**estar de moda**	**el estilo**
exagerado, exagerada	**mediano, mediana**	**probarse**
anunciar	**encontrar**	**en realidad**

Write the Spanish vocabulary word below each picture. If there is a word or phrase, copy it in the space provided. Be sure to include the article for each noun.

inmediatamente	**me parece que**	**¿Qué te parece?**
recientemente	**el cheque de viajero**	

Nombre ________________________ Hora ____________

Fecha ____________________

Vocabulary Check, Sheet 1

Tear out this page. Write the English words on the lines. Fold the paper along the dotted line to see the correct answers so you can check your work.

la entrada ____________________

la ganga ____________________

el letrero ____________________

la liquidación ____________________

el mercado ____________________

la salida ____________________

el cajero, la cajera ____________________

el cheque (personal) ____________________

el cheque de viajero ____________________

el cupón de regalo ____________________

en efectivo ____________________

el precio ____________________

la marca ____________________

la talla ____________________

Fold In ←

Vocabulary Check, Sheet 2

Tear out this page. Write the Spanish words on the lines. Fold the paper along the dotted line to see the correct answers so you can check your work.

entrance ____________

bargain ____________

sign ____________

sale ____________

market ____________

exit ____________

cashier ____________

(personal) check ____________

traveler's check ____________

gift certificate ____________

cash ____________

price ____________

brand ____________

size ____________

Fold In ←

Tear out this page. Write the English words on the lines. Fold the paper along the dotted line to see the correct answers so you can check your work.

algodón ______________

cuero ______________

lana ______________

seda ______________

tela sintética ______________

apretado, apretada ______________

flojo, floja ______________

mediano, mediana ______________

estar de moda ______________

encontrar ______________

anunciar ______________

escoger ______________

probarse ______________

Fold In ←

Tear out this page. Write the Spanish words on the lines. Fold the paper along the dotted line to see the correct answers so you can check your work.

cotton ____________

leather ____________

wool ____________

silk ____________

synthetic fabric ____________

tight ____________

loose ____________

medium ____________

to be in fashion ____________

to find ____________

to announce ____________

to choose ____________

to try on ____________

Fold In ←

To hear a complete list of the vocabulary for this chapter, go to Disc 1, Track 4 on the Guided Practice Audio CD or go to www.phschool.com and type in the Web Code jdd-0299. Then click on **Repaso del capítulo.**

Preterite of regular verbs (p. 110)

- Use the preterite tense to talk about actions that were completed in the past. To form the preterite tense of a regular verb, add the preterite endings to the stem of the verb.
- Here are the preterite forms for the verbs **mirar** (to look), **aprender** (to learn), and **escribir** (to write):

yo	**miré** **aprendí** **escribí**	nosotros/nosotras	**miramos** **aprendimos** **escribimos**
tú	**miraste** **aprendiste** **escribiste**	vosotros/vosotras	**mirasteis** **aprendisteis** **escribisteis**
usted/él/ella	**miró** **aprendió** **escribió**	ustedes/ellos/ellas	**miraron** **aprendieron** **escribieron**

A. Write the infinitive form of the underlined verb for each sentence. Follow the model.

Modelo Yo aprendí a leer. *Infinitive:* aprender

1. Tú miraste el letrero. *Infinitive:* ____________
2. Mi papá escribió un cheque. *Infinitive:* ____________
3. Las chicas aprendieron mucho en la clase. *Infinitive:* ____________
4. Nosotros escribimos el libro. *Infinitive:* ____________

B. Choose the verb from the word bank that best completes each sentence.

miró	**aprendieron**	**escribí**	**miré**	**aprendimos**

1. Uds. ____________ a leer en la escuela.
2. Yo no ____________ la carta.
3. Carlos y yo ____________ el inglés.
4. Rafael no ____________ el precio de la camisa.
5. Ayer yo ____________ la tele.

Preterite of regular verbs (*continued*)

- Note that **-ar** and **-er** verbs that have a stem change in the present tense do not have a stem change in the preterite.

  Present tense: **Siempre te pruebas la camisa antes de comprarla.**
  You always try the shirt on before you buy it.

  Preterite tense: **Ayer no te probaste la camisa.**
  Yesterday you didn't try on the shirt.

C. Complete the following paragraph by filling in each blank with the preterite form of **probar** or **encontrar** in parentheses.

La semana pasada yo fui al centro comercial, pero yo no ______________ (**encuentro** / **encontré**) una camiseta de mi talla porque soy grande. Mi mamá también buscó la camiseta ayer pero no la ______________ (**encuentra** / **encontró**). Recientemente, me ______________ (**pruebo** / **probé**) una camiseta apretada y no me gustó. Esta mañana nosotros ______________ (**encontramos** / **encontraron**) una camiseta floja. ¡Qué bien, por fin ______________ (**encuentro** / **encontré**) mi camiseta!

- Verbs that end in **-car, -gar,** and **-zar** have a spelling change in the **yo** form of the preterite.

buscar	**c→qu**	**yo busqué**
pagar	**g→gu**	**yo pagué**
almorzar	**z→c**	**yo almorcé**

D. Read the following conversation. Then, write the **yo** form of the verb in parentheses to complete each sentence.

1. JUAN: ¿Buscaste una camisa nueva?
   EMILIO: Sí, yo (buscar) ______________ una camisa nueva.
2. JUAN: ¿Pagaste la camisa en efectivo?
   EMILIO: Sí, yo (pagar) ______________ en efectivo.
3. JUAN: ¿Almorzaste con Elena en el restaurante?
   EMILIO: Sí, yo (almorzar) ______________ con Elena.

Demonstrative adjectives (p. 114)

Demonstrative adjectives show how close something is to the speaker. Here's a chart that compares the three demonstrative adjectives:

Singular		Plural	
este/esta	*this*	**estos/estas**	*these*
ese/esa	*that*	**esos/esas**	*those*
aquel/aquella	*that one over there*	**aquellos/aquellas**	*those over there*

A. Write the equivalent word(s) in English for each underlined demonstrative adjective. Follow the model.

Modelo Me gustan aquellas camisas blancas. *English:* *those over there*

1. Yo prefiero estas camisas rojas. *English:* ______________
2. A mí me gusta esta gorra roja. *English:* ______________
3. Yo quiero comprar esos zapatos. *English:* ______________
4. A mi madre le gusta esa blusa elegante. *English:* ______________

B. Look at the pictures of clothing below. Then, answer the question by circling the correct demonstrative adjective for each article of clothing. The smallest article of clothing is the farthest away. Follow the model.

Modelo

—¿Qué falda prefieres?
—Prefiero (**esta** / **(aquella)**) falda.

1. 

—¿Qué camisa prefieres?
—Prefiero (**esa** / **esta**) camisa.

2. 

—¿Qué pantalones prefieres?
—Prefiero (**estos** / **aquellos**) pantalones.

3. 

—¿Qué traje prefieres?
—Prefiero (**ese** / **este**) traje.

Using adjectives as nouns (p. 116)

- When you compare two similar things, you can avoid repetition by dropping the noun and using the *article* + the *adjective* for the second thing.

  ¿Cuál prefieres, el vestido apretado o el flojo? *Which do you prefer, the tight dress or the loose one?*

  Prefiero el flojo. *I prefer the loose one.*

A. Answer the questions using each underlined adjective as a noun. Follow the model.

Modelo —¿Pagaste el precio alto o el bajo?
—Pagué el bajo.

1. —¿Compraste la blusa clara o la oscura?
   —Compré ______ ______.
2. —¿Probaste los zapatos caros o los baratos?
   —Probé ______ ______.
3. —¿Encontraste el vestido grande o el mediano?
   —Encontré ______ ______.
4. —¿Te gustan los jeans apretados o los flojos?
   —Me gustan ______ ______.
5. —¿Quieres el número uno o el dos?
   —Quiero ______ ______.

B. Now, answer the questions using the other adjectives.

1. ¿Compraste la blusa clara o la oscura?
   Compré ______ ______.
2. ¿Probaste los zapatos caros o los baratos?
   Probé ______ ______.
3. ¿Encontraste el vestido grande o el mediano?
   Encontré ______ ______.
4. ¿Te gustan los jeans apretados o los flojos?
   Me gustan ______ ______.
5. ¿Quieres el número uno o el dos?
   Quiero ______ ______.

Lectura: Los jeans (pp. 118–119)

A. The reading in your textbook is about the history of jeans. Before you read the selection, think about and answer the following questions.

1. Do you like to wear jeans? Why? ____________

2. Why are jeans popular with many students? ____________

B. The second section from your textbook reading is about jeans and one of its inventors, Levi Strauss. Read the selection and answer the questions. Use the ***Hints*** to help you answer the questions.

> *Un poco de historia*
> *Levis Strauss, un joven alemán, llegó a los Estados Unidos con su familia en 1847 a la edad de 18 años. Después de trabajar algunos años con su familia, Strauss viajó a California para abrir una tienda de ropa y accesorios.*
> *Esta tienda se convirtió en un negocio próspero durante los siguientes 20 años, y Strauss se hizo rico.*

1. What type of store did Strauss open in California? ***Hint:*** Look for the words **una tienda de.**

____

2. What happened over the next 20 years? ***Hint:*** Look for the words **próspero** and **rico.**

____

C. Now, look at the dates and events from the life of Levi Strauss and answer the following questions.

1847: Levi Strauss llegó a los Estados Unidos.
1872: Recibió una carta de Jacob Davis que le explicó un proceso para hacer más fuertes los pantalones. Ellos pidieron la patente de este proceso.
1873: Recibieron la patente y empezaron a fabricar *waist overalls.*

1. When did Levi Strauss arrive in the United States?
   a. 1873 b. 1847
2. Before Levi Strauss and Jacob Davis began to make waist overalls, they needed a
   a. patent. b. letter.
3. When Strauss and Davis received the patent, they began to
   a. make waist overalls. b. explain the process.

Presentación escrita (p. 121)

Task: You received $200 for your birthday and have just purchased some articles of clothing. Write an e-mail to your friend describing your shopping trip.

A. Before you write the e-mail, it would be helpful to organize the information about your purchases. Fill in the table below. The first line is done for you.

	¿Qué compraste?	¿Dónde...?	¿Cuánto pagaste?
1.	*camiseta*	*en el centro comercial*	*$20*
2.			
3.			

B. Answer the following questions about your shopping trip. You can look back at your answers in **part A** to help you.

1. ¿Qué compraste?

   Yo ____________________.

2. ¿Dónde compraste la ropa?

   Yo ____________________.

3. ¿Cuánto pagaste?

   Yo ____________________.

4. ¿Por qué compraste esta ropa?

   Yo ____________________.

C. Use the answers to the questions in **parts A** and **B** to write an e-mail to your friend below. You may use the following model.

> *¡Hola Pedro! Yo recibí $200 en mi cumpleaños. Yo compré ropa en el centro comercial. Compré una camiseta de algodón. Yo pagué $20. Luego, compré una chaqueta de cuero. Pagué $120 por la chaqueta. La chaqueta está de moda y me gusta mucho. ¿Qué te parece mi ropa? Adiós, Antonio.*

____

____

____

____

D. Check your e-mail for spelling, forms of the preterite, and agreement.

Nombre ______ Hora ______

Fecha ______

Vocabulary Flash Cards, Sheet 1

Write the Spanish vocabulary word below each picture. If there is a word or phrase, copy it in the space provided. Be sure to include the article for each noun.

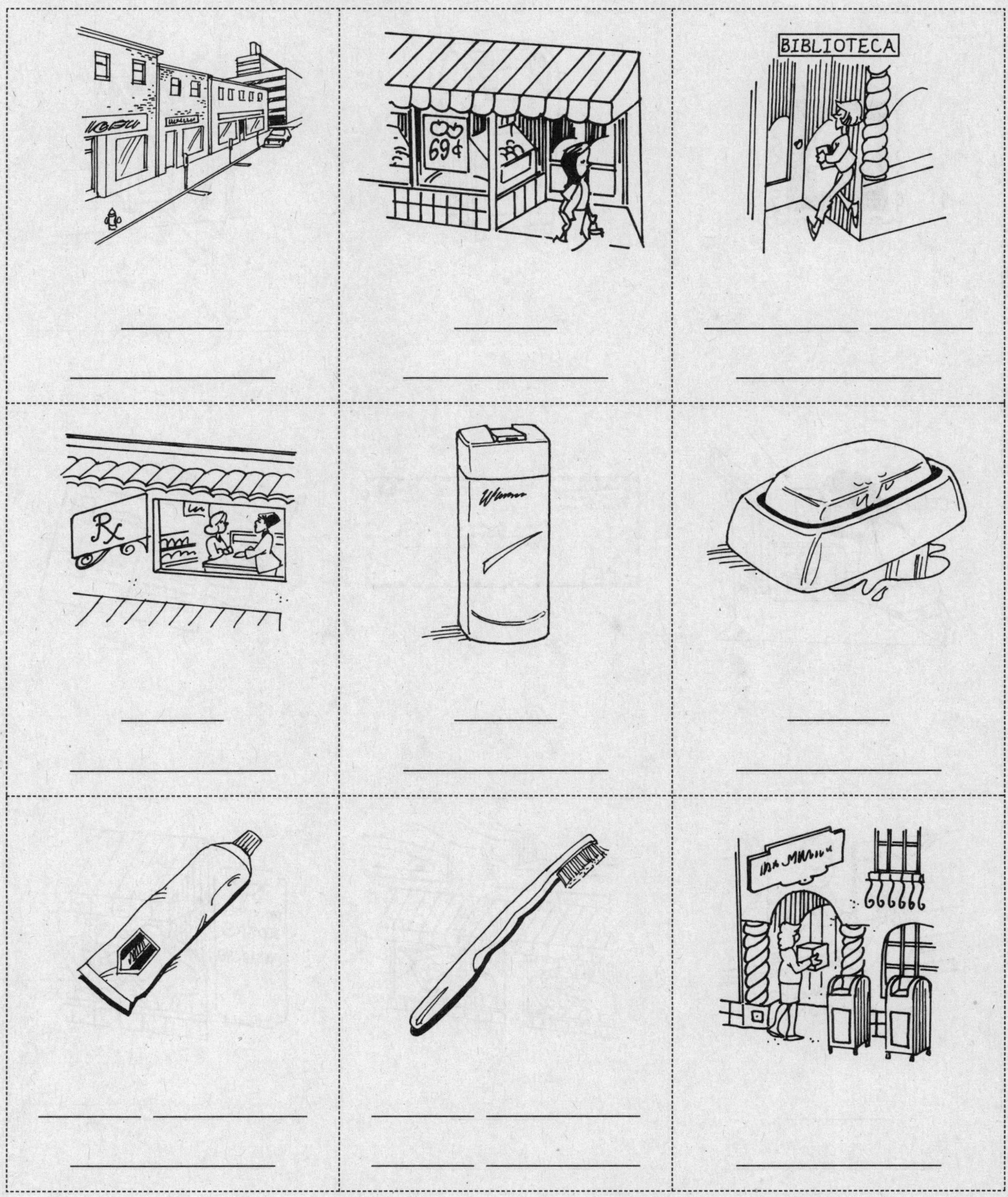

Nombre ____________ Hora ____________

Fecha ____________

Vocabulary Flash Cards, Sheet 2

Write the Spanish vocabulary word below each picture. If there is a word or phrase, copy it in the space provided. Be sure to include the article for each noun.

Realidades 2

Capítulo 3A

Nombre ______ Hora ______

Fecha ______

Vocabulary Flash Cards, Sheet 3

Write the Spanish vocabulary word below each picture. If there is a word or phrase, copy it in the space provided. Be sure to include the article for each noun.

DR. VICTORIA ROJAS CAMACHO		

Write the Spanish vocabulary word below each picture. If there is a word or phrase, copy it in the space provided. Be sure to include the article for each noun.

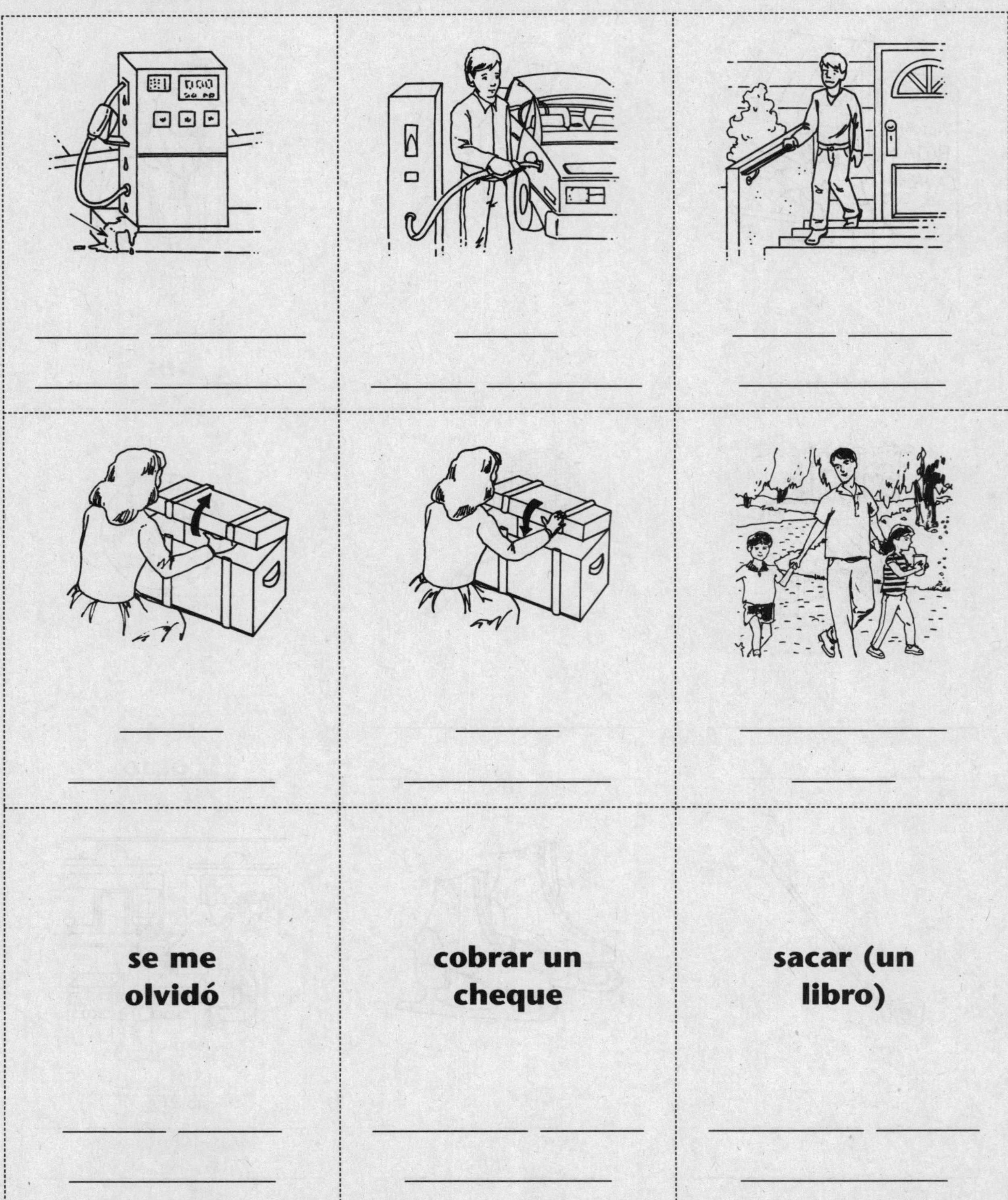

se me olvidó	**cobrar un cheque**	**sacar (un libro)**

Realidades 2

Capítulo 3A

Nombre ____________ Hora ____________

Fecha ____________

Vocabulary Flash Cards, Sheet 5

Write the Spanish vocabulary word below each picture. If there is a word or phrase, copy it in the space provided. Be sure to include the article for each noun.

caramba ________	**casi** ________	**¡Cómo no!** ________ ________
en seguida ________ ________	**hasta** ________	**por** ________
pronto ________	**Hasta pronto.** ________ ________	**quedarse** ________

Write the Spanish vocabulary word below each picture. If there is a word or phrase, copy it in the space provided. Be sure to include the article for each noun.

todavía ____________	**varios, varias** ____________, ____________	**cerrar** ____________
la gasolina ______ ____________	______ ____________	______ ____________
______ ____________	______ ____________	______ ____________

Nombre ______ Hora ______

Fecha ______

Vocabulary Check, Sheet 1

Tear out this page. Write the English words on the lines. Fold the paper along the dotted line to see the correct answers so you can check your work.

la farmacia ______

el supermercado ______

el banco ______

el centro ______

la estación de servicio ______

enviar ______

el sello ______

la tarjeta ______

el buzón ______

todavía ______

cerrar ______

cuidar a ______

devolver (un libro) ______

Hasta pronto. ______

ir a pie ______

Fold In

Tear out this page. Write the Spanish words on the lines. Fold the paper along the dotted line to see the correct answers so you can check your work.

pharmacy ______________

supermarket ______________

bank ______________

downtown ______________

service station ______________

to send ______________

stamp ______________

card ______________

mailbox ______________

still ______________

to close ______________

to take care of ______________

to return (a book) ______________

See you soon. ______________

to go on foot ______________

Fold In ←

Realidades 2 | Nombre ______ | Hora ______

Capítulo 3A | Fecha ______ | **Vocabulary Check, Sheet 3**

Tear out this page. Write the English words on the lines. Fold the paper along the dotted line to see the correct answers so you can check your work.

la carta ______

echar una carta ______

el correo ______

el equipo deportivo ______

el palo de golf ______

los patines ______

la pelota ______

la raqueta de tenis ______

el cepillo de dientes ______

el champú ______

el jabón ______

la pasta dental ______

caramba ______

casi ______

Fold In ←

Tear out this page. Write the Spanish words on the lines. Fold the paper along the dotted line to see the correct answers so you can check your work.

letter	______________
to mail a letter	______________
post office	______________
sports equipment	______________
golf club	______________
skates	______________
ball	______________
tennis racket	______________
toothbrush	______________
shampoo	______________
soap	______________
toothpaste	______________
good gracious	______________
almost	______________

Fold In ←

To hear a complete list of the vocabulary for this chapter, go to Disc 1, Track 5 on the Guided Practice Audio CD or go to www.phschool.com and type in the Web Code jdd-0389. Then click on **Repaso del capítulo**.

Direct object pronouns (p. 138)

- A direct object tells who or what receives the action of the verb. Direct objects may represent people or things.
- To avoid repeating a direct object noun, you can replace it with a direct object pronoun.
  ¿Martín echó la carta ayer? (**La carta** is the direct object.)
  No, la echó hoy. (**La** is the direct object pronoun. It replaces the word **carta**.)
- Here are the direct object pronouns you have already used:

Singular	Plural
lo it, him, you *(masculine formal)*	**los** them, you *(masculine formal)*
la it, her, you *(feminine formal)*	**las** them, you *(feminine formal)*

A. Write the direct object pronoun that replaces the underlined words. Follow the model.

Modelo ¿Quién cobró el cheque? *lo*

1. ¿Cuándo llenaste el tanque del coche? ________
2. ¿Vas a enviar las tarjetas a la tía? ________
3. ¿Sacaron los libros de la biblioteca? ________
4. ¿Él cerró la estación de servicio? ________

B. Write the direct object from the word bank that matches the underlined direct object pronoun in the answers.

las pelotas	el palo de golf	la raqueta de tenis	los patines

1. ¿Dónde está ____________? No lo veo.
2. ¿Tienes ____________? Sí, sí la tengo.
3. ¿Dónde están ____________? No los encuentro.
4. ¿Tienes ____________? Yo no las tengo.

Realidades 2 | Nombre ______ | Hora ______

Capítulo 3A | Fecha ______ | **Guided Practice Activities 3A-2**

Irregular preterite verbs: *ir, ser* (p. 140)

- The preterite forms of **ser** (to be) and **ir** (to go) are the same. Usually the context of the verb is what makes the meaning clear:

  Mi doctora fue la Dra. Serrano. *My doctor was Dr. Serrano.*
  Yo fui a la farmacia. *I went to the pharmacy.*
  (In English, *to go* is generally followed by the preposition *to.* In Spanish, **ir** is generally followed by the preposition **a.**)

- Here are the preterite forms of **ser** and **ir**:

yo	**fui**	nosotros/nosotras	**fuimos**
tú	**fuiste**	vosotros/vosotras	**fuisteis**
usted/él/ella	**fue**	ustedes/ellos/ellas	**fueron**

A. Decide whether the infinitive of the underlined verb is **ser** or **ir**. Then, write your choice in the blank provided. Follow the models.

Modelos Esta mañana Magda fue al supermercado. *ir*

Nuestra visita con el dentista fue por una hora. *ser*

1. Por la mañana fuimos a la farmacia. ______
2. La comedia fue muy divertida. ______
3. El consultorio fue muy aburrido. ______
4. Fui a la tienda de equipo deportivo. ______
5. Las clases fueron interesantes. ______
6. Por la tarde fuimos al centro. ______

Irregular preterite verbs: *ir, ser* (*continued*)

B. Write the correct form of the verb within parentheses. Follow the model.

Modelo Rafael y Hernando no fueron (ir) al consultorio ayer.

1. Anoche yo __________ (ir) al centro.
2. Luego, Marcela y yo __________ (ir) a cobrar un cheque.
3. La noche __________ (ser) divertida.
4. Y tú ¿adónde __________ (ir)?
5. La tarde __________ (ser) aburrida.

Irregular preterite verbs: *hacer, tener, estar, poder* (p. 142)

- The preterite of the irregular verbs **hacer** (to do) and **tener** (to have) follow a similar pattern.

yo	**hice** **tuve**	nosotros/nosotras	**hicimos** **tuvimos**
tú	**hiciste** **tuviste**	vosotros/vosotras	**hicisteis** **tuvisteis**
usted/él/ella	**hizo** **tuvo**	ustedes/ellos/ellas	**hicieron** **tuvieron**

A. Laura is asking Daniel about the chores he and his family had to do yesterday. Complete the dialogue with the correct form of the verb within parentheses.

1. LAURA: ¿Qué __________ (**hicieron / hizo**) tú y tu familia ayer?
   DANIEL: Nosotros __________ (**tuvimos / tuvieron**) que ir al centro.
2. LAURA: ¿Qué __________ (**hizo / hice**) tu papá?
   DANIEL: Él __________ (**tuve / tuvo**) que enviar una carta.
3. LAURA: ¿Qué __________ (**hiciste / hizo**) tu mamá?
   DANIEL: Ella __________ (**tuvo / tuve**) que devolver un libro.
4. DANIEL: Y tú Laura, ¿qué __________ (**hizo / hiciste**) en la noche?
   LAURA: Yo __________ (**tuve / tuviste**) que cuidar a mi hermanito.

Irregular preterite verbs: *hacer, tener, estar, poder* (continued)

- Like the verbs **hacer** and **tener**, the verbs **estar** (to be) and **poder** (to be able) are also irregular in the preterite.
- Here are the preterite forms of **estar** and **poder**:

yo	estuve	nosotros/nosotras	estuvimos
tú	estuviste	vosotros/vosotras	estuvisteis
usted/él/ella	estuvo	ustedes/ellos/ellas	estuvieron

yo	pude	nosotros/nosotras	pudimos
tú	pudiste	vosotros/vosotras	pudisteis
usted/él/ella	pudo	ustedes/ellos/ellas	pudieron

B. Write the missing endings of the preterite forms of **estar** and **poder** in the chart.

yo	1. estuv_____ pude	nosotros/nosotras	estuvimos 5. pud_____
tú	estuviste 2. pud_____	vosotros/vosotras	estuvisteis pudisteis
usted/él/ella	3. estuv_____ 4. pud_____	ustedes/ellos/ellas	6. estuv_____ pudieron

C. Complete each sentence below with verbs from the word bank.

hicimos	**estuve**	**pudimos**	**estuvieron**	**tuvimos**

1. El fin de semana pasado yo __________ en casa.
2. Mi hermano Camilo y yo __________ que hacer una tarjeta para nuestro tío Frank.
3. Nos divertimos mucho, pero casi no __________ terminarla a tiempo.
4. Después eché la tarjeta al buzón y por la noche, nosotros __________ la cena.
5. ¿Dónde __________ ustedes el fin de semana?

Go Online WEB CODE jdd-0306
PHSchool.com

Lectura: La unidad en la comunidad internacional (pp. 146–147)

You will be reading about **Ciudades Hermanas Internacional** or the Sister Cities International Program in your textbook.

A. Headings are a way of organizing ideas in a reading. Look at the following headings from your textbook reading to help you complete the activity.

Ciudades Hermanas Internacional
¡Quiero tener una ciudad hermana!
Intercambio económico
Intercambio cultural
Intercambio educativo

According to the headings, write **L** (for **Lectura**) next to the sentence below if it is something you might find in your reading. Write **N** (for **No**) next to the sentence if it is something you might not find in the reading.

1. El programa de "Ciudades Hermanas Internacional" es para los equipos deportivos. ________
2. La misión de "Ciudades Hermanas Internacional" es el intercambio y la cooperación. ________
3. Las ciudades hermanas pueden tener intercambios educativos, económicos y culturales. ________
4. Cómo tener una ciudad hermana. ________
5. Las ciudades hermanas no pueden ser de diferentes países. ________

B. Read the following excerpt from the reading in your textbook. Try to determine the main idea of the excerpt and place a ✓ next to it.

¡Quiero tener una ciudad hermana!
Cualquier ciudad en los Estados Unidos puede tener una ciudad hermana. Primero es necesario encontrar otra ciudad extranjera. Esta ciudad puede tener alguna relación con la ciudad original.

1. It is difficult for people in the United States to find a sister city. ________
2. People in the United States can easily find a sister city. ________

Presentación oral (p. 149)

Task: Pretend you need to prepare for a trip to Mérida, Mexico. You will visit some Mayan ruins and the beach in Cancún. Remember that it will be very hot and humid.

A. Complete the following chart. Write **Sí** in the middle column, **¿Lo necesitas?**, if you need the item, or **No** if you do not need the item. Then, place a ✓ in the right column, **¿Lo tienes?**, if you already have the item.

Ropa	¿Lo necesitas?	¿Lo tienes?
pantalones cortos	______	______
camisetas	______	______
abrigo	______	______
traje de baño	______	______
sombrero para el sol	______	______
botas	______	______
cepillo de dientes	______	______

B. Review your answers in **part A**. List three items that you need but that you already have at home.

______________________ ______________________ ______________________

C. Pretend you already went shopping for the items you did not have. In the left column, list those items you had to buy for your trip. In the right column, write down where you bought them. The first one is done for you.

Tuve que comprar...	¿Dónde?
pantalones cortos	*el almacén*
______	______
______	______
______	______

D. Use the information in **parts B** and **C** to talk about your trip preparation. The following sentences are provided as a model. You may want to also bring in and show props like articles of clothing.

> *Para mi viaje a México necesito camisetas, pero ya las tengo.*
> *Tuve que comprar unos pantalones cortos en el almacén...*

Nombre ______ Hora ______

Fecha ______ **Vocabulary Flash Cards, Sheet 1**

Write the Spanish vocabulary word below each picture. If there is a word or phrase, copy it in the space provided. Be sure to include the article for each noun.

Realidades 2 | Nombre ______ | Hora ______

Capítulo 3B | Fecha ______ | **Vocabulary Flash Cards, Sheet 2**

Write the Spanish vocabulary word below each picture. If there is a word or phrase, copy it in the space provided. Be sure to include the article for each noun.

Write the Spanish vocabulary word below each picture. If there is a word or phrase, copy it in the space provided. Be sure to include the article for each noun.

________	________	**¡Basta!** ________
De acuerdo. ____ ________	**dejar** ________	**Déjame en paz.** ________ ____ ______
despacio ________	**estar seguro, segura** ____ ______, ________	**Me estás poniendo nervioso, nerviosa.** ____ ______ ________ ________, ________

Nombre ____________ Hora ____________

Fecha ____________

Vocabulary Flash Cards, Sheet 4

Write the Spanish vocabulary word below each picture. If there is a word or phrase, copy it in the space provided. Be sure to include the article for each noun.

peligroso, peligrosa ____________, ____________	**quitar** ____________	**tener cuidado** ____________ ____________
ya ____________	**aproximadamente** ____________	**¿Cómo se va...?** ____________ ____________ ____________
complicado, complicada ____________, ____________	**cruzar** ____________	**desde** ____________

Write the Spanish vocabulary word below each picture. If there is a word or phrase, copy it in the space provided. Be sure to include the article for each noun.

hasta	**por**	**quedar**
seguir	**tener prisa**	**la avenida**
la cuadra	**en medio de**	**parar**

Write the Spanish vocabulary word below each picture. If there is a word or phrase, copy it in the space provided. Be sure to include the article for each noun.

pasar ____________	**el conductor, la conductora** ______ ________, ______ ________	**esperar** ____________
manejar ____________	**el metro** ______ ____________	______ ____________

Realidades 2 | Nombre ________ | Hora ________

Capítulo 3B | Fecha ________ | **Vocabulary Check, Sheet 1**

Tear out this page. Write the English words on the lines. Fold the paper along the dotted line to see the correct answers so you can check your work.

la avenida ________

el camión ________

la carretera ________

el conductor, la conductora ________

el tráfico ________

el cruce de calles ________

la cuadra ________

la esquina ________

la estatua ________

la fuente ________

el peatón ________

el permiso de manejar ________

la plaza ________

el policía, la policía ________

el puente ________

Fold In ←

Tear out this page. Write the Spanish words on the lines. Fold the paper along the dotted line to see the correct answers so you can check your work.

avenue ________

truck ________

highway ________

driver ________
____

traffic ________

intersection ________

block ________

corner ________

statue ________

fountain ________

pedestrian ________

driver's license ________

plaza ________

police officer ________

bridge ________

Fold In ←

Realidades 2 | Nombre ______ | Hora ______

Capítulo 3B | Fecha ______ | **Vocabulary Check, Sheet 3**

Tear out this page. Write the English words on the lines. Fold the paper along the dotted line to see the correct answers so you can check your work.

ancho, ancha ______

¡Basta! ______

De acuerdo. ______

dejar ______

Déjame en paz. ______

despacio ______

esperar ______

peligroso, peligrosa ______

tener cuidado ______

ya ______

cruzar ______

parar ______

pasar ______

quedar ______

Fold In ←

Vocabulary Check, Sheet 4

Tear out this page. Write the Spanish words on the lines. Fold the paper along the dotted line to see the correct answers so you can check your work.

wide ______

Enough! ______

OK. Agreed. ______

to leave, to let ______

Leave me alone. ______

slowly ______

to wait ______

dangerous ______

to be careful ______

already ______

to cross ______

stop ______

to pass, to go ______

to be located ______

Fold In ←

To hear a complete list of the vocabulary for this chapter, go to Disc 1, Track 6 on the Guided Practice Audio CD or go to www.phschool.com and type in the Web Code jdd-0399. Then click on **Repaso del capítulo.**

Direct object pronouns: *me, te, nos* (p. 166)

- Remember that you can replace a direct object noun with a direct object pronoun.
- The pronouns **lo, la, los,** and **las** can refer to people, places, or things. The pronouns **me, te, nos,** and **os** refer only to people, not to places or things.
- Here are all the direct object pronouns.

Singular		Plural	
me	me	**nos**	us
te	me *(familiar)*	**os**	you *(familiar)*
lo	it, him, you *(masculine formal)*	**los**	them, you *(masculine formal)*
la	it, her, you *(feminine formal)*	**las**	them, you *(feminine formal)*

A. Read the following exchanges between Pedro and Lola. In each sentence, underline the direct object pronoun. Follow the model.

Modelo PEDRO: ¿Te habló Lucas por teléfono anoche?
LOLA: No, no me habló por teléfono.

1. PEDRO: ¿Los ayudas a ir hasta la plaza?
   LOLA: Sí, yo los ayudo.
2. PEDRO: ¿Me llevas mañana, Lola?
   LOLA: Sí, te llevo, Pedro.
3. PEDRO: ¿Nos esperan aquí?
   LOLA: Sí, los esperamos aquí.
4. PEDRO: Y tus tijeras, ¿las dejaste en la escuela?
   LOLA: Sí, las dejé allá.
5. PEDRO: ¿Los buscaste a Ricardo y Enrique en la esquina?
   LOLA: Sí, los busqué allá.
6. PEDRO: ¿Me ayudas con la tarea?
   LOLA: Sí, te ayudo.
7. PEDRO: Ella es la conductora, ¿la vas a seguir?
   LOLA: No, no la voy a seguir.

Direct object pronouns (*continued*)

- Remember that in Spanish the subject and the verb ending tell who does the action. The direct object pronoun indicates who receives the action:
  ¿Me escuchas, por favor?
  Can you listen to me please?

B. Read the sentences and decide who is *doing* the action. Then write **X** in the appropriate column. Pay attention to the underlined verb ending. The first one is done for you.

	yo	tú	él/ella	nosotros/nosotras	ustedes/ellos/ellas
1. No te entiendo.	X				
2. Laura te lleva en el coche.					
3. Quieres llevarnos al centro.					
4. Te dejamos en la esquina.					
5. La esperaron en la plaza.					

C. Read the sentences and decide who is *receiving* the action. Then write **X** in the appropriate column. Pay attention to the underlined object pronoun. The first one is done for you.

	yo	tú	él/ella	nosotros/nosotras	ustedes/ellos/ellas
1. No te entiendo.		X			
2. Laura te lleva en el coche.					
3. Quieres llevarnos al centro.					
4. Las dejamos en la esquina.					
5. La esperaron temprano.					

D. Read the sentences and the underlined words. Then, fill in the blanks with the appropriate direct object pronouns.

1. ¿Ves la señal de parada? ¡Tienes que parar!
Sí, sí. _____ veo.

2. ¿Tienes el permiso de manejar?
Sí, _____ tengo.

3. ¿Llevas los materiales a la escuela?
No, no _____ llevo.

4. ¿Elena invitó a tus hermanas y a ti?
Sí, ella _____ invitó.

Go Online WEB CODE jdd-0314
PHSchool.com

Irregular affirmative *tú* commands (p. 168)

- Some verbs have irregular forms for the affirmative **tú** commands. To form the command, take the **yo** form of the present tense and drop the ending **-go.**

infinitive	*yo* form	command form
poner	pon**go**	**pon**
tener	ten**go**	**ten**
decir	di**go**	**di**
salir	sal**go**	**sal**
venir	ven**go**	**ven**

A. Complete the following sentences with the **tú** command of the verb in parentheses. Follow the model.

Modelo (**Salir**) Sal del coche sucio.

1. (**Tener**) __________ tu nuevo permiso de manejar.
2. ¡Miguel, (**venir**) __________ rápido; el tren va a salir!
3. (**Decir**) __________ tu nombre al policía.
4. (**Poner**) __________ el libro en la mesa.

- The verbs **hacer, ser,** and **ir** also have irregular **tú** commands:

hacer: **haz**	ser: **sé**	ir: **ve**

B. Complete the following exchanges with the **tú** command of the verb in parentheses. Follow the model.

Modelo ELISA: ¿Cómo llego a la fiesta, Mamá?
MAMÁ: ¡(**Ir**) Ve en un coche!

1. CARLOS: ¿No se dónde queda la plaza. ¿Qué hago?
MAMÁ: ¡(**Hacer**) __________ una pregunta!
2. PATTY: ¿Qué debo hacer para no recibir multas de la policía?
RUTH: (**Ser**) __________ una buena conductora.
3. ALBERTO: ¿Cómo llego a la Avenida Juárez?
LOLA: ¡(**Ir**) __________ en el metro!

Present progressive: irregular forms (p. 171)

- Remember that you form the present progressive by using **estar** + the present participle:

  Estoy hablando con Lucia.

- Some verbs have irregular present participle forms. To form the present participle of **-ir** stem-changing verbs, the **e** in the stem of the infinitive changes to **i**, and then the **o** in the stem changes to **u**:

decir → **diciendo**	pedir → **pidiendo**	repetir → **repitiendo**
servir → **sirviendo**	seguir → **siguiendo**	dormir → **durmiendo**

A. Choose the verb from the word bank that best completes each sentence. The first one is done for you.

diciendo	durmiendo	pidiendo	repitiendo	sirviendo

1. Tú estás *sirviendo* una comida buena.
2. Teresa no entiende y está ______________ su pregunta.
3. Los niños están ______________ sus nombres.
4. El bebé está ______________.
5. Yo estoy ______________ ayuda.

- To form the present participle of the following **-er** verbs, add **-yendo** instead of **-iendo**:

creer → **creyendo**	leer → **leyendo**	traer → **trayendo**

B. Read the following sentences and circle the correct present progressive form of the verb.

1. Los estudiantes están (**trayendo** / **traiendo**) sus tareas.
2. Nosotras estamos (**leyendo** / **leiendo**) un libro.
3. Mario está (**traiendo** / **trayendo**) la comida.
4. Tú estás (**creyendo** / **creindo**) en mí.

Lectura: ¿Qué es manejar a la defensiva? (pp. 174–175)

A. The reading in your textbook is about defensive driving habits. You will need to understand the meaning of some important words in the reading which you may not know. Sometimes you can use context clues to guess the meaning of unknown words. Read the following sentences and answer the questions.

> *Manejar bien requiere muchos años de práctica. Si puedes practicar todos los días después de obtener tu permiso de manejar de estudiante, es mejor porque así vas adquiriendo experiencia.*

1. In the first sentence, what words tell you what **requiere** means?

____

2. What do you think **vas adquiriendo experiencia** means? How do you know?

____

B. This excerpt is taken from the first section of your textbook reading. Read the excerpt and find the meaning of the words below by using context clues. Circle the choice that best describes the meaning of each word.

> *¿Qué es manejar a la defensiva?*
> *Manejar a la defensiva quiere decir practicar buenos hábitos para no tener colisiones u otra clase de accidentes.*
>
> *Distracciones al manejar*
> *Un buen conductor siempre maneja con atención y se concentra en la carretera, sin pensar en otras cosas que pueden ser distracciones.*

1. Colisiones:
   a. clase de accidentes
   b. clase de gestos

2. Concentrarse:
   a. poner libros en la mochila
   b. poner atención

C. Imagine that you are driving a car. You want to reassure your passenger that you know about safe driving habits. Circle the word in parentheses that best completes each sentence about driving defensively.

1. Estoy (**manejando** / **vistiendo**) con atención.
2. La carretera es estrecha, por eso estoy (**siguiendo** / **poniendo**) mucha atención.
3. No estoy (**diciendo** / **leyendo**) en el coche.
4. No estoy (**manejando** / **durmiendo**).
5. Estoy (**siguiendo** / **durmiendo**) las señales de tráfico.

Presentación escrita (p. 177)

Task: Pretend that you have received your first driver's license. Make a poster that reminds your classmates of safe driving practices and important traffic signs.

A. Look at the traffic signs below. Then, write the meaning of each sign in English in the middle column and in Spanish in the right column.

	English	Spanish
1. ALTO		
2.		
3.		

B. From the following list, write the word describing the meaning of each traffic light color.

seguir **parar** **manejar con cuidado**

rojo ____________, amarillo ____________, verde ____________

C. The following are two actions a driver should take to drive safely. Think about two other actions for safe driving which you have read about in the chapter. Then write them below.

1. manejar despacio por calles estrechas
2. tener cuidado cerca de las señales de tráfico
3. ____________
4. ____________

D. Read through your answers in **parts A, B,** and **C.** Decide which information to use to make a poster about safe driving practices. Be sure to include drawings or photos of traffic signs and some of the safe driving practices.

E. Share your poster with a partner who will check the following:

____ Does the poster present important and accurate information?
____ Is the visual representation clear and easy to understand?
____ Is there anything to add, change, or correct?

Write the Spanish vocabulary word below each picture. If there is a word or phrase, copy it in the space provided. Be sure to include the article for each noun.

Nombre ______ Hora ______

Fecha ______

Vocabulary Flash Cards, Sheet 2

Write the Spanish vocabulary word below each picture. If there is a word or phrase, copy it in the space provided. Be sure to include the article for each noun.

______ ______ ______ ______	______ ______	______ ______
______ ______	______ ______	Los Angelitos ______ ______ ______
______ ______	______ ______	**de niño, de niña** ______ ______, ______ ______

Realidades 2 | Nombre ____ | Hora ____

Capítulo 4A | Fecha ____ | **Vocabulary Flash Cards, Sheet 3**

Write the Spanish vocabulary word below each picture. If there is a word or phrase, copy it in the space provided. Be sure to include the article for each noun.

de vez en cuando	**mentir**	**obedecer**
ofrecer	**permitir**	**por lo general**
todo el mundo	**de pequeño, de pequeña**	**la verdad**

Write the Spanish vocabulary word below each picture. If there is a word or phrase, copy it in the space provided. Be sure to include the article for each noun.

consentido, consentida __________, __________	**desobediente** __________	**generoso, generosa** __________, __________
obediente __________	**tímido, tímida** __________, __________	**travieso, traviesa** __________, __________
coleccionar __________	**el mundo** _____ __________	**portarse bien/mal** __________ __________

Realidades 2 | Nombre ______ | Hora ______

Capítulo 4A | Fecha ______ | **Vocabulary Check, Sheet 1**

Tear out this page. Write the English words on the lines. Fold the paper along the dotted line to see the correct answers so you can check your work.

los bloques ______

la colección ______

la cuerda ______

el dinosaurio ______

la muñeca ______

el muñeco ______

el oso de peluche ______

el tren eléctrico ______

el triciclo ______

el pez ______

la tortuga ______

la guardería infantil ______

el patio de recreo ______

el vecino, la vecina ______

Fold In ←

Tear out this page. Write the Spanish words on the lines. Fold the paper along the dotted line to see the correct answers so you can check your work.

blocks ______________

collection ______________

rope ______________

dinosaur ______________

doll ______________

action figure ______________

teddy bear ______________

electric train ______________

tricycle ______________

fish ______________

turtle ______________

daycare center ______________

playground ______________

neighbor ______________

Fold In ←

Realidades 2 | Nombre ______ | Hora ______

Capítulo 4A | Fecha ______ | **Vocabulary Check, Sheet 3**

Tear out this page. Write the English words on the lines. Fold the paper along the dotted line to see the correct answers so you can check your work.

coleccionar ______

molestar ______

pelearse ______

saltar (a la cuerda) ______

mentir ______

obedecer ______

permitir ______

portarse bien / mal ______

de niño, de niña ______

de vez en cuando ______

Fold In ←

Nombre ______ Hora ______

Fecha ______

Vocabulary Check, Sheet 4

Tear out this page. Write the Spanish words on the lines. Fold the paper along the dotted line to see the correct answers so you can check your work.

to collect	______
to bother	______
to fight	______
to jump (rope)	______
to lie	______
to obey	______
to permit, to allow	______
to behave well/badly	______
as a child	______
once in a while	______

Fold In ←

To hear a complete list of the vocabulary for this chapter, go to Disc 1, Track 7 on the Guided Practice Audio CD, or go to www.phschool.com and type in the Web Code jdd-0489. Then click on **Repaso del capítulo.**

The imperfect tense: regular verbs (p. 194)

- The imperfect tense is used to talk about actions that happened repeatedly in the past.

  Rafael caminaba y Ramiro corría en el parque.
  Rafael used to walk and Ramiro used to run in the park.
- Here are the regular forms of **-ar, -er,** and **-ir** verbs in the imperfect tense:

	jugar	hacer	vivir
yo	jug**aba**	hac**ía**	viv**ía**
tú	jug**abas**	hac**ías**	viv**ías**
usted / él / ella	jug**aba**	hac**ía**	viv**ía**
nosotros / nosotras	jug**ábamos**	hac**íamos**	viv**íamos**
vosotros / vosotras	jug**abais**	hac**íais**	viv**íais**
ustedes / ellos / ellas	jug**aban**	hac**ían**	viv**ían**

- These expressions can cue you to use the imperfect: **generalmente, por lo general, a menudo, muchas veces, de vez en cuando, todos los días, nunca.**

A. Write the infinitive form of each underlined verb. The first one is done for you.

1. Pedro jugaba con muñecos. *jugar*
2. De pequeña, Fernanda molestaba a los vecinos. ____________
3. Mis vecinos coleccionaban trenes eléctricos. ____________
4. Por lo general, tú obedecías a tus padres. ____________
5. Yo ofrecía mis bloques a mi prima cuando ella nos visitaba. ____________
6. Nuestros padres no nos permitián saltar a la cuerda en la casa. ____________
7. De vez en cuando, corriámos en la plaza. ____________
8. Todos vivíamos en la misma ciudad. ____________

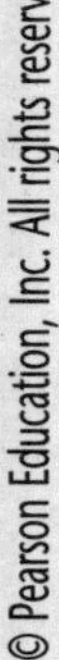

The imperfect tense: regular verbs (*continued*)

B. Complete the sentences below to describe what people *used to do.* Choose the verb from the word bank that best completes each sentence. Follow the model.

dormía	**leías**	**molestaba**
coleccionaban	**se peleaban**	**jugábamos**

Modelo Mario *saltaba* a la cuerda.

1. Ellos ______________ dinosaurios en la escuela primaria.

2. Ellas ______________ todos los días.

3. Nosotros ______________ al tenis los domingos.

4. Yo siempre ______________ con el despertador en la mesita.

5. Alicia siempre ______________ a su hermana.

6. Tú ______________ en la biblioteca los fines de semana.

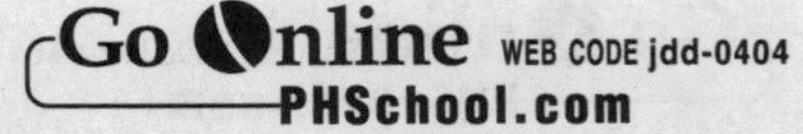

The imperfect tense: irregular verbs (p. 196)

- There are only three irregular verbs in the imperfect tense: **ir, ser,** and **ver.** Here are their forms:

	ir	**ser**	**ver**
yo	**iba**	**era**	**veía**
tú	**ibas**	**eras**	**veías**
usted / él / ella	**iba**	**era**	**veía**
nosotros / nosotras	**íbamos**	**éramos**	**veíamos**
vosotros / vosotras	**ibais**	**erais**	**veíais**
ustedes / ellos / ellas	**iban**	**eran**	**veían**

A. Write the infinitive of the underlined verb in each sentence. Use the chart above to help you. Follow the model.

Modelo Clara y Nubia eran mis amigas. *ser*

1. Por lo general, yo veía a mis primas. ____________
2. Mis primos nunca iban conmigo al mercado. ____________
3. Mis hermanos y yo éramos muy traviesos. ____________
4. ¿Tú veías muchas películas? ____________

B. Complete the following exchanges between a boy and his grandmother. Use the imperfect form of the verb in parentheses. Follow the model.

Modelo NIETO: Abuelita, ¿tú y tus hermanos iban a la escuela todos los días?

ABUELA: Claro, nosotros **(ir)** *íbamos* a la escuela todos los días.

1. NIETO: Oye Abuelita, ¿mi mamá era muy traviesa de niña?

   ABUELA: ¡Sí, tu mamá **(ser)** ____________ muy traviesa!

2. NIETO: ¿Ustedes veían los videos en casa?

   ABUELA: Sí, nosotros generalmente **(ver)** ____________ los videos en casa.

3. NIETO: De niña, ¿ibas a la guardería infantil?

   ABUELA: No, yo **(ir)** ____________ a la casa de mis tíos.

Indirect object pronouns (p. 199)

- An indirect object tells *to whom* or *for whom* something is done.

  Julio siempre les escribe cartas a sus amigos.
- Indirect object pronouns can replace an indirect object.

  Julio escribió una carta a Susana.

  Julio le escribió una carta.
- Indirect object pronouns, especially **le** and **les**, can also be used with an indirect object.

  Julio le escribió una carta a Susana.
- Here are the forms of the indirect object pronouns:

Singular	Plural
me (to / for) me	**nos** (to / for) us
te (to / for) you *(familiar)*	**os** (to / for) you *(familiar)*
le (to / for) him, her, you *(formal)*	**les** (to / for) them, you *(formal)*

- Indirect object pronouns are placed before the verb or attached to the infinitive.

  Mi abuela nunca me quería dar dinero en mi cumpleaños.
  Mi abuela nunca quería darme dinero en mi cumpleaños.

A. Look at the underlined word in each sentence. If it is an indirect object pronoun, write **Sí**. If it is not, write **No**.

1. Yo le pido a mamá una muñeca. ______
2. Mamá me da un oso de peluche. ______
3. Carlos y yo le ofrecemos unos chocolates. ______
4. Claudia va a comprarnos ropa. ______
5. Roberto les ofrece el triciclo a sus hermanas. ______

B. Circle the appropriate indirect object pronoun in parentheses to complete each sentence. The first one is done for you.

1. Generalmente mi abuela (**nos** / **me**) compraba muchos juguetes a nosotros.
2. Mamá y yo siempre (**le** / **nos**) dábamos tarjetas bonitas a la tía.
3. Yo (**te** / **le**) ofrecía dulces a ti en la escuela primaria.
4. Tú siempre (**les** / **te**) dabas osos de peluche a mis hermanas.

Lectura: El grillo y el jaguar (pp. 202–203)

Making predictions is a useful strategy to help prepare you for a reading.

A. The reading in your textbook is a fable from Mexico. Look at the title of the reading and the pictures. Using the fables you know as guide, list three things that you think might happen in the reading.

1. ______
2. ______
3. ______

B. In the following paragraph from the reading, the jaguar challenges the cricket to a race. Read the paragraph and circle the option that describes what you think will happen.

> *—Vamos a hacer una carrera hasta aquella roca enorme que está por donde empiezan las montañas. Si llegas primero, te perdono todo y puedes seguir cantando, pero si llego primero yo, te prohíbo cantar.*

1. El grillo gana la carrera y puede seguir cantando.
2. El jaguar gana la carrera y el grillo no puede cantar.

C. Write the letter of the answer that best completes each sentence based on the fable **El grillo y el jaguar.**

1. Los personajes principales *(main characters)* de esta fábula son: ______
   - **a.** El grillo y el jaguar
   - **b.** El jaguar y el jardin
   - **c.** El grillo y el lago

2. El problema de esta fábula es: ______
   - **a.** El grillo quiere correr tan rápidamente como el jaguar.
   - **b.** El jaguar quiere cantar.
   - **c.** Al jaguar no le gusta la canción del grillo.

3. La moraleja *(moral)* de esta fábula es: ______
   - **a.** El grillo gana porque corre más rápidamente.
   - **b.** El grillo gana porque el jaguar es simpático.
   - **c.** El grillo gana porque es más inteligente.

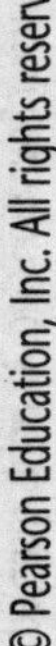

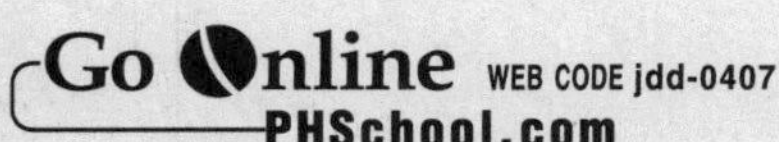

Presentación oral (p. 205)

Task: Describe what you were like when you were a small child and draw a series of pictures that illustrate your sentences.

A. Think about what you were like when you were a small child, what things you used to do, and what things you weren't allowed to do. Then complete the following sentences.

1. Cuando era niño(a), era _______________ y _______________.
2. Yo jugaba con _______________.
3. Me gustaba jugar _______________.
4. Yo tenía que _______________.
5. Mis padres no me permitían _______________.

B. On a separate sheet of paper, make a drawing or cut out pictures from a magazine to illustrate each sentence from **part A.** Number your pictures 1 to 5.

C. Use your sentences from **part A** and your drawings from **part B** to prepare your presentation. You can practice your presentation with a partner. Make sure that:

- your sentences describe the pictures in order
- you use complete sentences
- you speak clearly so that you can be understood

D. Talk about what you were like when you were a child. Use your pictures during the presentation. You can follow the model.

> *De niño(a) yo era obediente. Yo jugaba con mis amigos. Me gustaba jugar con mi triciclo. Yo tenía que portarme bien. Mis padres no me permitían saltar en la cama.*

E. Your teacher will probably grade you on the following:

- the amount of information you communicate
- how easy it is to understand you
- the quality of visuals

Realidades 2

Capítulo 4B

Nombre ______ Hora ______

Fecha ______

Vocabulary Flash Cards, Sheet 1

Write the Spanish vocabulary word below each picture. If there is a word or phrase, copy it in the space provided. Be sure to include the article for each noun.

Realidades 2

Capítulo 4B

Nombre ______ Hora ______

Fecha ______

Vocabulary Flash Cards, Sheet 2

Write the Spanish vocabulary word below each picture. If there is a word or phrase, copy it in the space provided. Be sure to include the article for each noun.

Realidades 2

Capítulo 4B

Nombre ____________________ Hora __________

Fecha ____________________

Vocabulary Flash Cards, Sheet 3

Write the Spanish vocabulary word below each picture. If there is a word or phrase, copy it in the space provided. Be sure to include the article for each noun.

______ ____________	______ ____________	______ ____________
llevarse bien, llevarse mal ______ ______, ______ ______	**felicitar** ____________	**los parientes** ______ ____________
alrededor de ______ ______	**la costumbre** ______ ____________	**divertirse** ____________

Realidades 2 | Nombre ____ | Hora ____

Capítulo 4B | Fecha ____ | **Vocabulary Flash Cards, Sheet 4**

Write the Spanish vocabulary word below each picture. If there is a word or phrase, copy it in the space provided. Be sure to include the article for each noun.

nacer	**la reunión**	**antiguo, antigua**
frecuentemente	**había**	**mientras (que)**
recordar	**el día festivo**	**¡Felicidades!**

Tear out this page. Write the English words on the lines. Fold the paper along the dotted line to see the correct answers so you can check your work.

el bebé, la bebé ______

el aniversario ______

la costumbre ______

el desfile ______

el día festivo ______

la fiesta de sorpresa ______

los fuegos artificiales ______

la reunión ______

los mayores ______

los modales ______

abrazar(se) ______

besar(se) ______

dar(se) la mano ______

Fold In ←

Tear out this page. Write the Spanish words on the lines. Fold the paper along the dotted line to see the correct answers so you can check your work.

baby ____________

anniversary ____________

custom ____________

parade ____________

holiday ____________

surprise party ____________

fireworks ____________

gathering ____________

grown-ups ____________

manners ____________

to hug ____________

to kiss ____________

to shake hands ____________

Fold In ←

Tear out this page. Write the English words on the lines. Fold the paper along the dotted line to see the correct answers so you can check your work.

despedirse (de) ______

saludar(se) ______

sonreír ______

contar (chistes) ______

llorar ______

reírse ______

reunirse ______

casarse (con) ______

charlar ______

cumplir años ______

hacer un picnic ______

nacer ______

regalar ______

recordar ______

Fold In ←

Vocabulary Check, Sheet 4

Tear out this page. Write the Spanish words on the lines. Fold the paper along the dotted line to see the correct answers so you can check your work.

to say goodbye (to) ________

to greet ________

to smile ________

to tell (jokes) ________

to cry ________

to laugh ________

to meet ________

to get married (to) ________

to chat ________

to have a birthday ________

to have a picnic ________

to be born ________

to give (a gift) ________

to remember ________

Fold In ←

To hear a complete list of the vocabulary for this chapter, go to Disc 1, Track 8 on the Guided Practice Audio CD, or go to www.phschool.com and type in the Web Code jdd-0499. Then click on **Repaso del capítulo.**

The imperfect tense: describing a situation (p. 219)

- The imperfect tense is also used to describe people, places, and situations in the past:

  La casa de mis abuelos era pequeña. Tenía dos dormitorios.
  My grandparents' house was small. It had two bedrooms.

A. Circle the correct form of the verb in parentheses that best completes the sentence. The first one is done for you.

1. El bebé (**lloraba** / **lloré**) en la reunión de la familia.
2. Los fuegos artificiales del parque siempre (**eran** / **era**) muy bonitos.
3. De niño, Pablo (**tenía** / **teníamos**) el pelo rubio.
4. A papá le (**gustan** / **gustaba**) contar chistes.
5. Los chicos charlaban en el patio de recreo cuando (**hacía** / **hacíamos**) calor.
6. La profesora (**teníamos** / **tenía**) muchos animales en su casa.
7. Mi amigo Sergio (**era** / **eran**) mi persona favorita.
8. Mis hermanas siempre (**estaba** / **estaban**) cansadas.

B. Complete the following sentences based on your own family or an imaginary family. Choose one of the expressions in the word bank for each sentence and write each verb in the correct imperfect form. Follow the model.

contar chistes	hacer picnics	charlar con los parientes
divertirse	jugar al fútbol	pasar tiempo con las amigos

Modelo Mi papá *contaba chistes*.

1. Mi mamá ______________________.
2. Mis padres ______________________.
3. Mi hermano / hermana ______________________.
4. Yo ______________________.

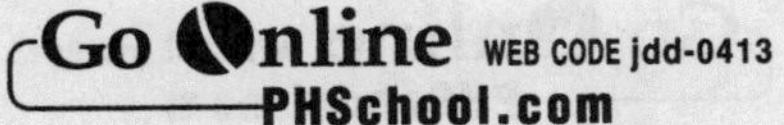
Go Online WEB CODE jdd-0413 PHSchool.com

The imperfect tense (*continued*)

- The imperfect is also used to talk about a past action or situation when no beginning or ending time is mentioned.

  Había mucha gente en la fiesta para el aniversario de mis padres.
  There were many people at the party for my parents' anniversary.

C. In the sentences below, Ana is talking about her childhood friend Dora. Read the sentences and circle the correct form of the verb. The first one is done for you.

1. Los sábados yo __________ al parque con Dora.
   a. iba b. fui
2. En el parque, yo le __________ chistes a mi amiga Dora.
   a. conté b. contaba
3. Dora __________ muy simpática. Ella sonreía y me abrazaba.
   a. era b. fue
4. Nosotras hacíamos un picnic cuando __________ buen tiempo.
   a. hizo b. hacía
5. Nosotros nos __________ con algunos amigos para los picnics.
   a. reunimos b. reuníamos
6. Dora y yo __________ a nuestros amigos frecuentemente.
   a. veíamos b. vimos
7. Mis hermanos también __________ al parque con nosotras.
   a. venían b. vino
8. Dora y su mamá __________ mucho por teléfono.
   a. hablamos b. hablaban
9. Mi mamá y Dora se __________ muy bien.
   a. llevaban b. llevarnos
10. Mis padres siempre __________ cuando veían a Dora.
    a. sonreían b. sonrieron

The imperfect tense (*continued*)

- The imperfect tense is also used to tell what someone was doing when something else happened (preterite):

  Mis parientes charlaban cuando mi mamá entró.
  My relatives were chatting when my mother came in.

D. Juan is asking Gloria about what happened at a party for Marta. Read the questions and answer by writing the correct form of the verb in parentheses. The first one is done for you.

1. JUAN: ¿Qué hacías tú cuando la fiesta empezó?

   GLORIA: Yo *hablaba* **(hablar)** por teléfono cuando la fiesta empezó.

2. JUAN: ¿Qué hacían tus parientes y tú cuando la fiesta empezó?

   GLORIA: Mis parientes y yo ____________ **(charlar)** cuando la fiesta empezó.

3. JUAN: ¿Qué hacía Marta cuando llegaron sus padres?

   GLORIA: Marta ____________ **(contar)** chistes cuando llegaron sus padres.

4. JUAN: ¿Qué hacía Marta cuando le dieron los regalos?

   GLORIA: Marta ____________ **(comer)** un pastel cuando le dieron los regalos.

5. JUAN: ¿Qué hacía la bebé de Marta cuando su abuela entró?

   GLORIA: La bebé ____________ **(jugar)** cuando su abuela entró.

6. JUAN: ¿Qué hacían los primos cuando llegó Ana?

   GLORIA: Los primos ____________ **(beber)** refrescos cuando llegó Ana.

7. JUAN: ¿Qué hacían Luisa y Mariana cuando la fiesta terminó?

   GLORIA: Luisa y Mariana ____________ **(bailar)** cuando la fiesta terminó.

8. JUAN: ¿Qué hacías tú cuando se fueron todos?

   GLORIA: Yo ____________ **(escribir)** sobre la fiesta cuando se fueron todos.

Reciprocal actions (p. 224)

- You can use **se** and **nos** to express the idea "(to) each other:"

  Luis y Jorge se felicitan.

  Luis and Jorge congratulate each other.

A. Write the correct form of the appropriate reflexive verb in the blank.

Modelo Elena y María *se pelean*.

1. Alicia y Cristina ______________.

2. Gregorio y Andrés ______________.

3. Daniel y Susi ______________ de Tomás.

4. Gloria y Francisco ______________.

5. Antonio y Clara ______________.

Go Online WEB CODE jdd-0414 PHSchool.com

Lectura: El seis de enero (pp. 228–229)

A. ***El seis de enero,*** or Three King's Day, is one of the most beloved holidays for children in the Hispanic world. Before this holiday arrives, children write letters to the **Reyes Magos** (Three Kings or Wise Men), just as many children in the U.S. would write to Santa Claus. Circle the things you would expect to find in a letter to the **Reyes Magos.**

1. Los niños dicen sus nombres.
2. Los niños dicen que se portan bien.
3. Los niños dicen que se portan mal.
4. Los niños dicen qué juguetes quieren.

B. Now read the following letter to the **Reyes Magos.** Answer the questions that follow.

> 4 de enero
>
> Queridos Reyes:
>
> Yo soy Carolina y quiero decirles que me porto bien con mami, papi, la maestra. Les escribo para pedirles una bicicleta rosada. Muchas gracias. Feliz año nuevo.
>
> Les quiere,
>
> Carolina

1. See if you can find in the letter any of the things that you circled in **part A.** List three of them in English.

   ______, ______, ______

2. ¿Qué regalo pide Carolina? ______
3. ¿De qué color es la bicicleta? ______

C. Imagine that you're writing to the **Reyes Magos** or to Santa Claus. Write about two gifts that you would like to have and tell why you want each.

Yo quiero ______ y ______.

Yo quiero ______ porque ______.

Yo quiero ______ porque ______.

Presentación escrita (p. 231)

Task: Some friends want to learn more about your favorite celebration or holiday. Write a paragraph describing such an event from your childhood.

A. Read the names of the following celebrations. Then, circle three of your favorite celebrations.

¿Qué celebrabas con tu familia?			
El Día de los Reyes Magos	El Día de la Madre	La Navidad *(Christmas)*	La Semana Santa *(Easter week)*
El Año Nuevo	Halloween	El Día del Padre	El Día de Acción de Gracias

B. Which of the celebrations or holidays from **part A** was your favorite when you were younger? Why was this your favorite celebration? Name the celebration and then give two reasons below.

______________ era mi celebración favorita porque ______________

y ______________.

C. Use the chart below to think about what happened during your favorite celebration. What did you use to do? Where did you get together? Who was there? Circle all the expressions that describe the celebration.

¿Qué hacían?	¿Dónde se reunían?	¿Quiénes estaban?
bailábamos había muchos regalos comíamos mucho	en nuestra casa en casa de los abuelos en casa de mis tíos	mis primos y parientes los amigos muchos niños

D. Now, use the imperfect tense to write a paragraph about your favorite celebration. The following is a model.

El Día de los Reyes Magos era mi celebración favorita. Lo celebraba con mi familia. Nosotros íbamos a la casa de los abuelos. Me gustaba mucho porque había muchos regalos. Siempre jugaba con mis primos.

E. Read your paragraph and check for correct spelling and vocabulary use. Share your paragraph with a partner, who should check the following:

____ Is the paragraph easy to understand?
____ Does it provide an interesting description of the event?
____ Is there anything you should add?
____ Are there any errors?

Realidades 2

Capítulo 5A

Nombre ______________________ Hora ____________

Fecha ______________________

Vocabulary Flash Cards, Sheet 1

Write the Spanish vocabulary word below each picture. If there is a word or phrase, copy it in the space provided. Be sure to include the article for each noun.

Write the Spanish vocabulary word below each picture. If there is a word or phrase, copy it in the space provided. Be sure to include the article for each noun.

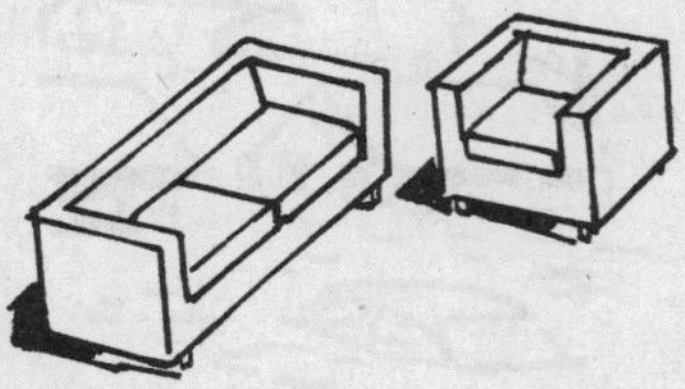

Write the Spanish vocabulary word below each picture. If there is a word or phrase, copy it in the space provided. Be sure to include the article for each noun.

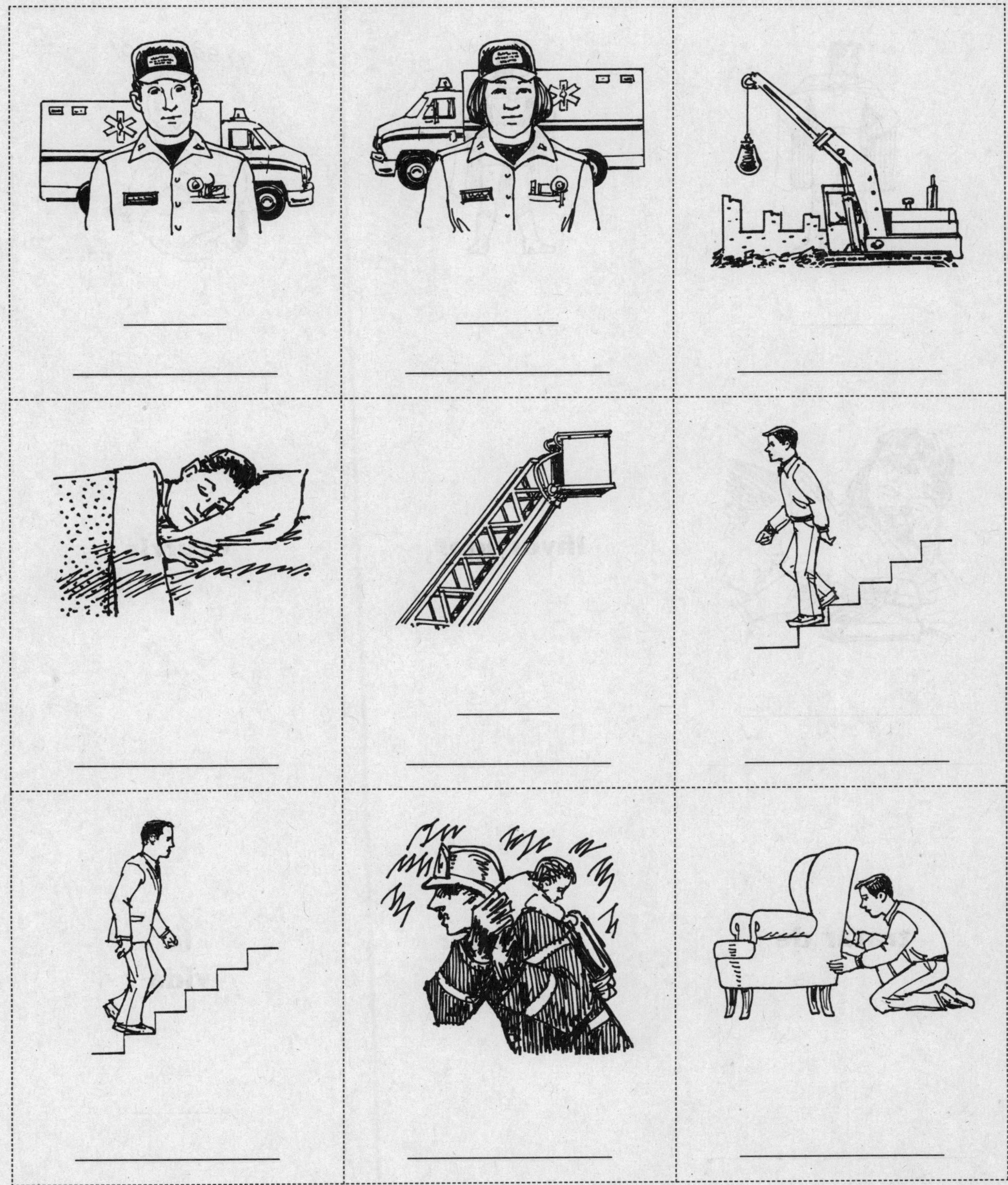

Realidades 2 Nombre ______ Hora ______

Capítulo 5A Fecha ______ **Vocabulary Flash Cards, Sheet 4**

Write the Spanish vocabulary word below each picture. If there is a word or phrase, copy it in the space provided. Be sure to include the article for each noun.

investigar

ocurrir

tratar de

comenzar

la vida

Nombre ______ Hora ______

Fecha ______ **Vocabulary Flash Cards, Sheet 5**

Write the Spanish vocabulary word below each picture. If there is a word or phrase, copy it in the space provided. Be sure to include the article for each noun.

escaparse ______	**muerto, muerta** ______, ______	**herido, herida** ______, ______
el herido, la herida ______ ______, ______ ______	**salvar** ______	**valiente** ______
vivo, viva ______, ______	**a causa de** ______ ______ ______	**asustado, asustada** ______, ______

Write the Spanish vocabulary word below each picture. If there is a word or phrase, copy it in the space provided. Be sure to include the article for each noun.

la causa	**de prisa**	**de repente**
gritar	**hubo**	**se murieron**
oír	**sin duda**	**el noticiero**

Write the Spanish vocabulary word below each picture. If there is a word or phrase, copy it in the space provided. Be sure to include the article for each noun.

afortunadamente ________	**la tormenta** ____ ________	**quemar(se)** ________
____ ________	____ ________	____ ________
____ ________	____ ________	____ ________

Realidades 2 | Nombre ____ | Hora ____

Capítulo 5A | Fecha ____ | **Vocabulary Check, Sheet 1**

Tear out this page. Write the English words on the lines. Fold the paper along the dotted line to see the correct answers so you can check your work.

llover ____

nevar ____

el terremoto ____

la tormenta ____

el artículo ____

el locutor,
la locutora ____

el noticiero ____

ocurrir ____

el reportero,
la reportera ____

apagar ____

el bombero,
la bombera ____

la escalera ____

escaparse ____

esconderse ____

Fold In ←

Realidades 2 | Nombre ______ | Hora ______

Capítulo 5A | Fecha ______

Vocabulary Check, Sheet 2

Tear out this page. Write the Spanish words on the lines. Fold the paper along the dotted line to see the correct answers so you can check your work.

to rain ______

to snow ______

earthquake ______

storm ______

article ______

announcer ______

newscast ______

to occur ______

reporter ______

to put out (fire) ______

firefighter ______

ladder ______

to escape ______

to hide (oneself) ______

Fold In ←

Realidades 2 Nombre _______________ Hora _______

Capítulo 5A Fecha _______________ **Vocabulary Check, Sheet 3**

Tear out this page. Write the English words on the lines. Fold the paper along the dotted line to see the correct answers so you can check your work.

el humo ____________________

el incendio ____________________

el paramédico, la paramédica ____________________

quemar(se) ____________________

el herido, la herida ____________________

rescatar ____________________

salvar ____________________

la vida ____________________

vivo, viva ____________________

afortunadamente ____________________

asustado, asustada ____________________

la causa ____________________

gritar ____________________

¡Socorro! ____________________

Fold In ←

Tear out this page. Write the Spanish words on the lines. Fold the paper along the dotted line to see the correct answers so you can check your work.

smoke ______

fire ______

paramedic ______

to burn (oneself), to burn up ______

injured person ______

to rescue ______

to save ______

life ______

living, alive ______

fortunately ______

frightened ______

cause ______

to scream ______

Help! ______

Fold In ←

To hear a complete list of the vocabulary for this chapter, go to Disc 2, Track 1 on the Guided Practice Audio CD, or go to www.phschool.com and type in the Web Code jdd-0589. Then click on **Repaso del capítulo**.

The imperfect tense: other uses (p. 248)

- You can use the imperfect tense to tell what time it was **(qué hora era)**, or what the weather was like **(qué tiempo hacía)** when something happened.

  Eran las cinco de la mañana cuando el huracán comenzó.

  It was five in the morning when the hurricane began.

A. Read the following sentences and circle the correct verb in parentheses. Follow the model.

Modelo ¿Qué hora era cuando terminó el noticiero?
(**Eran** / **Fueron**) las diez de la noche.

1. ¿Qué tiempo hacía cuando te levantaste?

   (**Llovía** / **Llovió**) mucho cuando me levanté.

2. ¿Qué tiempo hacía cuando saliste de casa?

   (**Nevó** / **Nevaba**) cuando salí de casa.

3. ¿Qué hora era cuando comenzó el huracán?

   (**Eran** / **Fueron**) las tres de la tarde cuando comenzó el huracán.

4. ¿Qué tiempo hacía cuando comenzó la inundación?

   (**Hubo** / **Había**) una tormenta de lluvia cuando comenzó la inundación.

5. ¿Qué hora era cuando viste el incendio?

   (**Era** / **Eran**) la una de la tarde cuando vi el incendio.

6. ¿Qué hora era cuando te acostaste?

   (**Eran** / **Era**) las nueve cuando me acosté.

7. ¿Qué tiempo hacía cuando llegaste a casa?

   (**Hacía** / **Hacían**) mal tiempo cuando llegué a casa.

8. ¿Qué hora era cuando tu hermano volvió a casa?

   (**Eran** / **Era**) las doce cuando mi hermano volvió a casa.

The imperfect tense: other uses (*continued*)

- The imperfect tense is also used to tell how a person was feeling when something happened.

  Anoche me acosté temprano porque tenía sueño.

  Last night I went to bed early because I was sleepy.

B. Look at the expressions in the word bank. Choose the expression that best completes each sentence. Follow the model.

estaban tristes	**tenía sueño**	**estaba cansado**	**estaban contentas**
tenías sed	**estaba asustada**	**estábamos nerviosos**	**tenía prisa**

Modelo Queríamos comer algo porque nosotros *teníamos* *hambre*.

1. Juanita gritó porque ella ________ ________.
2. Después de rescatar al gato, Luisa y Victoria ________ ________.
3. Tú tomaste mucha agua porque ________ ________.
4. Salí temprano porque yo ________ ________.
5. Cuando llegamos al edificio de apartamentos, nosotros ________ ________.
6. Cuando apagaron el incendio, el bombero ________ ________.
7. María se acostó temprano porque ________ ________.
8. Los paramédicos lloraban porque ________ ________.

C. Complete the sentences in the first column by choosing a phrase from the second column. Write the letter of the appropriate phrase in the blank.

1. Miguel estudiaba mucho y... ______.
2. La mujer bajaba las escaleras lentamente porque... ______.
3. Los niños hacían ejercicio todos los días y... ______.
4. Nosotros oíamos la música de los vecinos y... ______.
5. Tú te escondiste en el edificio porque... ______.

a. era una noche oscura.
b. después ellos tenían sed.
c. tenías miedo de las explosiones.
d. no quería salir con nosotros.
e. estábamos cansados de oírla.

Go Online WEB CODE jdd-0504
PHSchool.com

Realidades 2 | Nombre ____________ Hora ____________

Capítulo 5A | Fecha ____________ **Guided Practice Activities 5A-3**

The imperfect tense: other uses (*continued*)

- Remember that **hubo** and **había** are forms of **haber**. Both words mean "there was" or "there were." Look at these rules:
- Use **hubo** to say that an event (such as a fire) took place.
  Hubo un incendio ayer.
- Use **había** to describe a situation in the past.
  Había mucho humo en el edificio.

D. Complete each sentence below with **hubo** or **había**.

1. ______________ un terremoto en esta ciudad.
2. ______________ poca gente en las calles.

3. ______________ muchos heridos.
4. ______________ un incendio a las siete de la mañana.

5. ______________ una inundación en la ciudad.
6. ______________ muchas casas destruidas.

E. Choose the verb from the word bank that best completes each sentence. The first one is done for you.

hubo	estábamos	gritaban	eran	sabía	tenía

Recuerdo que (1.) ___hubo___ un terremoto en la ciudad. (2.) ____________ las seis de la tarde. Algunas personas (3.) ____________. Todos (4.) ____________ muy asustados. Yo no (5.) ____________ qué hacer. Yo (6.) ____________ mucho miedo.

The preterite of the verbs *oír, leer, creer,* and *destruir* (p. 250)

- The verbs **oír, leer, creer,** and **destruir** are irregular in the preterite. Here are their preterite forms.

yo	**oí**	**leí**	**creí**	**destruí**
tú	**oíste**	**leíste**	**creíste**	**destruiste**
usted/él/ella	**oyó**	**leyó**	**creyó**	**destruyó**
nosotros/nosotras	**oímos**	**leímos**	**creímos**	**destruimos**
vosotros/vosotras	**oísteis**	**leísteis**	**creísteis**	**destruisteis**
ustedes/ellos/ellas	**oyeron**	**leyeron**	**creyeron**	**destruyeron**

A. Read the sentences below and look at the underlined verbs. Write an **X** in either the **Present** or the **Preterite** column, according to the tense of the underlined verb. The first one is done for you.

	Present	Preterite
1. Anoche oí un grito en la casa.	______	X
2. Ella oye al locutor por la radio.	______	______
3. ¿Tú crees que la gente se escapó?	______	______
4. Nosotros creímos al reportero.	______	______
5. El incendio destruyó el edificio de apartamentos.	______	______
6. Anoche Amalia leyó el artículo del terremoto.	______	______

B. In the following sentences, circle the correct form of the verb in parentheses.

1. Ayer tú (**oí** / **oíste**) el noticiero en la radio.
2. Mis padres (**creyeron** / **creíste**) las noticias.
3. El huracán (**destruyó** / **destruí**) las casas.
4. Los bomberos (**oyó** / **oyeron**) la explosión.
5. El incendio (**destruyó** / **destruyeron**) los muebles.

Lectura: Desastre en Valdivia, Chile (pp. 256–257)

A. Read the two paragraphs below about three disasters in Valdivia, Chile, from the reading in your textbook. Then answer the questions that follow.

> *A las seis y dos minutos de la mañana, el 21 de mayo de 1960, una gran parte del país sintió el primer terremoto. El próximo día, el 22 de mayo a las tres y diez de la tarde, otro terremoto más intenso. . .ocurrió.*
>
> *Unos minutos después del desastroso terremoto, llegó un tsunami que destruyó lo poco que quedaba en la ciudad y en las pequeñas comunidades. La gran ola de agua se levantó destruyendo a su paso casas, animales, botes y, por supuesto, muchas vidas humanas.*

1. Cognates are words that are very similar to words you may already know in English. What do you think these words mean?

a. tsunami ____________ **d.** simplemente ____________

b. intensidad ____________ **e.** registrado ____________

c. epicentro ____________ **f.** desastroso ____________

2. ¿A qué hora ocurrió el primer terremoto? ¿Y el segundo?

____

3. Escribe tres cosas que destruyó el tsunami.

____

B. Read the following rules from your textbook reading about what to do and not to do during an earthquake. Place an **X** next to the things you *should not* do.

Si estás en un edificio durante un terremoto:

1. Debes mantener la calma. ______

2. Debes mantenerte cerca de las ventanas. ______

3. Debes utilizar los elevadores. ______

Si estás fuera de un edificio durante un terremoto:

4. Debes estar lejos de los postes de energía eléctrica. ______

5. Debes ir a un edificio alto. ______

Presentación oral (p. 259)

Task: You and a partner will role-play an interview about an imaginary fire that happened in your town or city. You will need to create a list of questions and answers for the interview. Use your lists during the interview.

A. Read the following phrases. Write **dónde** if the phrase describes *where* the fire happened. Write **cuándo** if it describes *when* it happened. Write **quién** if it names people *who* were involved. Write **por qué** if it describes *why* it happened. Follow the model.

Modelo problema eléctrico *por qué*

1. en una escuela ______
2. ayer por la noche ______
3. una explosión ______
4. muchos niños ______
5. a las cinco de la mañana ______
6. un cable eléctrico ______
7. en un edificio ______
8. algunas personas ______

B. Use the information from **part A** or make up your own to answer the following questions about the fire. The first one is done for you.

1. ¿Dónde fue el incendio? *El incendio fue en un edificio.*
2. ¿Cuándo ocurrió? ______
3. ¿Quiénes estaban allí? ______
4. ¿Por qué ocurrió? ______

C. Use the questions and your answers from **part B** to practice for the interview.

D. Your teacher will tell you which role to play. Listen to your partner's questions or answers and keep the interview going. Remember that you should ask or tell "when," "where," and "why" the imaginary fire occurred and "who" was involved. Complete the paragraph below to start the interview.

Anoche hubo un incendio en ______. Los bomberos estuvieron allí ______. ______ se salvaron. El incendio ocurrió porque ______.

Nombre ____________________ Hora ________

Fecha ____________________

Vocabulary Flash Cards, Sheet 1

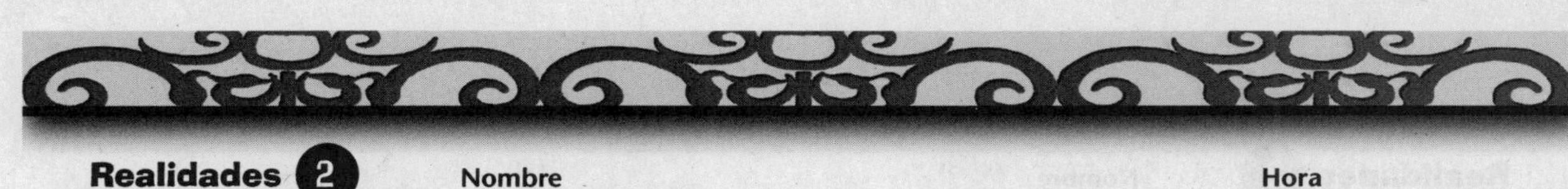

Write the Spanish vocabulary word below each picture. If there is a word or phrase, copy it in the space provided. Be sure to include the article for each noun.

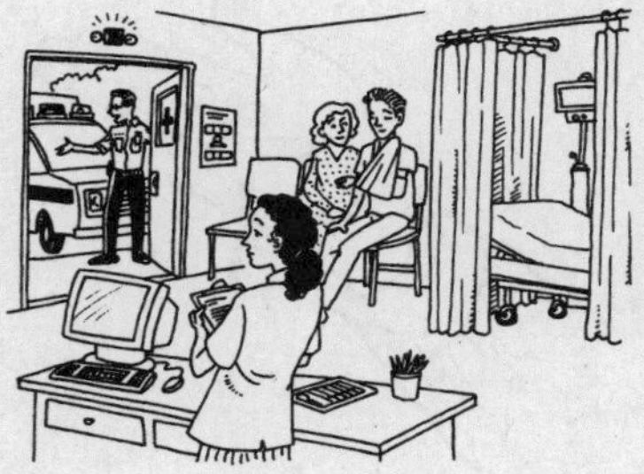

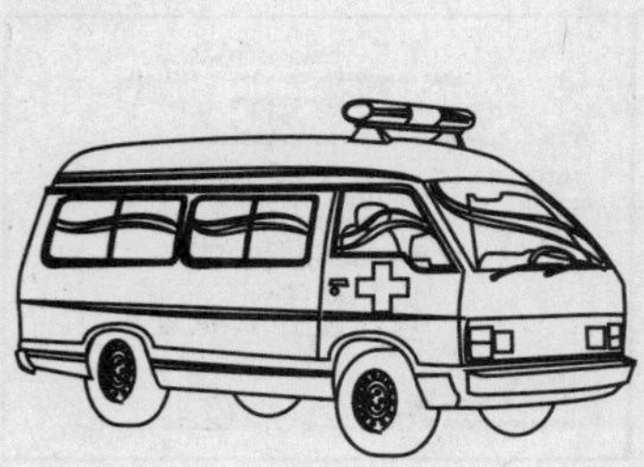

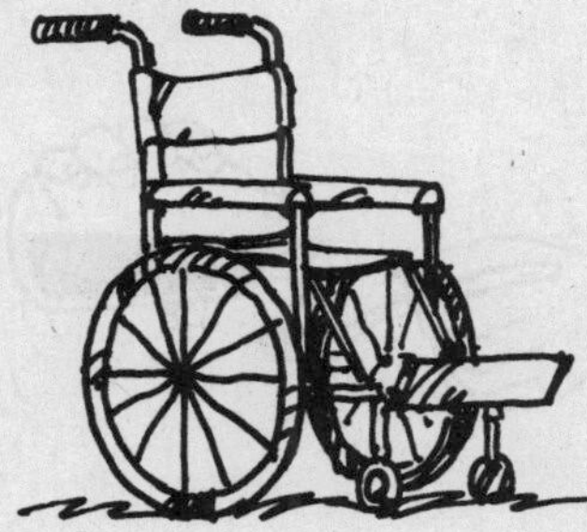

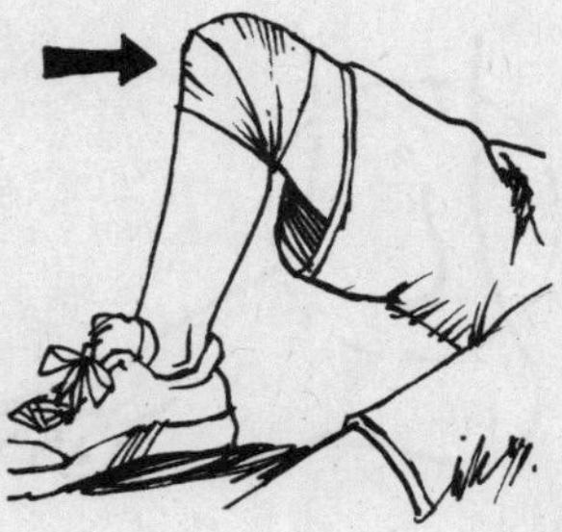

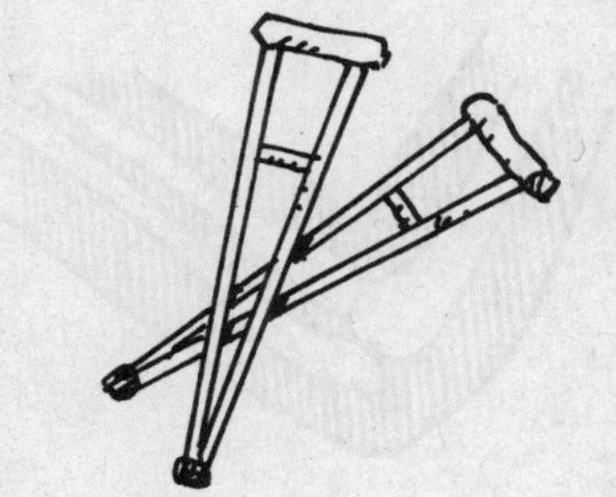

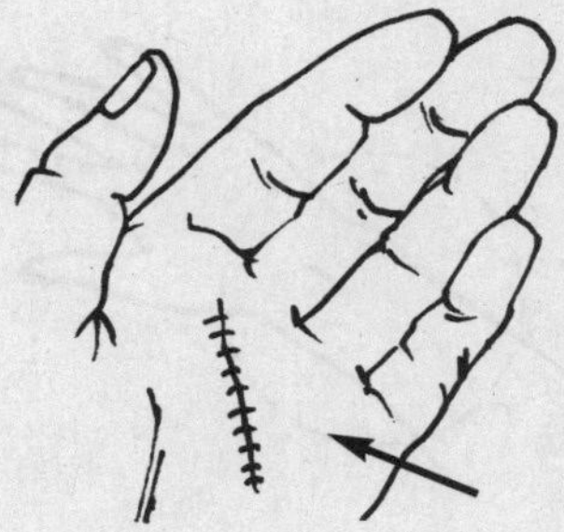

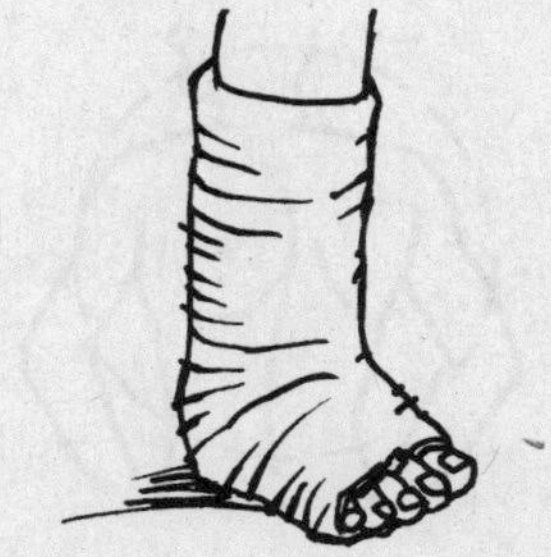

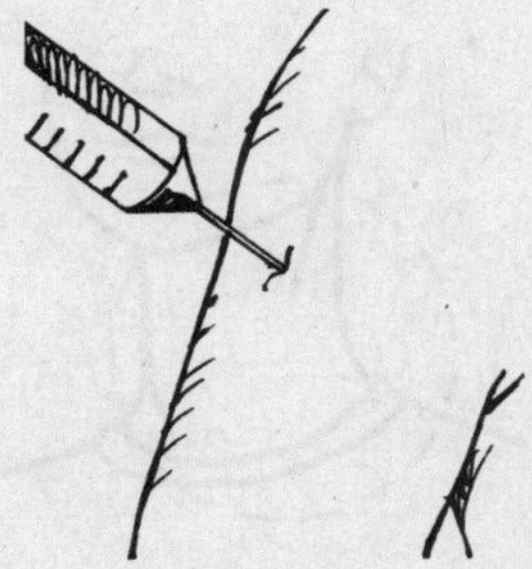

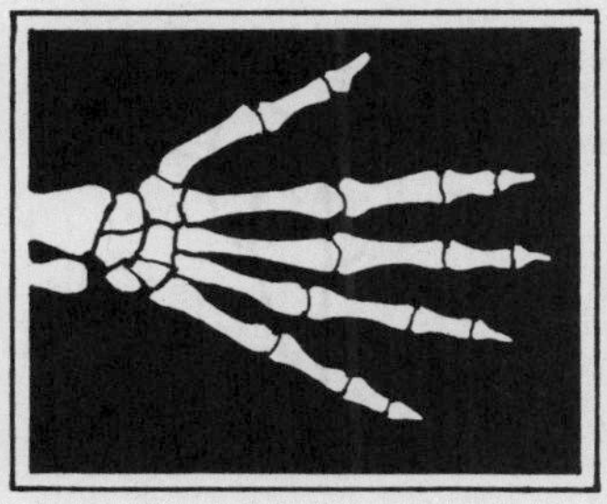

Write the Spanish vocabulary word below each picture. If there is a word or phrase, copy it in the space provided. Be sure to include the article for each noun.

Realidades 2

Capítulo 5B

Nombre ______ Hora ______

Fecha ______

Vocabulary Flash Cards, Sheet 3

Write the Spanish vocabulary word below each picture. If there is a word or phrase, copy it in the space provided. Be sure to include the article for each noun.

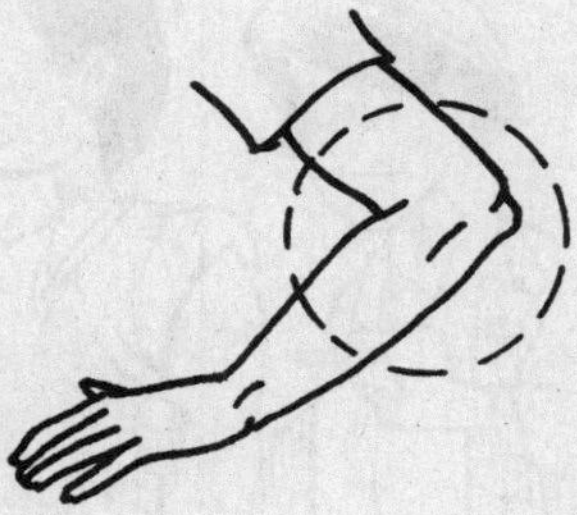

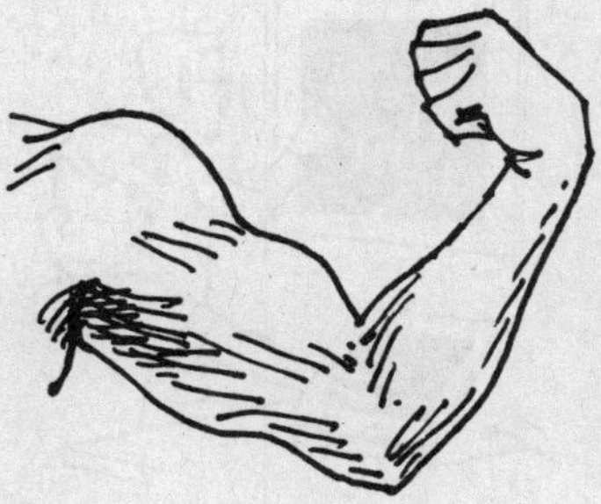

Realidades 2 | Nombre | Hora

Capítulo 5B | Fecha | **Vocabulary Flash Cards, Sheet 4**

Write the Spanish vocabulary word below each picture. If there is a word or phrase, copy it in the space provided. Be sure to include the article for each noun.

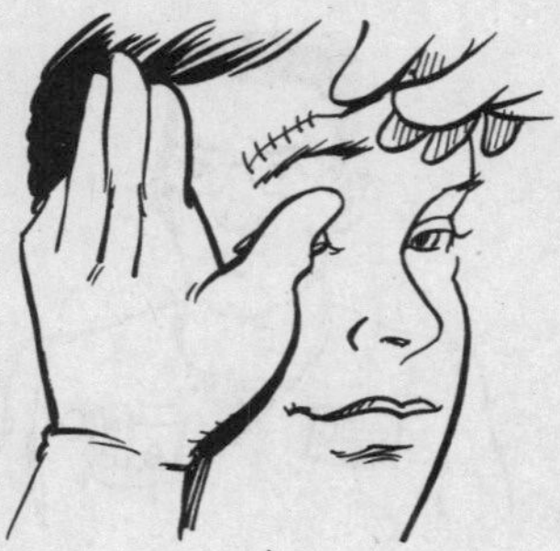

doler

pobrecito, pobrecita

Write the Spanish vocabulary word below each picture. If there is a word or phrase, copy it in the space provided. Be sure to include the article for each noun.

la sangre	**recetar**	**roto, rota**
me caigo	**el accidente**	**te caes**
se cayeron	**cortarse**	**¿Qué te pasó?**

Vocabulary Flash Cards, Sheet 6

Write the Spanish vocabulary word below each picture. If there is a word or phrase, copy it in the space provided. Be sure to include the article for each noun.

torcerse	**sentirse**	**moverse**
¡Qué lástima!		

Realidades 2 Nombre Hora

Capítulo 5B Fecha **Vocabulary Check, Sheet 1**

Tear out this page. Write the English words on the lines. Fold the paper along the dotted line to see the correct answers so you can check your work.

el enfermero, la enfermera ______

la inyección ______

la medicina ______

las pastillas ______

las puntadas ______

la radiografía ______

la receta ______

la sala de emergencia ______

la sangre ______

la venda ______

el yeso ______

el accidente ______

la ambulancia ______

cortarse ______

lastimarse ______

Fold In ←

Realidades 2 | Nombre ______ | Hora ______

Capítulo 5B | Fecha ______ | **Vocabulary Check, Sheet 2**

Tear out this page. Write the Spanish words on the lines. Fold the paper along the dotted line to see the correct answers so you can check your work.

nurse ______

injection, shot ______

medicine ______

pills ______

stitches ______

X-ray ______

prescription ______

emergency room ______

blood ______

bandage ______

cast ______

accident ______

ambulance ______

to cut oneself ______

to hurt oneself ______

Fold In

Realidades 2 Nombre _______________ Hora _______

Capítulo 5B Fecha _______________ **Vocabulary Check, Sheet 3**

Tear out this page. Write the English words on the lines. Fold the paper along the dotted line to see the correct answers so you can check your work.

romperse _______________

torcerse _______________

tropezar (con) _______________

el codo _______________

el cuello _______________

la espalda _______________

el hombro _______________

el hueso _______________

la muñeca _______________

el músculo _______________

la rodilla _______________

el tobillo _______________

pobrecito, pobrecita _______________

Fold In ←

Realidades 2

Capítulo 5B

Nombre ____________ Hora ____________

Fecha ____________

Vocabulary Check, Sheet 4

Tear out this page. Write the Spanish words on the lines. Fold the paper along the dotted line to see the correct answers so you can check your work.

to break, to tear ____________

to twist, to sprain ____________

to trip (over) ____________

elbow ____________

neck ____________

back ____________

shoulder ____________

bone ____________

wrist ____________

muscle ____________

knee ____________

ankle ____________

poor thing ____________

Fold In ←

To hear a complete list of the vocabulary for this chapter, go to Disc 2, Track 2 on the Guided Practice Audio CD, or go to www.phschool.com and type in the Web Code jdd-0599. Then click on **Repaso del capítulo.**

Irregular preterites: *venir, poner, decir,* and *traer* (p. 274)

- The verbs **venir, poner, decir,** and **traer** have a similar pattern in the preterite as that of **estar, poder,** and **tener**. They have irregular stems.

Infinitive	Stem
decir	dij-
estar	estuv-
poder	pud-
poner	pus-
tener	tuv-
traer	traj-
venir	vin-

Irregular Preterite Endings	
-e	-imos
-iste	-isteis
-o	-ieron, -eron

A. Look at the drawings showing what happened to Diego. Then, read the sentences and write the infinitive of the underlined verb next to each sentence. The first one has been done for you.

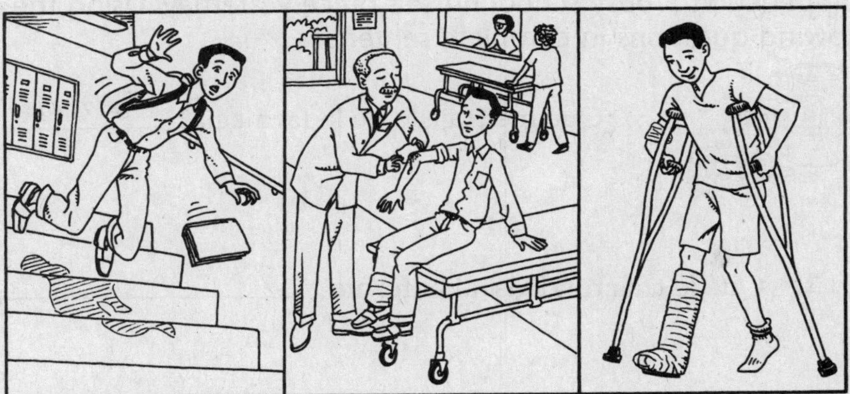

1. Ayer Diego tuvo un accidente. *tener*
2. Él tuvo que ir a la sala de emergencia. ________
3. Enrique estuvo con él en el hospital. ________
4. Diego no pudo moverse por dos horas. ________
5. Después el enfermero le puso una venda en el brazo. ________
6. Diego tuvo que caminar con muletas. ________

Irregular preterites: *venir, poner, decir,* and *traer* (*continued*)

B. The following actions happened in the past. Choose the answer that best completes each sentence and write it in the space provided. Follow the model.

Modelo Los enfermeros me *pusieron* una inyección.
a. pusieron b. ponen

1. Mi mamá y papá me ________________ una silla de ruedas.
   a. traen b. trajeron
2. El enfermero me ________________ que debo tomar una pastilla para el dolor.
   a. dijo b. dijeron
3. Mi hermano ________________ a la sala de emergencia.
   a. vino b. va
4. ¡Qué lástima que tú no ________________ venir con mi hermano!
   a. pudiste b. pudo

C. Tell what happened at a busy school nurse's office yesterday. Using the drawings, answer the following questions in complete sentences.

Modelo ¿Qué me trajiste de la farmacia? *Te traje la medicina.*

1. ¿Qué le trajeron Uds. al enfermo? ________________
2. ¿Qué le puso la enfermera a Carlos? ________________
3. ¿Adónde viniste tú? ________________
4. ¿Qué dije cuando me lastimé? ________________

¡Ay!

Imperfect progressive and preterite (p. 277)

- You can use the imperfect progressive tense to describe something that was happening over a period of time. The imperfect progressive uses the imperfect tense of **estar** + the present participle:

  Teresa estaba leyendo.
  Teresa was reading.

A. The following drawings and sentences show what people were doing yesterday. Circle the verbs in the imperfect progressive. Follow the model.

Modelo A las seis de la mañana, Mario (estaba caminando) con muletas.

1. A las ocho y media de la mañana, mi hermano estaba sacando una radiografía.

2. A las once de la mañana, mis amigos y yo estábamos esperando la ambulancia.

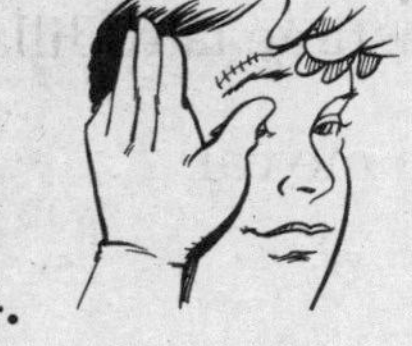

3. A las tres de la tarde, la Dra. Carrillo estaba escribiendo una receta.

4. A las seis de la tarde, usted estaba ayudando a Javier.

5. A las siete y media de la noche, tú estabas poniendo una inyección.

Imperfect progressive and preterite (*continued*)

- When you use pronouns with the imperfect progressive, you can put them before **estar** or attach them to the participle:

  Yo me estaba sirviendo. *or:* **Yo estaba sirviéndome.**

B. Rewrite the sentences below by putting the underlined object pronoun before the conjugated form of **estar.** Follow the model.

Modelo Mariana estaba vistiéndose. *Mariana se estaba vistiendo.*

1. Yo estaba durmiéndome. ______
2. Cristina y Julia estaban sintiéndose mal. ______
3. Tú estabas duchándote. ______
4. Nosotros estábamos levantándonos. ______

- You can use the imperfect progressive and the preterite in the same sentence. The imperfect progressive describes what was happening while the preterite tells about something specific that happened or that interrupted an action.

  Ella estaba corriendo cuando se lastimó el tobillo.
  She was running when she hurt her ankle.

C. The following sentences describe actions that took place in the past. Complete the sentences with the imperfect progressive tense of the verb in parentheses. The first one is done for you.

1. Lupe *se* *estaba* *vistiendo* **(vestirse)** cuando sintió dolor en la espalda.
2. Ricardo y Raúl ______ ______ **(leer)** el mapa cuando chocaron con otro peatón.
3. Tú ______ ______ **(examinar)** las puntadas cuando te tropezaste.
4. Eugenia y yo ______ ______ **(caminar)** cuando me lastimé la rodilla.
5. Yo ______ ______ **(pedir)** una silla de ruedas cuando me caí.

Go Online WEB CODE jdd-0514 PHSchool.com

Lectura: Mejorar la salud para todos (pp. 282–283)

A. The articles in your textbook reading are about health campaigns. A good strategy for understanding these articles is to look for cognates. The following words are cognates from the reading. Say each word in Spanish aloud and then write the letter of the English word that matches it.

1. ______ internacional **a.** international **b.** internal
2. ______ institución **a.** institution **b.** inspiration
3. ______ promover **a.** protect **b.** promote
4. ______ prevención **a.** prevention **b.** preview
5. ______ voluntarios **a.** volume **b.** volunteers

B. The following are quotes from the reading in your textbook. Read what was said by the singers Luis Enrique and Mercedes Sosa. Then, circle the option that best completes each sentence.

> *"La vida nos pone a prueba (test) día a día, con momentos buenos y malos. Es nuestra responsabilidad tomar las decisiones correctas. ¡Dile no a las drogas y dile sí a la vida, siempre!" –Luis Enrique*
>
> *"No les falles a tus chicos, llévalos a vacunar (to be vaccinated). Así pueden estar completamente protegidos y darle ¡Gracias a la vida!" –Mercedes Sosa*

1. Luis Enrique habla sobre
   a. la prevención del uso de las drogas.
   b. la vacunación.
2. Mercedes Sosa habla sobre
   a. la donación de sangre.
   b. la vacunación.

C. Look at this title from one of the articles in your textbook. Then, read the sentences which follow and write **L** (for **Lectura**) if it's something you read in the title. Write **N** (for **No**) if it's something you didn't read.

> *Cuerpo de la Paz y Medical Aid for Children of Latin America (MACLA) ayudan a niños que requieren cirugía plástica.*

1. MACLA significa *Medical Aid for Children of Latin America.* ______
2. Cuerpo de la Paz y MACLA ayudan a niños que requieren cirugía plástica. ______
3. Los niños son de Europa. ______

Presentación escrita (p. 285)

Task: Imagine you have to report an accident you saw. Organize your ideas before you write the report.

A. Describe what you were doing when the accident occurred. Choose an activity from the list below. Then, circle the activity.

¿Qué estabas haciendo?

1. Estaba saliendo de la escuela.
2. Estaba jugando con mis amigos.
3. Estaba hablando con la profesora.

B. This chart can help you organize information about the accident: What happened? When did it happen? Who was hurt? Who helped? Circle one option in each column.

¿Qué pasó?	¿Cuándo ocurrió?	¿Quién se lastimó?	¿Quiénes ayudaron?
un árbol se cayó un coche chocó con algo una ventana se rompió	por la mañana por la tarde por la noche	un estudiante un profesor una señora	los estudiantes los bomberos una enfermera la policía

C. Now, use your answers from **parts A and B** to complete a report of the accident.

Yo ______________________ cuando vi un accidente. ______________________

______________________ y ______________________ se lastimó.

______________________ lo / la ayudó.

D. Read through your report to check for spelling, correct verb usage, vocabulary, and clarity.

E. Share the report with a partner who should check the following:

_____ Is the report easy to understand?

_____ Is the information in a clear, logical order?

_____ Is there anything to add to give more information?

_____ Are there any errors?

Vocabulary Flash Cards, Sheet 1

Write the Spanish vocabulary word below each picture. If there is a word or phrase, copy it in the space provided. Be sure to include the article for each noun.

Realidades 2 Nombre ______ Hora ______

Capítulo 6A Fecha ______ **Vocabulary Flash Cards, Sheet 2**

Write the Spanish vocabulary word below each picture. If there is a word or phrase, copy it in the space provided. Be sure to include the article for each noun.

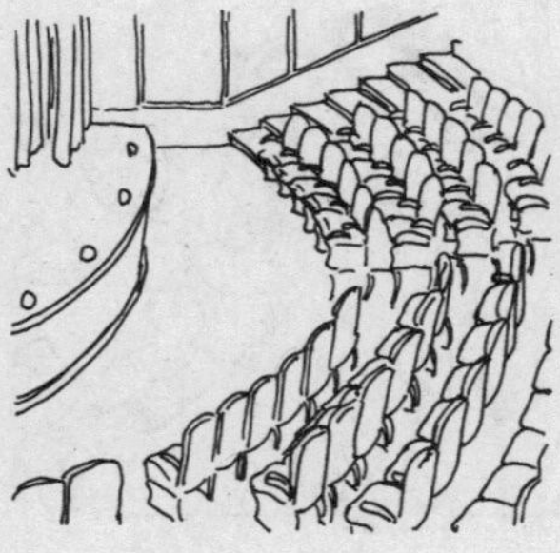

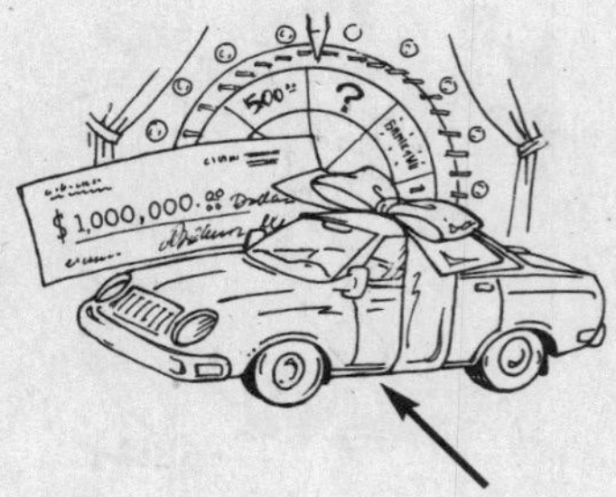

Realidades 2 Nombre Hora

Capítulo 6A Fecha **Vocabulary Flash Cards, Sheet 3**

Write the Spanish vocabulary word below each picture. If there is a word or phrase, copy it in the space provided. Be sure to include the article for each noun.

Write the Spanish vocabulary word below each picture. If there is a word or phrase, copy it in the space provided. Be sure to include the article for each noun.

enojado, enojada	**furioso, furiosa**	**agitado, agitada**
al final	**la competencia**	**fenomenal**
la liga	**por . . . vez**	**resultar**

Write the Spanish vocabulary word below each picture. If there is a word or phrase, copy it in the space provided. Be sure to include the article for each noun.

último, última _______________, _______________	**aburrirse** _______________	**enojarse** _______________
volverse loco, loca __________ ________, ________	**dormirse** _______________	**morirse** _______________
los campeones ________ _______________	**competir** _______________	**entrevistar** _______________

Realidades 2

Capítulo 6A

Nombre ____________________ Hora ____________

Fecha ____________________

Vocabulary Flash Cards, Sheet 6

Write the Spanish vocabulary word below each picture. If there is a word or phrase, copy it in the space provided. Be sure to include the article for each noun.

poponerse + adjective		

Nombre ____________ Hora ____________

Fecha ____________

Vocabulary Check, Sheet 1

Tear out this page. Write the English words on the lines. Fold the paper along the dotted line to see the correct answers so you can check your work.

aplaudir ____________

competir ____________

la competencia ____________

al final ____________

fenomenal ____________

resultar ____________

último, última ____________

el auditorio ____________

el comentario ____________

entrevistar ____________

el público ____________

aburrirse ____________

alegre ____________

emocionado, emocionada ____________

enojado, enojada ____________

Fold In

Realidades 2 | Nombre ______ | Hora ______

Capítulo 6A | Fecha ______ | **Vocabulary Check, Sheet 2**

Tear out this page. Write the Spanish words on the lines. Fold the paper along the dotted line to see the correct answers so you can check your work.

to applaud ______

to compete ______

competition ______

at the end ______

phenomenal ______

to result, to turn out ______

last, final ______

auditorium ______

commentary ______

to interview ______

audience ______

to get bored ______

happy ______

excited, emotional ______

angry ______

Fold In ←

Realidades 2 Nombre ____ Hora ____

Capítulo 6A Fecha ____ **Vocabulary Check, Sheet 3**

Tear out this page. Write the English words on the lines. Fold the paper along the dotted line to see the correct answers so you can check your work.

el aficionado, la aficionada ____

el atleta, la atleta ____

el campeonato ____

el empate ____

el jugador, la jugadora ____

perder ____

el tanteo ____

el concurso de belleza ____

el premio ____

la reina ____

el presentador, la presentadora ____

agitado, agitada ____

furioso, furiosa ____

dormirse ____

Fold In ←

Tear out this page. Write the Spanish words on the lines. Fold the paper along the dotted line to see the correct answers so you can check your work.

fan ____________

athlete ____________

championship ____________

tie ____________

player ____________

to lose ____________

score ____________

beauty contest ____________

prize ____________

queen ____________

presenter ____________

agitated ____________

furious ____________

to fall asleep ____________

Fold In ←

To hear a complete list of the vocabulary for this chapter, go to Disc 2, Track 3 on the Guided Practice Audio CD or go to www.phschool.com and type in the Web Code jdd-0689. Then click on **Repaso del capítulo.**

Preterite of *-ir* stem-changing verbs (p. 302)

- In the preterite, verbs ending in **-ir**, like **preferir, pedir,** and **dormir,** have stem changes but only in the **usted/él/ella** and **ustedes/ellos/ellas** forms. The **e** changes to **i,** and the **o** to **u.**

  Mi mamá se durmió durante la película.
  Mis padres prefirieron ver el concurso de belleza.
  En la liga compitieron los mejores equipos de México.
- Here are the preterite forms of **preferir, pedir,** and **dormir.**

preferir (e → i)		pedir (e → i)		dormir (o → u)	
preferí	preferimos	pedí	pedimos	dormí	dormimos
preferiste	preferisteis	pediste	pedisteis	dormiste	dormisteis
prefirió	**prefirieron**	**pidió**	**pidieron**	**durmió**	**durmieron**

- Note the special spelling of the preterite forms of **reír:**
  reí, reíste, rió, reímos, reísteis, rieron
- Here are other **-ir** verbs with stem changes in the preterite tense:
  Verbs like **preferir: divertirse, mentir, sentirse**
  Verbs like **pedir: competir, despedirse, repetir, seguir, servir, vestirse**
  Verbs like **dormir: morir**
  Verbs like **reír: sonreír**

A. Complete the following sentences with the correct form of the verb in parentheses. The first one is done for you.

1. Carlos ___prefirió___ **(prefirió / prefieren)** asistir al partido el sábado.
2. Las niñas se ______ **(durmió / durmieron)** en el auditorio.
3. Usted ______ **(pidió / pedimos)** una entrevista al entrenador.
4. Ustedes ______ **(preferir / prefirieron)** ver este partido.
5. Las presentadoras ______ **(pidió / pidieron)** a los voluntarios al final del programa.
6. Tomás se ______ **(durmió / duermen)** antes de la competencia.
7. El campeón ______ **(pidió / pedí)** un millón de dólares.
8. Lucía ______ **(preferimos / prefirió)** entrevistar al público.

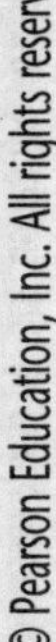

Preterite of *-ir* stem-changing verbs (*continued*)

B. Use the correct verb form from the word list to complete each sentence. The first one is done for you.

repitió	**siguieron**	**reímos**	**vistieron**	**mintío**	**competiste**
divertí	**sonrió**	**sintieron**	**despidió**	**servimos**	**prefirieron**

1. Millones de aficionados ___*siguieron*___ al jugador.
2. La reina _______________ mucho cuando ganó el concurso de belleza.
3. Pilar y yo nos _______________ de los chistes que contó el presentador.
4. Al final, la reina de belleza se _______________ del público.
5. El entrenador y su equipo se _______________ de rojo y blanco.
6. La presentadora _______________ el tanteo para el público.
7. Ustedes se _______________ alegres al final del partido.
8. Yo me _______________ mucho en el campeonato.
9. La reportera dice que el jugador _______________; él no rescató a la señora.
10. Tú no _______________ en el campeonato del año pasado.
11. Nosotros _______________ una comida fantástica a los jugadores.
12. Ustedes _______________ ver el partido en la tele.

Go Online WEB CODE jdd-0604
PHSchool.com

Preterite of *-ir* stem-changing verbs (*continued*)

C. Sergio and Patricia went out on a Saturday night. Look at the pictures and choose the appropriate verb from the word bank that matches each picture. Then, write the correct preterite form of each verb. Follow the model.

reírse	servir	preferir	pedir	seguir

Modelo Sergio y Patricia se *se divirtieron* mucho.

1. Una tarde, Sergio y Patricia salieron a comer. Ellos ______ por la calle Miraflores.

2. Sergio y Patricia ______ espaguetis.

3. El camarero les ______ una comida muy buena.

4. Después de la cena, Sergio y Patricia ______ ir al cine.

5. Sergio y Patricia ______ mucho.

Other reflexive verbs (p. 305)

- Some reflexive verbs do not have the meaning of a person doing an action to or for himself or herself. These reflexive verbs describe a change. We say that someone "gets" or "becomes" something. Examples of these verbs are:

aburrirse	*to get bored*	**enojarse**	*to become angry*
casarse	*to get married*	**ponerse (furioso, -a; alegre;...)**	*to become (furious, happy, . . .)*
divertirse	*to have fun*	**volverse loco, -a**	*to go crazy*
dormirse	*to fall asleep*		

Ramiro se aburrió durante la película. *Ramiro got bored during the movie.*
Lalo se enojó al final del partido. *Lalo became angry at the end of the game.*

A. Read the following sentences. Then, look at the underlined words in each sentence and write the English equivalent for those words. Follow the model.

Modelo María se casa el domingo. gets (is getting) married

1. Me puse alegre porque María se va a casar. ______
2. Mis hermanos se enojan cuando su equipo pierde. ______
3. Ayer, mis primos y yo nos divertimos durante el campeonato. ______
4. Juan se durmió durante el partido de ayer. ______
5. Yo no voy a las competencias porque me aburro. ______

B. Circle the correct verb in parentheses to complete the paragraph. The first one is done for you.

Ayer mi hermano y yo vimos un partido de fútbol en la televisión. Yo (**me aburrí** / **te aburriste**) mucho y mi hermano (**te enojaste** / **se enojó**). Entonces yo (**nos pusimos** / **me puse**) furiosa y mi hermano (**se rió** / **se rieron**). Después, yo (**se durmió** / **me dormí**). Cuando yo (**me desperté** / **nos despertamos**) mi hermano no estaba. Lo busqué y busqué. Casi (**me volví** / **se volvieron**) loca. Al fin lo encontré: ¡dormido, debajo de su cama!

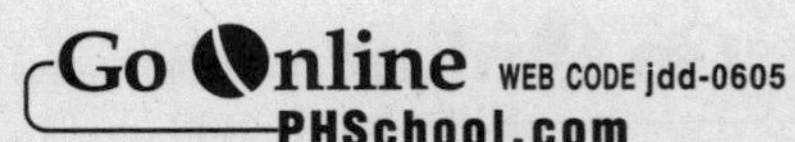

Lectura: Los Juegos Panamericanos (pp. 310–311)

A. The reading in your textbook is about the **Juegos Panamericanos** or Pan-American Games, a sports event similar to the Summer Olympics. Using what you know about the Summer Olympics can help you understand the reading. See if you can answer the questions below.

1. What are the Summer Olympics? ______
2. Who can participate in these Olympics? ______
3. What are five sports featured in the Summer Olympics? ______, ______, ______, ______, ______

B. Read the following excerpts from your textbook reading. Then look at the list below. Write what you think the words mean in English.

> *Todos los países de las Américas pueden mandar atletas a competir. Aproximadamente el 80 por ciento de los deportes de los Juegos Panamericanos se juegan en las Olimpíadas.*
>
> *Se convirtió en un héroe nacional de Ecuador cuando ganó otra vez la medalla de oro...*

1. todos los países ______ ______
2. el 80 por ciento ______ ______
3. deportes ______
4. héroe ______
5. nacional ______
6. medalla de oro ______ ______

C. Now read the sentences below. Based on the excerpts in **part B,** write **Sí** if the sentence tells something that happens during the Pan-American Games. Write **No** if it doesn't happen during these Games.

1. Todos los países del mundo pueden participar en estos Juegos. ______
2. Las personas que participan en estos Juegos son atletas. ______
3. Todos los deportes de los Juegos Panamericanos también se juegan en las Olimpíadas. ______
4. El mejor atleta o equipo de cada deporte gana una medalla de oro. ______

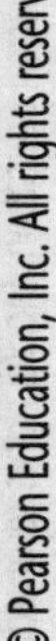

Presentación oral (p. 313)

Task: Prepare a review of your favorite television program and present it to your class.

A. Complete the following sentences about your favorite television program. Circle one option from the word lists for each sentence.

una comedia	**la telenovela**
un programa deportivo	**una película de detectives**
un programa de concursos	**un programa de dibujos animados**

1. Mi programa favorito es ______________________.

niños	**mayores**	**niños y mayores**

2. Este programa es para ______________________.

me río mucho	**me enojo mucho**
me siento emocionado(a)	**me vuelvo loco(a)**

3. Cuando veo este programa ______________________.

interesante	**divertido**	**fenomenal**	**alegre**

4. Este programa es ______________________.

B. Now use the information from **part A** to complete the following sentences.

1. Mi programa favorito se llama ____________ y es ____________.

2. Este programa es para ______________________.

3. Cuando veo este programa ______________________.

4. Este programa es ______________________.

C. Use the sentences from **parts A** and **B** to practice your oral presentation. Go through the presentation several times. Try to:

- include all the information in the sentences
- use complete sentences and speak clearly

D. Give your presentation about the television program to a partner.

Write the Spanish vocabulary word below each picture. If there is a word or phrase, copy it in the space provided. Be sure to include the article for each noun.

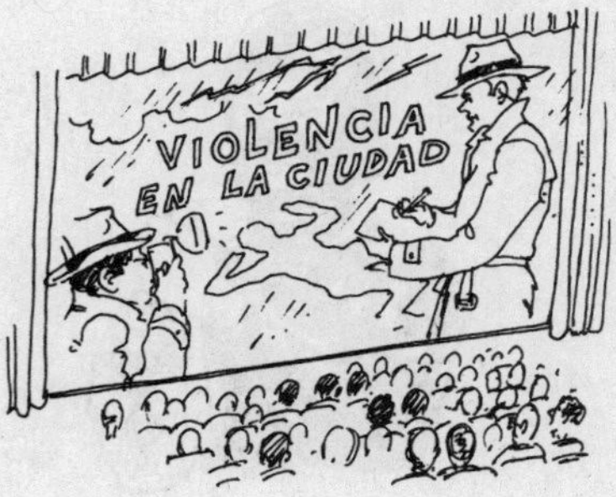

VIOLENCIA EN LA CIUDAD

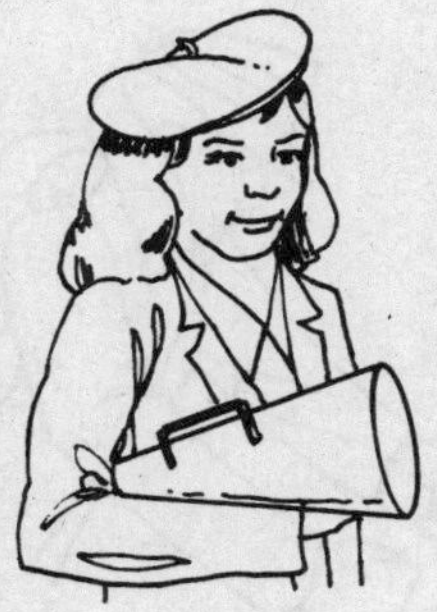

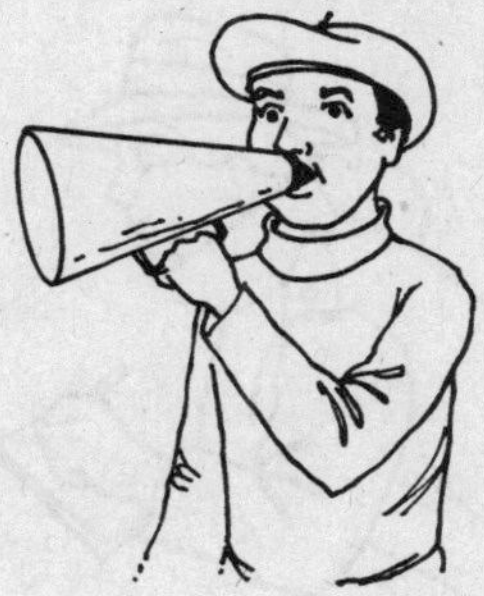

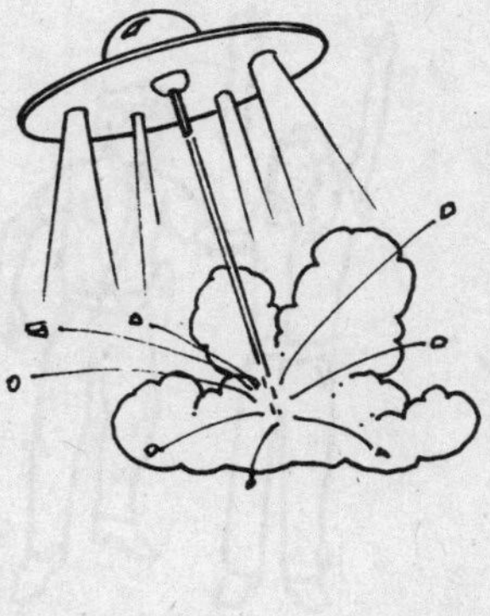

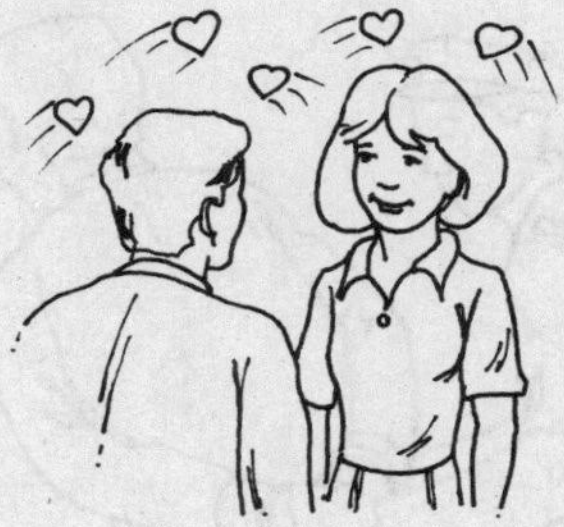

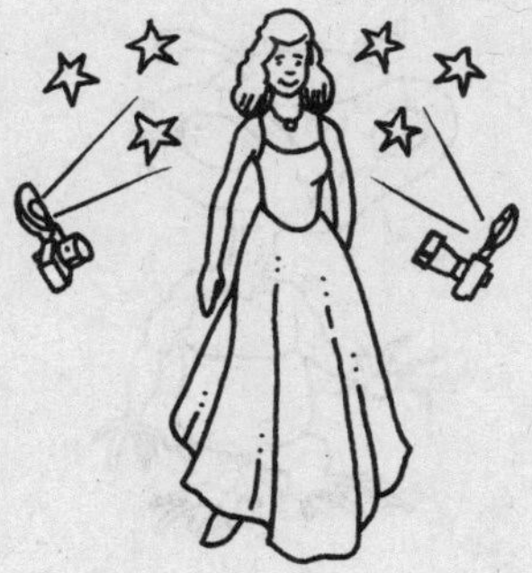

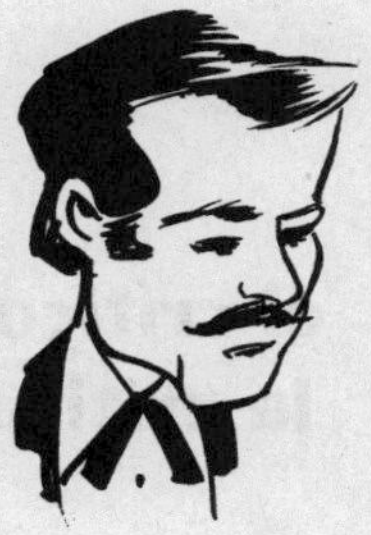

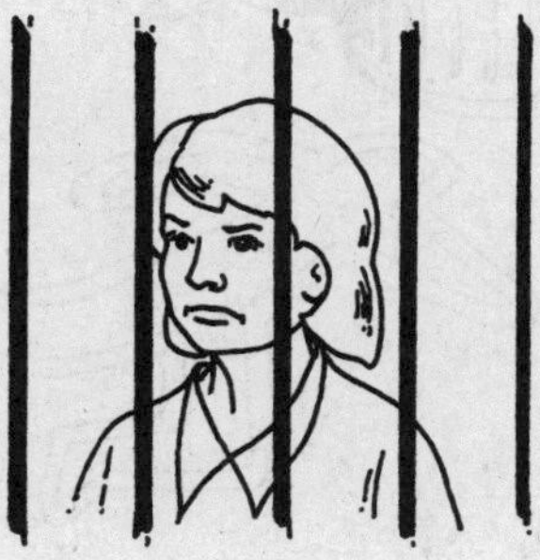

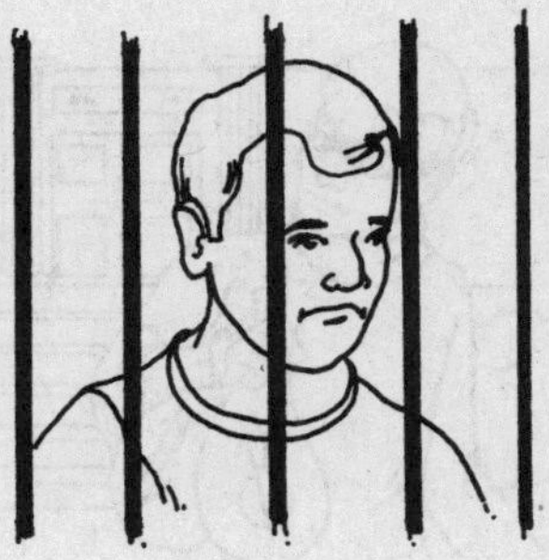

Realidades 2 | Nombre ______ | Hora ______

Capítulo 6B | Fecha ______ | **Vocabulary Flash Cards, Sheet 2**

Write the Spanish vocabulary word below each picture. If there is a word or phrase, copy it in the space provided. Be sure to include the article for each noun.

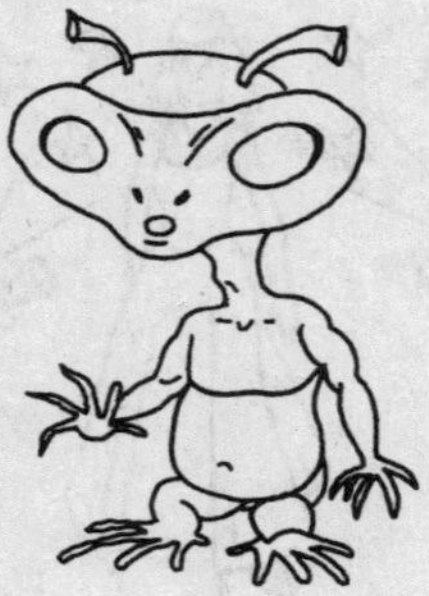

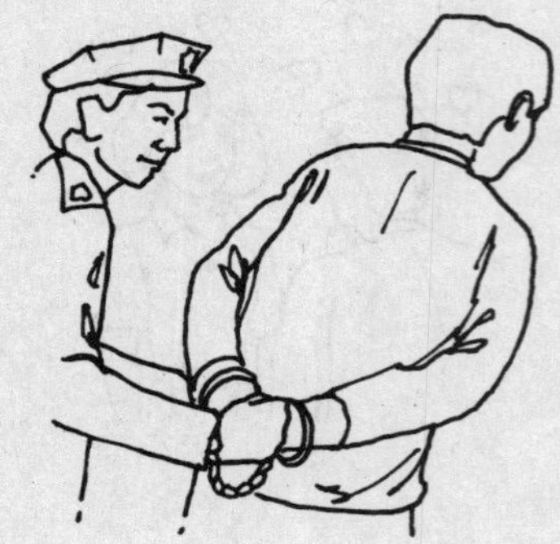

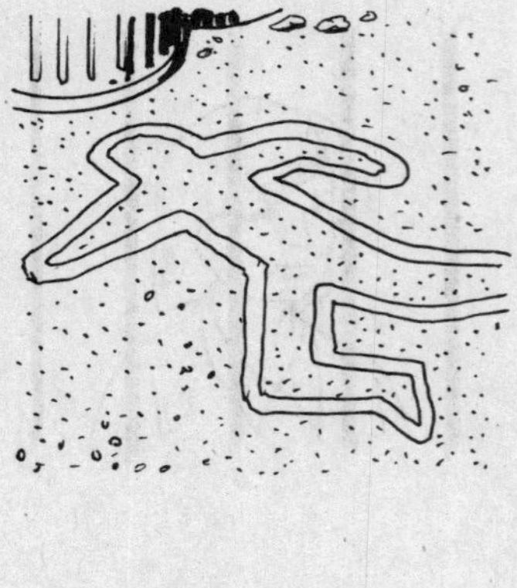

______ ______	______ ______	______ ______
______ ______ ______	______	______
______	______ ______	**el crítico, la crítica** ______ ______, ______ ______

Nombre _______________ Hora _______

Fecha _______________ **Vocabulary Flash Cards, Sheet 3**

Write the Spanish vocabulary word below each picture. If there is a word or phrase, copy it in the space provided. Be sure to include the article for each noun.

fascinar	**el fracaso**	**he visto**
has visto	**matar**	**¿Qué tal es . . .?**
recomendar	**será**	**tener éxito**

Realidades 2 Nombre _______ Hora _______

Capítulo 6B Fecha _______ **Vocabulary Flash Cards, Sheet 4**

Write the Spanish vocabulary word below each picture. If there is a word or phrase, copy it in the space provided. Be sure to include the article for each noun.

tratarse de	**la violencia**	**la actuación**
el argumento	**la dirección**	**alquilar**
hacer el papel de	**el personaje principal**	**no...todavía**

Write the Spanish vocabulary word below each picture. If there is a word or phrase, copy it in the space provided. Be sure to include the article for each noun.

enamorarse (de)	**(estar) enamorado, enamorada de**	**el crimen**
la ladrona	**la escena**	**estar basado, basada en**
el papel		

Realidades 2 | Nombre ______________ Hora ______

Capítulo 6B | Fecha ______________

Vocabulary Flash Cards, Sheet 6

Realidades 2 | Nombre | Hora

Capítulo 6B | Fecha | **Vocabulary Check, Sheet 1**

Tear out this page. Write the English words on the lines. Fold the paper along the dotted line to see the correct answers so you can check your work.

alquilar ______

el amor ______

arrestar ______

capturar ______

el (la) criminal ______

enamorarse (de) ______

robar ______

tener éxito ______

el fracaso ______

tratarse de ______

he visto ______

el director, la directora ______

la escena ______

el papel ______

la víctima ______

Fold In ←

Realidades 2 | Nombre ______ | Hora ______

Capítulo 6B | Fecha ______

Vocabulary Check, Sheet 2

Tear out this page. Write the Spanish words on the lines. Fold the paper along the dotted line to see the correct answers so you can check your work.

to rent ______

love ______

to arrest ______

to capture ______

the criminal ______

to fall in love (with) ______

to rob, to steal ______

to succeed, to be successful ______

failure ______

to be about ______

I have seen ______

director ______

scene ______

role ______

victim ______

Fold In ←

Realidades 2 Nombre Hora

Capítulo 6B Fecha **Vocabulary Check, Sheet 3**

Tear out this page. Write the English words on the lines. Fold the paper along the dotted line to see the correct answers so you can check your work.

la estrella (del cine) ______

el (la) detective ______

el galán ______

el ladrón, la ladrona ______

la película de acción ______

los efectos especiales ______

el (la) extraterrestre ______

la actuación ______

el argumento ______

el crimen ______

matar ______

el crítico, la crítica ______

fascinar ______

¿Qué tal es…? ______

Fold In

Vocabulary Check, Sheet 4

Tear out this page. Write the Spanish words on the lines. Fold the paper along the dotted line to see the correct answers so you can check your work.

(movie) star ______

detective ______

leading man ______

thief ______

action film ______

special effects ______

alien ______

acting ______

plot ______

crime ______

to kill ______

critic ______

to fascinate ______

How is (it)...? ______

Fold In ←

To hear a complete list of the vocabulary for this chapter, go to Disc 2, Track 4 on the Guided Practice Audio CD or go to www.phschool.com and type in the Web Code jdd-0699. Then click on **Repaso del capítulo.**

Verbs that use indirect object pronouns (p. 328)

- Verbs that use indirect object pronouns, such as **aburrir, doler, encantar, fascinar, gustar,** and **importar,** use a similar construction:

  indirect object pronoun + verb + subject.

  Le + encantan + las películas de acción.
  He likes action movies.

- You can use **a** + a noun or a pronoun with these verbs for emphasis or clarification:

  A Rodrigo le gustan las flores. or: ***A él* le gustan las flores.**
  Rodrigo likes flowers. or: *He likes flowers.*

(A mí)	**me**	(A nosotros/a nosotras)	**nos**
(A ti)	**te**	(A vosotros/a vosotras)	**os**
(A usted/A él/A ella)	**le**	(A ustedes/A ellos/A ellas)	**les**

A. Look at the pictures and read the sentences. Choose the appropriate ending from the word bank to complete each sentence.

me encantan las películas románticas	**te aburre el galán**
le gustan las películas sobre extraterrestres	**le queda bien el vestido**

1. A él ______________________________
______________________________.
2. A ti ______________________________
______________________________.
3. A mí ______________________________
______________________________.
4. A la estrella del cine ______________________________
______________________________.

The present perfect (p. 331)

Use the present perfect tense to tell what a person has done.

- To form this tense, use present-tense forms of **haber** + the past participle:

  Hemos alquilado dos películas.
  We have rented two movies.

- To form the past participle of a verb, drop the ending of the infinitive and add **-ado** for **-ar** verbs and **-ido** for **-er** and **-ir** verbs.

he	alquilado	**hemos**	alquilado
has	alquilado	**habéis**	alquilado
ha	alquilado	**han**	alquilado

- Most verbs that have two vowels together in the infinitive have a written accent on the **í** of the past participle:

  caer → caído **oír → oído**

A. Write the past participle form of the following verbs. Follow the model.

Modelo comer *comido*

1. estudiar ____________
2. hablar ____________
3. vivir ____________
4. tener ____________
5. leer ____________
6. traer ____________
7. caer ____________
8. oír ____________

B. Use the correct form of **haber** and the past participle of the verb in parentheses to complete the sentences below. The first one is done for you.

1. El personaje principal se **(caer)** *ha* *caído*.
2. ¿Tú ____________ ____________ **(oír)** de qué se trata la película?
3. Yo ____________ ____________ **(leer)** un artículo sobre el galán de la película.
4. Nosotros ____________ ____________ **(traer)** una revista de cine.

Realidades 2 | Nombre ____________________ | Hora ________

Capítulo 6B | Fecha ____________________ | **Guided Practice Activities 6B-3**

The present perfect (*continued*)

- These verbs have irregular past participles:

decir → *dicho*	**poner → *puesto***
escribir → *escrito*	**romper → *roto***
hacer → *hecho*	**ver → *visto***
morir → *muerto*	**volver → *vuelto***

- When you use object or reflexive pronouns with the present perfect, the pronoun goes right before the form of **haber:**

  ¿Has visto la película? Sí, la he visto.
  Have you seen the movie? Yes, I have seen it.

C. Look at the following verbs. Write **I** (for Irregular) if the verb has an irregular past participle form. If not, write **R** (for Regular). Follow the model.

Modelo alquilar ___R___

1. volver ____________
2. hacer ____________
3. escribir ____________
4. comer ____________
5. devolver ____________
6. vivir ____________
7. ver ____________
8. caer ____________

D. The following sentences describe a movie. Use the present perfect form of the verb in parentheses to complete the sentences. Follow the model.

Modelo Yo ___he___ ___visto___ **(ver)** una película policíaca.

1. El director ____________ ____________ **(decir)** que el argumento es malo.
2. Nadie ____________ ____________ **(morir)** en esta escena.
3. Luis y Damián ____________ ____________ **(hacer)** los papeles de las víctimas.
4. Nosotras ____________ ____________ **(escribir)** el argumento para la película.
5. El crítico ____________ ____________ **(volver)** a recomendar esa película.
6. ¿Tú ____________ ____________ **(poner)** el coche en la última escena?
7. La estrella ____________ ____________ **(romper)** el vaso otra vez.

The present perfect (*continued*)

E. Marta is talking about movies. Rewrite her statements by replacing the underlined words with the pronoun in parentheses and placing it before the form of **haber** for each sentence. Follow the model.

Modelo Yo he alquilado __la película__. (la)

____

1. Los detectives han arrestado **a las ladronas.** (las)

____

2. Los actores han leído la escena **al director.** (le)

____

3. El galán ha capturado **a los extraterrestres.** (los)

____

4. El director ha pedido ayuda **a nosotros.** (nos)

____

5. La estrella del cine ha visto **la película.** (la)

____

6. El ladrón ha robado las revistas **a ellos.** (les)

____

7. La directora ha escrito **el argumento.** (lo)

____

8. El crítico ha dicho su opinión **a mí.** (me)

____

Go Online WEB CODE jdd-0614
PHSchool.com

Lectura: La cartelera del cine (pp. 336–337)

A. Reading the title and subtitles first in the reading can give you an idea of the "big picture." To organize your ideas, circle the best option, **a.** or **b.**, for the following sentences.

1. This reading is about
   a. movies. **b.** sports.
2. Each section has a summary and a
   a. comedy. **b.** review.

B. Read the following excerpt from your textbook reading. Then answer the questions below.

> *El señor de los anillos 2: Las dos torres*
> *EE. UU., Nueva Zelandia 2002 | Clasificación: B | Director: Peter Jackson | Actores: Elijah Wood, Ian McKellen, Viggo Mortensen, Liv Tyler, Cate Blanchett*

1. ¿Cómo se llama la segunda parte de la película?
   ____
2. ¿Quién es el director de *El señor de los anillos*?
   ____
3. ¿En qué año se hizo la película?
   ____
4. ¿Cuál es la clasificación de la película?
   ____

C. Read the following ***Crítica*** section for ***El ataque de los clones.*** Circle the answer that best completes each of the statements below.

> *Esta película es muy comercial. Lo más interesante es el uso de los efectos especiales. El argumento es horrible. Es muy difícil de entender y no es muy lógico. Por los efectos especiales, le doy 10/10. Por el argumento, sólo le doy 5/10.*

1. El crítico de *El ataque de los clones* piensa que la película es
   a. espectacular. **b.** comercial.
2. Al crítico le gustan
   a. los efectos especiales. **b.** los actores.
3. El crítico dice que la película es
   a. difícil de entender. **b.** fenomenal.

Presentación escrita (p. 339)

Task: Think about and write a good movie idea for a class contest. Describe the main characters, the plot, and the scenes. Then draw a few scenes from the movie.

A. Fill in the blanks with information about the kind of movie you would like to write. You can choose an option from the list, or make up your own.

1. Me gustaría escribir ______________________________.
   una película de acción | una película romántica | un drama
   una película de ciencia ficción | una película policíaca | una comedia
   una película de horror

2. Los personajes principales de mi película pueden ser ______________.
   ladrones y policías | una familia y sus amigos
   extraterrestres | criminales

B. Read the following plot descriptions to get ideas for your movie. You can use these descriptions or make up your own. Then write a brief outline of your plot below.

- Los personajes desean encontrar algo que alguien escondió hace muchos años.
- Los extraterrestres vienen a visitarnos.
- Unos ladrones roban una pintura *(painting)* de un museo y la policía los busca.

____

____

____

____

C. In the following boxes, sketch four scenes from the movie plot you described in **part B.**

D. Read through your plot description, and check for spelling, correct verb usage, and vocabulary. Share this description with your partner who will check that it is complete, clear, and presented in a logical order.

Write the Spanish vocabulary word below each picture. If there is a word or phrase, copy it in the space provided. Be sure to include the article for each noun.

Realidades 2 | Nombre ______ | Hora ______

Capítulo 7A | Fecha ______ | **Vocabulary Flash Cards, Sheet 2**

Write the Spanish vocabulary word below each picture. If there is a word or phrase, copy it in the space provided. Be sure to include the article for each noun.

Paella

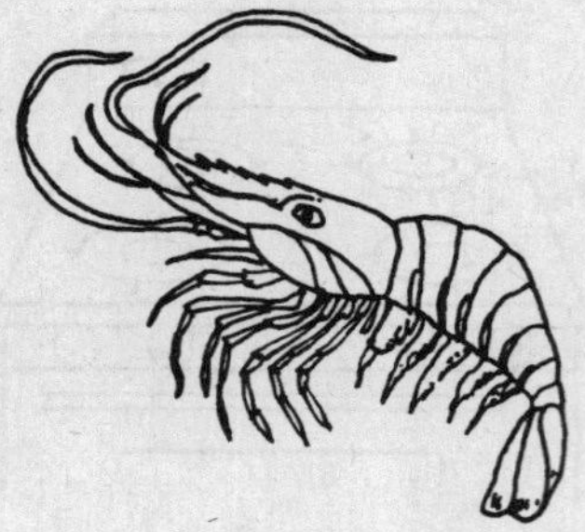

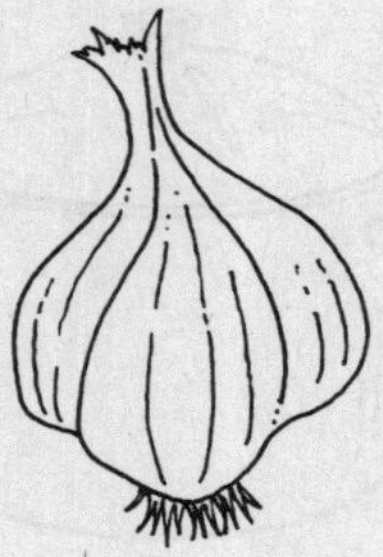

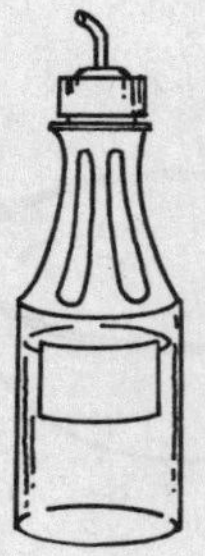

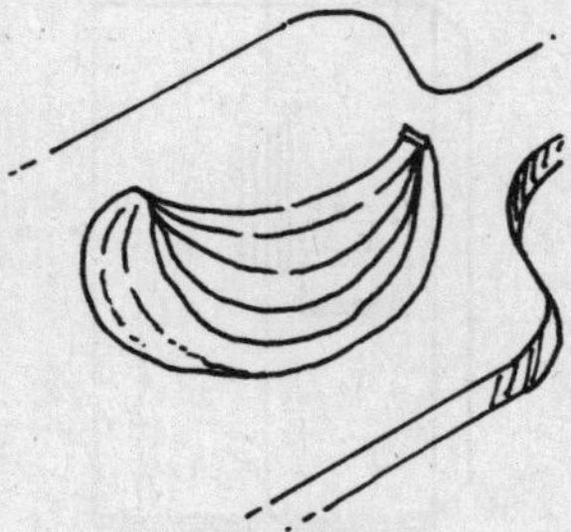

Write the Spanish vocabulary word below each picture. If there is a word or phrase, copy it in the space provided. Be sure to include the article for each noun.

Write the Spanish vocabulary word below each picture. If there is a word or phrase, copy it in the space provided. Be sure to include the article for each noun.

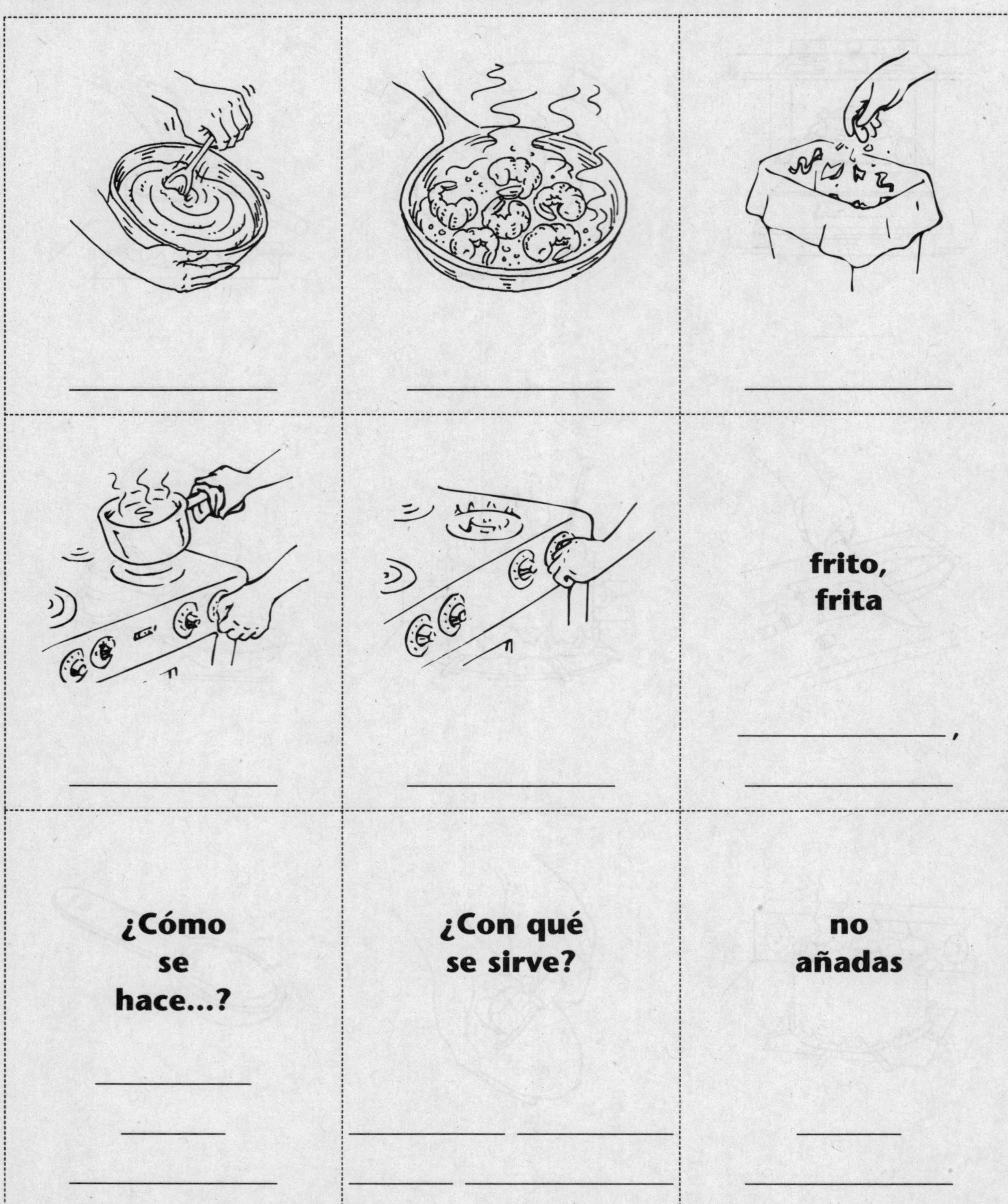

Vocabulary Flash Cards, Sheet 5

Write the Spanish vocabulary word below each picture. If there is a word or phrase, copy it in the space provided. Be sure to include the article for each noun.

dejar	**no dejes**	**olvidarse de**
no te olvides de	**no tires**	**se puede**
No hables.	**No comas.**	**No escribas.**

Write the Spanish vocabulary word below each picture. If there is a word or phrase, copy it in the space provided. Be sure to include the article for each noun.

congelado, congelada _______________, _______________	**enlatado, enlatada** _______________, _______________	**fresco, fresca** _______________, _______________
caliente _______________	_______ _______________	_______ _______________
_______ _______________	_______ _______________	_______ _______________

Nombre ______ Hora ______

Fecha ______

Vocabulary Check, Sheet 1

Tear out this page. Write the English words on the lines. Fold the paper along the dotted line to see the correct answers so you can check your work.

la salsa ______

el aceite ______

el ajo ______

la olla ______

el refrigerador ______

el fuego ______

caliente ______

el horno ______

añadir ______

tirar ______

freír ______

mezclar ______

probar ______

la receta ______

olvidarse de ______

Fold In ←

Tear out this page. Write the Spanish words on the lines. Fold the paper along the dotted line to see the correct answers so you can check your work.

salsa, sauce ______

cooking oil ______

garlic ______

pot ______

refrigerator ______

fire, heat ______

hot ______

oven ______

to add ______

to spill, to throw away ______

to fry ______

to mix ______

to taste, to try ______

recipe ______

to forget about/to ______

Fold In ←

Realidades 2

Capítulo 7A

Nombre ______ Hora ______

Fecha ______

Vocabulary Check, Sheet 3

Tear out this page. Write the English words on the lines. Fold the paper along the dotted line to see the correct answers so you can check your work.

el caldo ______

la estufa ______

el fregadero ______

el pedazo ______

la sartén ______

calentar ______

hervir ______

el ingrediente ______

picar ______

apagar ______

dejar ______

encender ______

fresco, fresca ______

Fold In

Tear out this page. Write the Spanish words on the lines. Fold the paper along the dotted line to see the correct answers so you can check your work.

broth ______________________

stove ______________________

sink ______________________

piece, slice ______________________

frying pan ______________________

to heat ______________________

to boil ______________________

ingredient ______________________

to chop ______________________

to turn off ______________________

to leave, to let ______________________

to turn on, to light ______________________

fresh ______________________

Fold In ←

To hear a complete list of the vocabulary for this chapter, go to Disc 2, Track 5 on the Guided Practice Audio CD or go to www.phschool.com and type in the Web Code jdd-0789. Then click on **Repaso del capítulo.**

Negative *tú* commands (p. 356)

- Negative commands are used to tell someone what *not* to do.
- To form negative **tú** commands, drop the **-o** of the present-tense **yo** form and add:
  -es for **-ar** verbs.
  usar → uso: No uses el microondas. *Don't use the microwave.*
  -as for **-er** and **-ir** verbs.
  encender → enciendo: No enciendas el horno. *Don't turn on the oven.*

A. Look at the pictures and read the sentences. Choose the correct words in parentheses to tell people what *not* to do. Follow the model.

Modelo Anita, no (**comer** / (**comas**)) todas las ((**frutas**) / **pizzas**).

1. No (**pongas** / **poner**) mucha sal en el (**sartén** / **caldo**).

2. No (**cortes** / **cortar**) el ajo en (**pedazos** / **mariscos**) tan pequeños.

3. No (**beber** / **bebas**) el café si está muy (**frito** / **caliente**).

4. No (**uses** / **usar**) tanto (**olla** / **aceite**).

5. No (**añadir** / **añadas**) el (**ajo** / **refrigerador**) ahora.

Negative *tú* commands (*continued*)

- With negative **tú** commands, some verbs such as **picar** (to chop), **pagar** (to pay), and **empezar** (to start) have spelling changes: **c** changes to **qu, g** changes to **gu,** and **z** changes to **c.**

  picar → no pi*qu*es **pagar → no pa*gu*es** **empezar → no empieces**
- Some verbs have irregular negative **tú** commands:

  dar → no des **estar → no estés**

  ir → no vayas **ser → no seas**

B. For each pair of sentences, write the negative **tú** command of the verb shown in the first sentence. Follow the model.

Modelo Pica el tomate. No *piques* el ajo.

1. Empieza la cena a las ocho. No ______ la cena a las siete.
2. Paga con dinero en efectivo. No ______ con tu tarjeta de crédito.
3. Pica las cebollas. No ______ los mariscos.
4. Almuerza a las dos. No ______ a las once.

C. For each of the following sentences, write the appropriate negative **tú** command of the verb in parentheses.

1. No **(dar)** ______ dulces a tu hermano antes del almuerzo.
2. No **(estar)** ______ en la cocina antes de la cena.
3. No **(ir)** ______ al mercado hoy.
4. No **(ser)** ______ tan desordenada.

D. Fill in the blanks with the appropriate negative **tú** command of a verb from the word bank.

ir	pagar	almorzar	estar

1. No ______ al restaurante. Hoy está cerrado.
2. No ______ solo. Almuerza con nosotros.
3. No ______ la cena. Mamá acaba de pagar.
4. No ______ impaciente. Vamos a cenar pronto.

Go Online WEB CODE jdd-0704
PHSchool.com

The impersonal *se* (p. 360)

- In Spanish, to say that people in general do a certain thing, you use **se** + the **usted/él/ella** or **ustedes/ellos/ellas** form of the verb. This is called the impersonal se.

  Aquí se sirve el pan tostado con mantequilla. *Here they serve the toast with butter.*
  Se come la sopa con tortillas. *Soup is eaten with tortillas.*

A. Look at the pictures and read the sentences that describe what people do in general when they prepare food. Choose the appropriate impersonal **se** expression from the word bank to complete each sentence.

se calienta en el microondas	**se come mucha fruta**	**se hace con sal y ajo**
se pica ajo	**se sirve con ensalada**	

1. En mi casa el pollo ______________________.
2. Para preparar la salsa ______________________.
3. El plato principal ______________________.
4. En mi casa ______________________.
5. La comida ______________________.

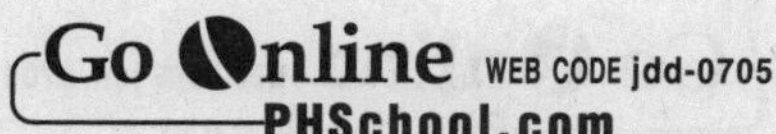

The impersonal *se* (*continued*)

B. Complete the following rules by circling the appropriate impersonal **se** expression to tell what is done or not done. Follow the model.

Modelo No (**se fríen** / **se pueden**) los camarones.

1. (**Se pela** / **Se sirve**) pan con mariscos.
2. (**Se calienta** / **Se tira**) el pan en el horno.
3. No (**se añade** / **se come**) sal a la sopa.
4. (**Se apaga** / **Se deja**) el ajo en la cocina.
5. No (**se encienden** / **se hierven**) los mariscos.

C. Complete the following recipe to prepare **arroz con mariscos** (rice with seafood). Use the impersonal **se** form of the verb in parentheses to complete each instruction. The first one is done for you.

Arroz con mariscos

1. *Se calienta* (calentar) el aceite en la sartén.
2. ______________ (preparar) los mariscos con sal.
3. ______________ (pelar) el ajo y ______________ (cortar) en pedazos.
4. ______________ (mezclar) los mariscos y el ajo.
5. ______________ (hervir) agua en una olla.
6. ______________ (añadir) arroz y sal al caldo.
7. ______________ (mezclar) los mariscos con el arroz.

Go Online WEB CODE jcd-0705
PHSchool.com

Lectura: Oda al tomate y Oda a la cebolla (pp. 364–365)

A. The poems in your textbook reading are about tomatoes and onions. What words would you use to describe a tomato or an onion? Write them below.

Tomato: ______________, ______________, ______________, ______________

Onion: ______________, ______________, ______________, ______________

B. These poems use many descriptive words to tell us about tomatoes and onions. Some of these words are listed below. Circle the letter of the English meaning of each word.

1.	**redonda**	**a.** small	**b.** round
2.	**clara**	**a.** clear	**b.** dark
3.	**pobres**	**a.** rich	**b.** poor
4.	**constelación**	**a.** condition	**b.** constellation
5.	**planeta**	**a.** planet	**b.** plantation

C. Look at the poem **"Oda a la cebolla"** below. Read it aloud and look back at your answers from **part B** if you need help with the meaning of certain words. Then, write **C (cierto)** or **F (falso)** for each sentence below.

(...) cebolla,
clara como un planeta,
y destinada
a relucir (shine),
constelación constante,
redonda rosa de agua
sobre la mesa
de las pobres gentes.

1. Según el poeta, la cebolla es como un planeta. ________

2. Una cebolla es también como un tomate. ________

3. *Redonda rosa de agua* quiere decir que es como una flor clara. ________

4. El poeta dice que todas las personas tienen la cebolla sobre su mesa. ________

Presentación oral (p. 367)

Task: Imagine you are a guest on a television cooking show. You will be telling the audience how to prepare your favorite main dish.

A. Write the name of your favorite dish below. Then place an *X* next to the ingredients in the chart that you need to prepare that dish.

Mi plato favorito es _______________.

Ingredientes			
____ huevos	____ caldo	____ carne	____ tomate
____ agua	____ pollo	____ lechuga	____ ajo
____ leche	____ sal	____ cebolla	____ pimienta
____ camarones	____ queso	____ aceite	____ mariscos

B. Use the ingredients you chose in **part A.** Think about the steps you would follow to prepare your dish. You can use the words from the list or others you have learned in this chapter.

se mezcla	se corta	se sirve	se pone	se añade

Now complete a recipe card. Include the name of the dish, the ingredients you need, and the steps to prepare this dish.

Nombre del plato: _______________

Ingredientes: _______________

Preparación: _______________

1. Primero, _______________
2. Luego, _______________
3. Después, _______________
4. Al final, _______________

C. Use your recipe card to practice your presentation. Remember to include the ingredients, describe the steps to prepare the dish, and to speak clearly.

Realidades 2

Capítulo 7B

Nombre ____________________ Hora ________

Fecha ____________________

Vocabulary Flash Cards, Sheet 1

Write the Spanish vocabulary word below each picture. If there is a word or phrase, copy it in the space provided. Be sure to include the article for each noun.

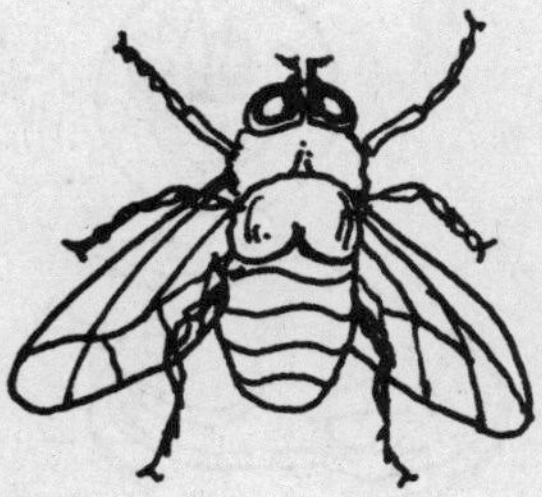

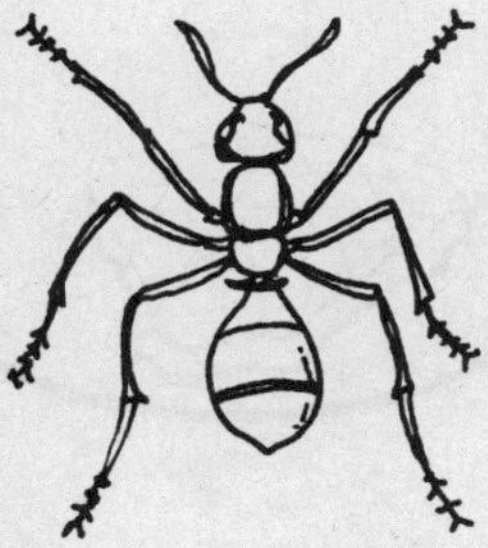

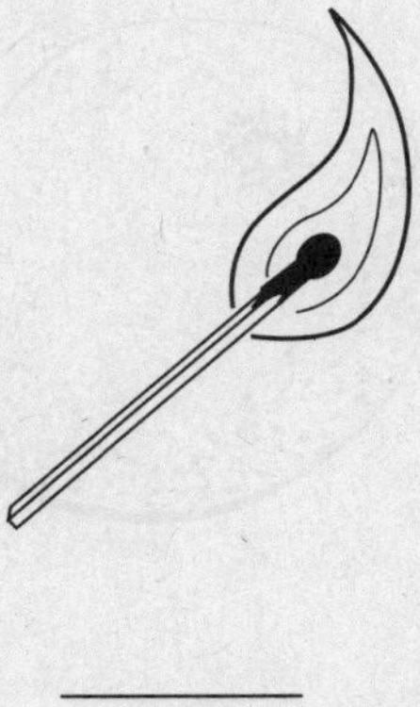

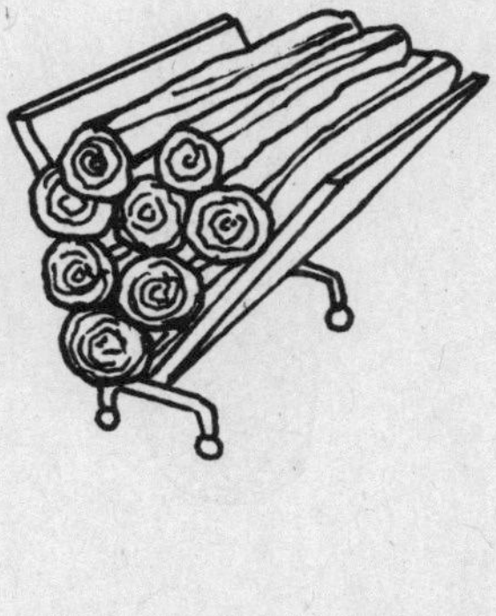

Write the Spanish vocabulary word below each picture. If there is a word or phrase, copy it in the space provided. Be sure to include the article for each noun.

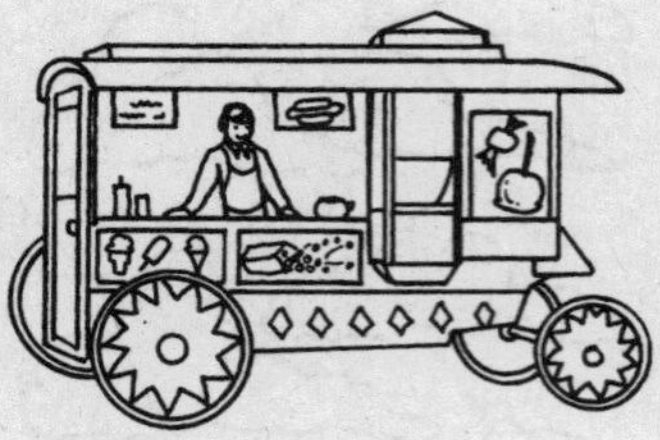

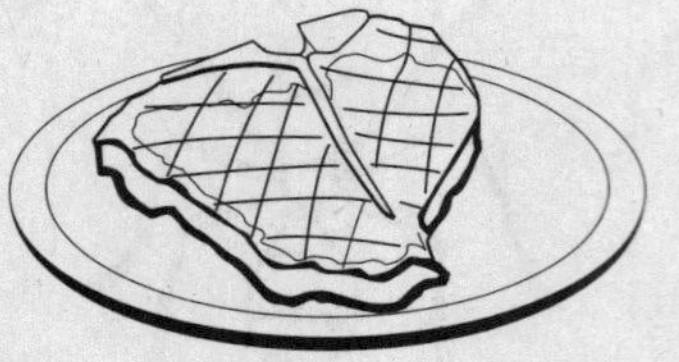

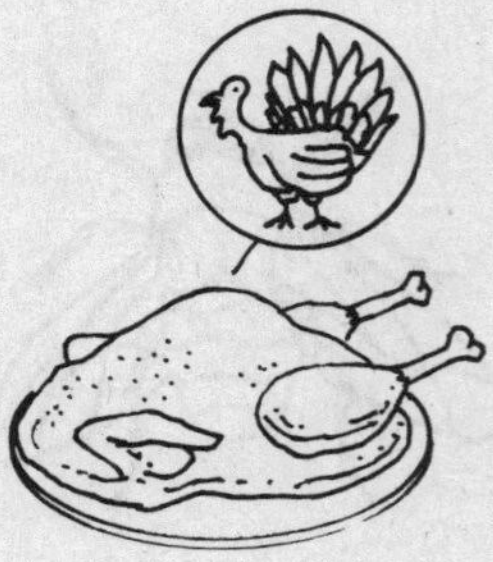

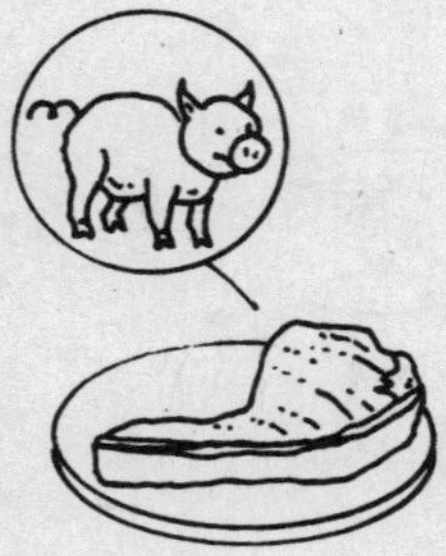

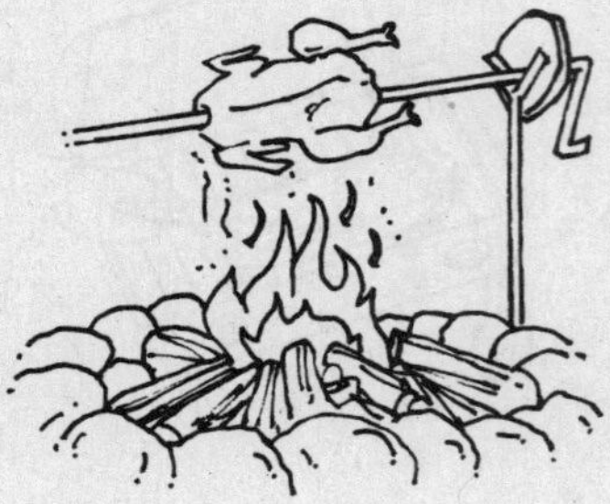

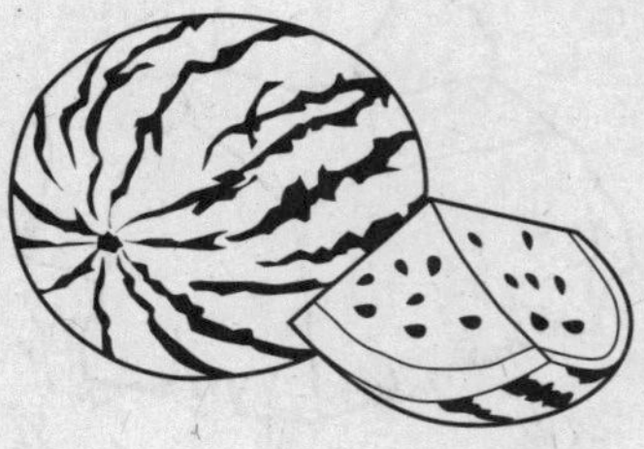

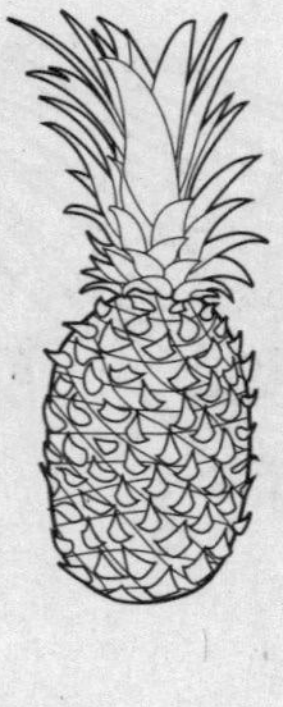

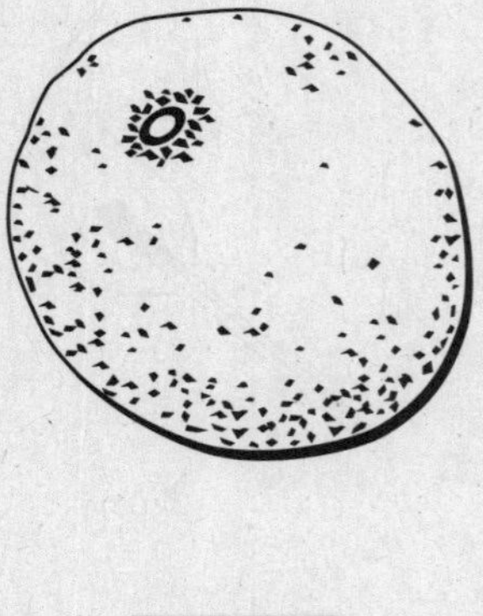

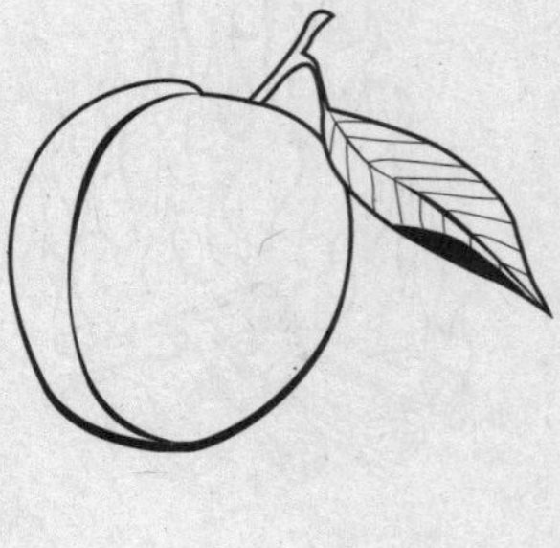

Realidades 2 Nombre Hora

Capítulo 7B Fecha **Vocabulary Flash Cards, Sheet 3**

Write the Spanish vocabulary word below each picture. If there is a word or phrase, copy it in the space provided. Be sure to include the article for each noun.

Realidades 2 Nombre _______________ Hora _______

Capítulo 7B Fecha _______________ **Vocabulary Flash Cards, Sheet 4**

Write the Spanish vocabulary word below each picture. If there is a word or phrase, copy it in the space provided. Be sure to include the article for each noun.

______ ____________	______ ____________	**seco, seca** ____________, ____________
____________	**mojado, mojada** ____________, ____________	**asado, asada** ____________, ____________
fuera (de) ________ ________	**dentro de** ________ ________	**el cielo** ______ ____________

Write the Spanish vocabulary word below each picture. If there is a word or phrase, copy it in the space provided. Be sure to include the article for each noun.

la harina	**dulce**	**grasoso, grasosa**
acompañar	**al aire libre**	**el suelo**
el sabor		

Realidades 2 | Nombre | Hora

Capítulo 7B | Fecha | **Vocabulary Flash Cards, Sheet 6**

Realidades 2 Nombre ______ Hora ______

Capítulo 7B Fecha ______ **Vocabulary Check, Sheet 1**

Tear out this page. Write the English words on the lines. Fold the paper along the dotted line to see the correct answers so you can check your work.

al aire libre ______

el cielo ______

dentro de ______

fuera (de) ______

la nube ______

la piedra ______

el aguacate ______

la chuleta de cerdo ______

los frijoles ______

la harina ______

el maíz ______

el sabor ______

dulce ______

picante ______

acompañar ______

Fold In ←

Tear out this page. Write the Spanish words on the lines. Fold the paper along the dotted line to see the correct answers so you can check your work.

outdoors ______

sky ______

inside ______

outside ______

cloud ______

rock ______

avocado ______

pork chop ______

beans ______

flour ______

corn ______

taste ______

sweet ______

spicy ______

to accompany ______

Fold In ←

Realidades 2 | Nombre ______ | Hora ______

Capítulo 7B | Fecha ______ | **Vocabulary Check, Sheet 3**

Tear out this page. Write the English words on the lines. Fold the paper along the dotted line to see the correct answers so you can check your work.

el sendero ______

el suelo ______

la fogata ______

el fósforo ______

la leña ______

a la parrilla ______

el puesto ______

asado, asada ______

asar ______

la carne de res ______

la cereza ______

la cesta ______

la mayonesa ______

la mostaza ______

Fold In ←

Tear out this page. Write the Spanish words on the lines. Fold the paper along the dotted line to see the correct answers so you can check your work.

trail _______________

ground, floor _______________

bonfire _______________

match _______________

firewood _______________

on the grill _______________

(food) stand _______________

grilled _______________

to grill, to roast _______________

steak _______________

cherry _______________

basket _______________

mayonnaise _______________

mustard _______________

Fold In ←

To hear a complete list of the vocabulary for this chapter, go to Disc 2, Track 6 on the Guided Practice Audio CD or go to www.phschool.com and type in the Web Code jdd-0799. Then click on **Repaso del capítulo.**

Usted and *ustedes* commands (p. 382)

- Use the **usted** command form to tell someone older than you what to do or what *not* to do. Use the **ustedes** form to tell a group of people what to do or what *not* to do.
- Affirmative and negative **usted** and **ustedes** commands have the same spelling changes and irregular forms as negative **tú** commands.
- The commands for **viajar** (to travel), **comer** (to eat), and **servir** (to serve) are shown below.

verbs ending in *-ar*			verbs ending in *-er*			verbs ending in *-ir*		
yo viajo	**usted**	**ustedes**	yo como	**usted**	**ustedes**	yo sirvo	**usted**	**ustedes**
	viaje	viajen		coma	coman		sirva	sirvan

A. Sra. Álvarez has some questions about camping. Tell her what to do. Circle the correct **usted** form in parentheses.

1. —¿Dónde pongo la cesta?
   —(**Ponga** / **Pongan**) la cesta en la mesa.
2. —¿Qué lugar busco para hacer la fogata?
   —(**Busquen** / **Busque**) un lugar seco para hacer la fogata.
3. —¿Con qué corto las chuletas?
   —(**Corten** / **Corte**) las chuletas con el cuchillo.
4. —¿Con qué sirvo las chuletas?
   —(**Sirvan** / **Sirva**) las chuletas con ensalada y papas.

B. Now, you and your friends have some questions for Sra. Álvarez. She will tell you what to do. Circle the correct **ustedes** command form in parentheses.

1. —¿Dónde dejamos los fósforos?
   —(**Dejen** / **Deje**) los fósforos en la cesta.
2. —¿Qué traemos para hacer la fogata?
   —(**Traigan** / **Traes**) leña, por favor.
3. —¿Vamos a esos árboles para buscar la leña?
   —Sí, (**vaya** / **vayan**) a esos árboles.
4. —¿Cortamos las chuletas de cerdo ahora?
   —Sí, (**corten** / **cortas**) las chuletas de cerdo.

Usted and *ustedes* commands (*continued*)

C. People are asking Rafael questions, and he is telling them what *not* to do. Look at the boldfaced verb in each question and complete Rafael's answer by using an **usted** or **ustedes** command form of the same verb. Follow the models.

Modelos

—Rafael, ¿**hacemos** el picnic aquí en el suelo?

—No, no *hagan* ustedes el picnic en el suelo.

—Rafael, ¿**dejo** las chuletas en la mesa?

—No, no *deje* usted las chuletas en la mesa.

1. —Rafael, ¿**dejo** la comida en casa?

   —No, no ____________ usted la comida en casa.

2. —Rafael, ¿**como** más salsa o no?

   —Por favor, ¡no ____________ usted más salsa!

3. —Rafael, ¿**dejamos** el maíz en la mesa?

   —No, no ____________ ustedes el maíz en la mesa.

4. —Rafael, ¿**hacemos** una fogata aquí?

   —No, no ____________ ustedes una fogata en un lugar mojado.

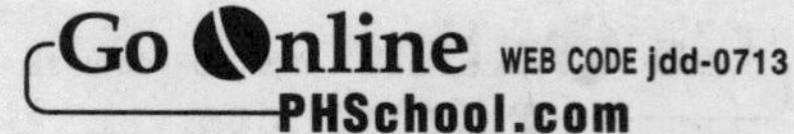

Usted and *ustedes* commands (*continued*)

- If you want to use a pronoun such as **lo, la, los,** or **las** with an affirmative command, attach it to the end of the command.

  —¿Dónde ponemos la leña? *Where do we put the firewood?*

  —Pónganla en un lugar seco. *Put it in a dry place.*

- If you want to use a pronoun with a negative command, put it right before the command.

  —¿Encendemos la fogata? *Should we light the fire?*

  —No, no la enciendan. *No, don't light it.*

D. Sr. Martínez is asking what to do with some things he brought for a barbecue. Read his questions and circle the pronoun **lo, la, los,** or **las** in the answers. Follow the models.

Modelos —¿Preparo el pollo?
—Sí, prepárelo a la parrilla.

—¿Uso las frutas?
—No, no las use para la ensalada.

1. —¿Busco las cerezas?
   —Sí, búsquelas en la cesta.
2. —¿Corto los aguacates?
   —No, no los corte.
3. —¿Traigo la leña?
   —No, no la traiga aquí.
4. —¿Enciendo el fósforo?
   —No, no lo encienda.
5. —¿Pongo las chuletas en la parrilla?
   —Sí, póngalas allí.
6. —¿Saco el cuchillo?
   —Sí, sáquelo de la cesta.
7. —¿Sirvo la piña?
   —Sí, sírvala con melón.
8. —¿Aso los frijoles?
   —No, no los ase.

Uses of *por* (p. 386)

The preposition **por** is used in many ways.

- To tell about time or distance: **Yo dormí por ocho horas.** *I slept for eight hours.*
- To tell about movement: **Vamos a caminar por el sendero.** *Let's walk along the path.*
- To tell about exchanging one thing for another: **No pagué mucho por la piña.** *I didn't pay much for the pineapple.*
- To tell about a reason: **Yo fui al mercado por unas cerezas.** *I went to the market for some cherries.*
- To tell about an action on someone's behalf: **Encendí la parrilla por Luisa.** *I lit the grill for Luisa.*
- To tell about a way of communication or transportation: **¿Vas a viajar por avión?** *Are you going to travel by plane?*

A. Each of these sentences below ends with an expression that uses **por.** Write the best ending for each sentence.

1. Caminen ______________________.
   a. por tren **b.** por el sendero
2. Yo dormí ______________________.
   a. por la camisa **b.** por dos horas
3. Daniel camina ______________________.
   a. por el parque **b.** por esos duraznos
4. Lupe va a la tienda ______________________.
   a. por avión **b.** por el periódico
5. Me gusta viajar ______________________.
   a. por dos tomates **b.** por avión
6. ¿Cuánto dinero pagaste ______________________?
   a. por el sendero **b.** por esa piña
7. Voy a preparar la carne ______________________.
   a. por mi hermano **b.** por teléfono

Go Online WEB CODE jdd-0714 PHSchool.com

Lectura: El Yunque (pp. 390–391)

A. You're going to read about a fantastic tropical park called **El Yunque.** What kind of things do you think you'll read about in the article? Add two more questions to the list about things you think the article may describe.

¿Dónde está el parque? ¿Qué hay en el parque? ¿Qué tipos de plantas hay?

________________, ________________, ________________

B. Read the following selections from the reading about **El Yunque.** As you read, find answers to some of the questions in **part A** and write them below.

El Yunque es una de las atracciones más visitadas de Puerto Rico.... Más de 240 especies de árboles coexisten con animales exóticos, como el coquí y la boa de Puerto Rico.

La mejor forma de explorar este parque es caminando por las varias veredas (paths) que pasan por el bosque.

1. ¿Dónde está el parque? El parque ésta en ________________.
2. ¿Qué hay en el parque? Hay ________________ ________________.
3. ¿Qué tipos de plantas hay? Hay ________________.

C. Look at the following advice from the reading about walking in **El Yunque.** After you read the selection, place a ✓ next to those sentences that are true.

Consejos para el caminante
1 Nunca camine solo. Siempre vaya acompañado.
2 Traiga agua y algo para comer.
3 Use repelente para insectos.
4 No abandone las veredas para no perderse (to get lost).
5 No toque (touch) las plantas del bosque.

1. Never walk alone in the park. ______
2. Don't take food or water with you. ______
3. Use insect repellent. ______
4. Don't walk along the paths. ______
5. Touch the plants in the forest. ______

Presentación escrita (p. 393)

Task: You will write and illustrate a poster on safety and fun at an outdoor cookout.

A. Read the list below and underline the sentences that tell about something you need for an outdoor cookout.

1. Se necesitan fósforos.
2. Se debe comprar carne.
3. Se debe buscar un lugar mojado.
4. Se necesita leña.
5. Se debe llevar regla y lápiz.
6. Se debe comprar agua o refrescos.
7. Se debe mirar una película.

B. Read the following sentences. Circle the numbers of the sentences that give good advice before, during, and after a cookout. This will help you choose what you will write.

1. Busquen un lugar seco para hacer la fogata.
2. Lleven sus videojuegos.
3. Compren carne para asar.
4. Tengan cuidado con la parrilla caliente.
5. Lleven repelente para mosquitos.
6. No jueguen cerca de un lago.
7. No tiren nada en el parque.
8. No apaguen la fogata antes de salir.

C. Using your answers from **parts A** and **B,** write a short paragraph. Mention how to stay safe and have fun before, during, and after the cookout. You may use the sentence starters below.

Antes de hacer una parrillada, ustedes necesitan ____________________.

El lugar debe ____________________.

Para hacer la fogata deben ____________________.

No jueguen ustedes con ____________________.

Antes de salir, ____________________.

D. Review the spelling and vocabulary on your poster. Check that your paragraph includes the appropriate commands and is easy to understand.

E. Use artwork to illustrate your sentences on the poster.

Realidades 2 | Nombre | Hora

Capítulo 8A | Fecha | **Vocabulary Flash Cards, Sheet 1**

Write the Spanish vocabulary word below each picture. If there is a word or phrase, copy it in the space provided. Be sure to include the article for each noun.

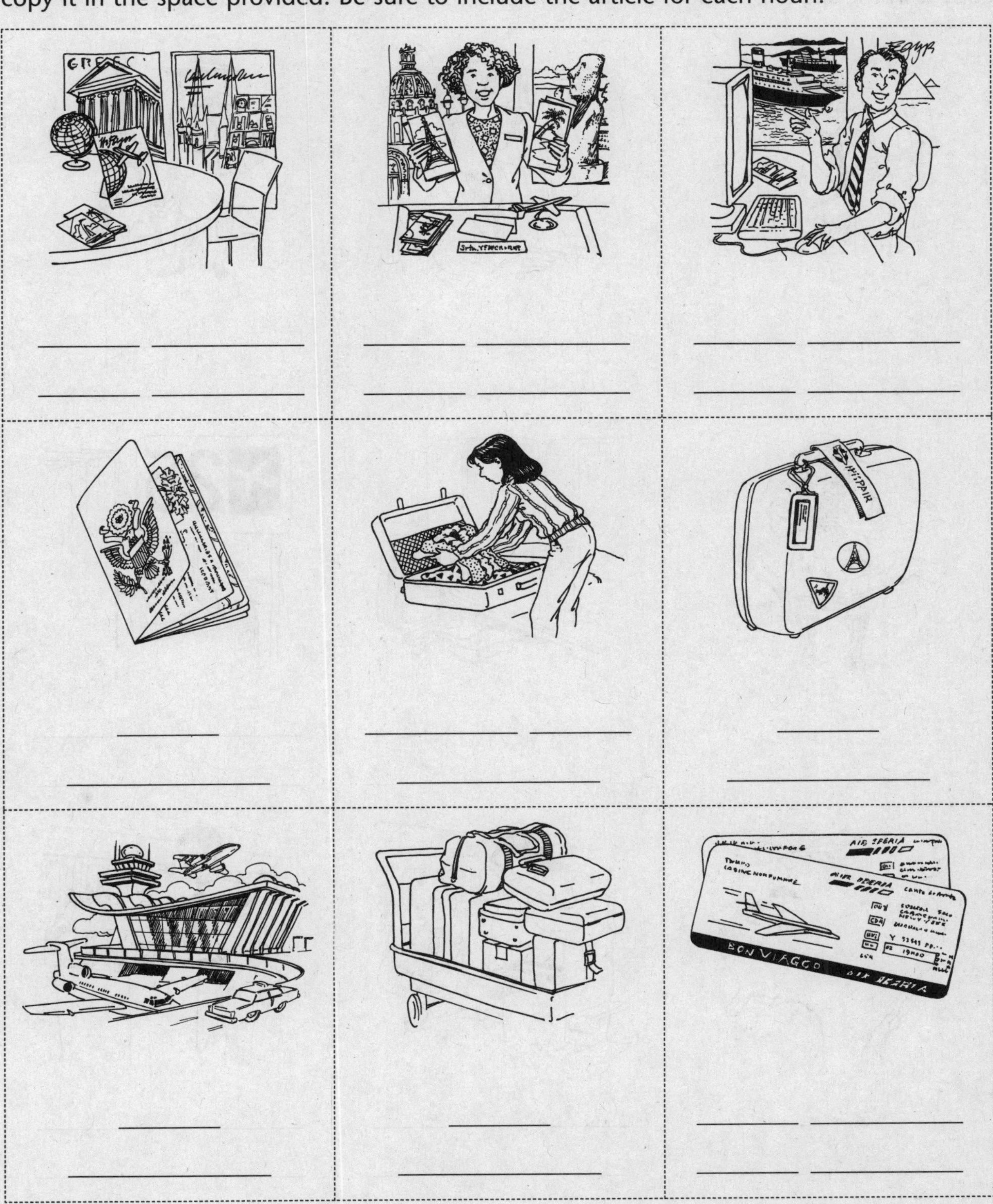

Nombre ______ Hora ______

Fecha ______

Vocabulary Flash Cards, Sheet 2

Write the Spanish vocabulary word below each picture. If there is a word or phrase, copy it in the space provided. Be sure to include the article for each noun.

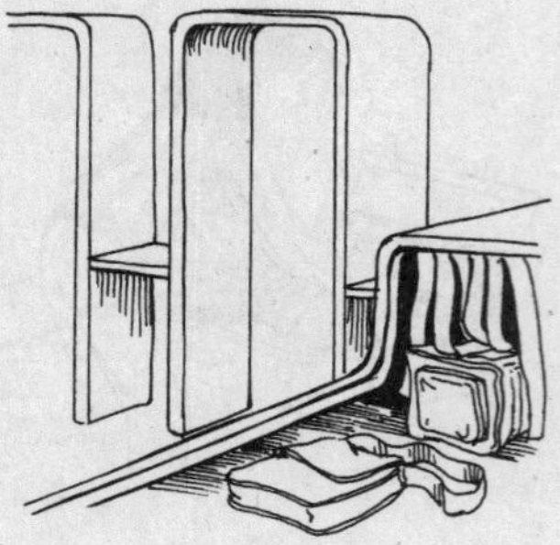

Write the Spanish vocabulary word below each picture. If there is a word or phrase, copy it in the space provided. Be sure to include the article for each noun.

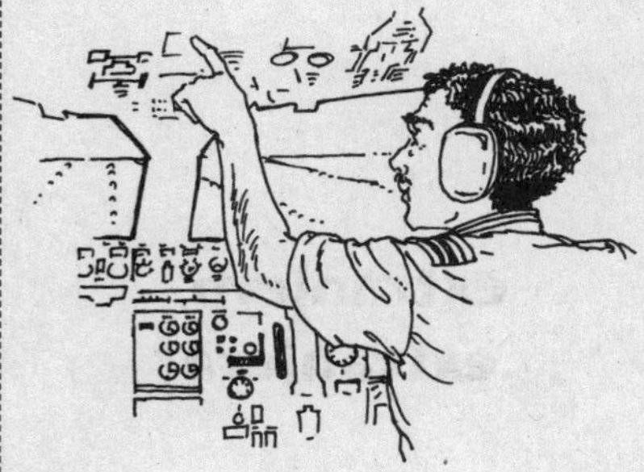

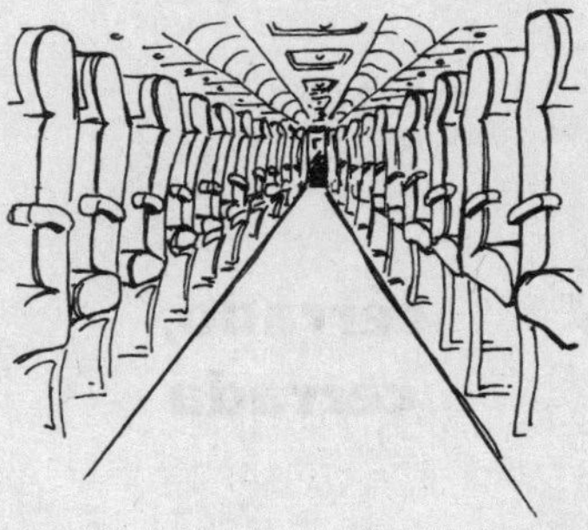

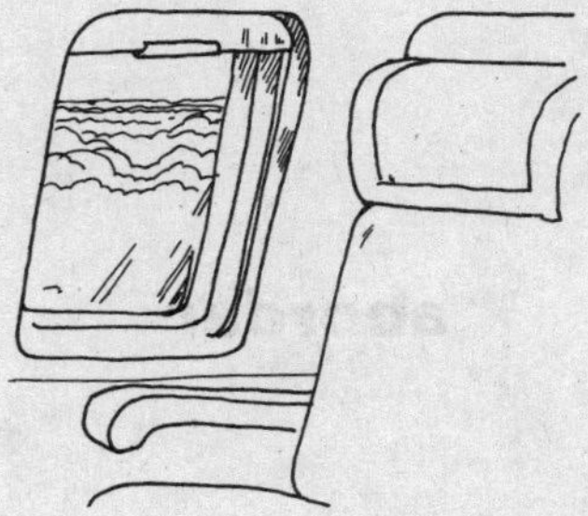

_______ ______________	_______ ______________	_______ ______________
_______ ______________	_______ ______________	_______ ______________
______________	17 _______ ______________	**abierto, abierta** ______________, ______________

Nombre ______________________ Hora ______________

Fecha ______________________ **Vocabulary Flash Cards, Sheet 4**

Write the Spanish vocabulary word below each picture. If there is a word or phrase, copy it in the space provided. Be sure to include the article for each noun.

cerrado, cerrada ______________, ______________	**extranjero, extranjera** ______________, ______________	**hacer un viaje** ________ ________ ________
planear ______________	**la reservación** ________ ______________	**abordar** ______________
con destino a ________ __________ ________	**de ida y vuelta** ________ ________ ________ __________	**directo, directa** ______________, ______________

Write the Spanish vocabulary word below each picture. If there is a word or phrase, copy it in the space provided. Be sure to include the article for each noun.

durar	**hacer escala**	**la línea aérea**
la llegada	**el retraso**	**la salida**
bienvenido, bienvenida	**insistir en**	**listo, lista**

Vocabulary Flash Cards, Sheet 6

Write the Spanish vocabulary word below each picture. If there is a word or phrase, copy it in the space provided. Be sure to include the article for each noun.

sugerir	**tendremos**	**tener paciencia**
la aduana	**el empleado, la empleada**	**facturar**

Realidades 2

Capítulo 8A

Nombre ______________________ Hora ____________

Fecha ____________________

Vocabulary Check, Sheet 1

Tear out this page. Write the English words on the lines. Fold the paper along the dotted line to see the correct answers so you can check your work.

la agencia de viajes ______________

el equipaje ______________

extranjero, extranjera ______________

hacer un viaje ______________

la maleta ______________

planear ______________

abordar ______________

la aduana ______________

el aeropuerto ______________

el anuncio ______________

de ida y vuelta ______________

la salida ______________

el vuelo ______________

abierto, abierta ______________

Fold In ←

Realidades 2 | Nombre ______ | Hora ______

Capítulo 8A | Fecha ______ | **Vocabulary Check, Sheet 2**

Tear out this page. Write the Spanish words on the lines. Fold the paper along the dotted line to see the correct answers so you can check your work.

travel agency ______

luggage ______

foreign ______

to take a trip ______

suitcase ______

to plan ______

to board ______

customs ______

airport ______

announcement ______

round-trip ______

departure ______

flight ______

open ______

Fold In ←

Realidades 2

Capítulo 8A

Nombre ______ Hora ______

Fecha ______

Vocabulary Check, Sheet 3

Tear out this page. Write the English words on the lines. Fold the paper along the dotted line to see the correct answers so you can check your work.

el pasaporte ______

la reservación ______

el turista, la turista ______

directo, directa ______

durar ______

el empleado, la empleada ______

la línea aérea ______

el pasajero, la pasajera ______

registrar ______

bienvenido, bienvenida ______

necesitar ______

permitir ______

preferir ______

cerrado, cerrada ______

Fold In ←

Tear out this page. Write the Spanish words on the lines. Fold the paper along the dotted line to see the correct answers so you can check your work.

passport ________

reservation ________

tourist ________

direct ________

to last ________

employee ________

airline ________

passenger ________

to inspect, to search *(luggage)* ________

welcome ________

to need ________

to allow, to permit ________

to prefer ________

closed ________

Fold In ←

To hear a complete list of the vocabulary for this chapter, go to Disc 2, Track 7 on the Guided Practice Audio CD or go to www.phschool.com and type in the Web Code jdd-0889. Then click on **Repaso del capítulo.**

Realidades 2

Capítulo 8A

Nombre ______ Hora ______

Fecha ______ Guided Practice Activities **8A-1**

The present subjunctive (p. 410)

- Use the subjunctive to say that one person influences the actions of another:

  Nosotros recomendamos que ustedes hablen con la empleada.

  We recommend that you speak with the employee.

- A sentence in the subjunctive has two parts, each with a different subject. The word **que** comes between the two parts. The first part uses the present indicative to recommend, suggest, prohibit, and so on. The second part uses the present subjunctive verb to say what the other person or people should or should not do, or what should or should not happen.

  Nosotros recomendamos que ustedes hablen con un agente de viajes.

  We recommend that you speak with a travel agent.

A. Read the following sentences, paying attention to the underlined part. Write **PI** (for Present Indicative) or **PS** (for Present Subjunctive) to identify the underlined part. The first one is done for you.

1. Isabel quiere que <u>nosotros estemos listos para abordar.</u> PS
2. <u>Yo deseo</u> que tú no registres las maletas. ______
3. <u>Yo quiero</u> que usted compre los boletos. ______
4. Ellos insisten en que <u>yo lleve el pasaporte.</u> ______
5. <u>Ella no permite</u> que yo facture las maletas. ______
6. Rosa necesita que <u>Pablo hable con el agente de viajes.</u> ______

B. Now, circle the subjunctive verb in each sentence. The first one is done for you.

1. Isabel quiere que nosotros (estemos) listos para abordar.
2. Yo deseo que tú no registres las maletas.
3. Yo quiero que usted compre los boletos.
4. Ellos insisten en que yo lleve el pasaporte.
5. Ella no permite que yo facture las maletas.
6. Rosa necesita que Pablo hable con el agente de viajes.

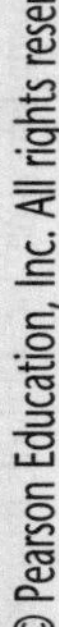

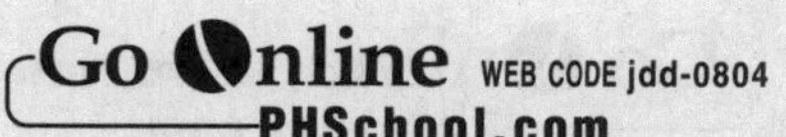
Go Online WEB CODE jdd-0804 PHSchool.com

The present subjunctive (*continued*)

- Some verbs that are often followed by **que** + subjunctive are:

  decir — preferir (**e → ie**)
  insistir en — querer (**e → ie**)
  necesitar — recomendar (**e → ie**)
  permitir — sugerir (**e → ie**)
  prohibir

  La empleada no permite que entres sin el pasaporte.
  The employee does not allow you to enter without a passport.

- You form the present subjunctive in the same way as you form negative **tú** commands and **usted/ustedes** commands. You drop the **-o** of the present-tense indicative **yo** form and add the present subjunctive endings. See the chart below:

hablar		aprender		escribir	
hable	habl**emos**	aprend**a**	aprend**amos**	escrib**a**	escrib**amos**
habl**es**	habl**éis**	aprend**as**	aprend**áis**	escrib**as**	escrib**áis**
habl**e**	habl**en**	aprend**a**	aprend**an**	escrib**a**	escrib**an**

C. Circle the verb in parentheses that best completes each sentence. The first one is done for you.

1. Yo insisto en que tú (**hables** / **habla**) con tu mamá antes del viaje.
2. Mario necesita que su hermano (**aprenda** / **aprendan**) a hacer la maleta.
3. Usted recomienda que yo (**escriba** / **escribo**) a la línea aérea.
4. Julia sugiere que usted (**hablen** / **hable**) con el agente de viajes.
5. Tú prefieres que los niños (**aprendan** / **aprende**) a leer los horarios en el aeropuerto.
6. Ellos quieren que nosotros (**escriben** / **escribamos**) nuestros nombres en las maletas.
7. Yo no permito que los estudiantes (**hablen** / **hable**) mucho durante el vuelo.
8. Ustedes necesitan que Julia y Mario (**escribas** / **escriban**) la hora de salida.

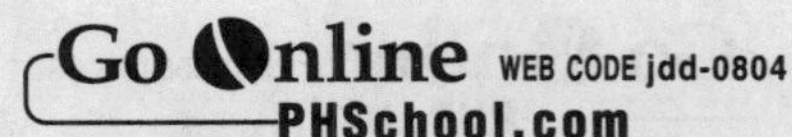

Nombre ______________________ Hora ______________

Fecha ______________________

The present subjunctive (*continued*)

- The present subjunctive has the same spelling changes and irregular **yo** form changes that you used with the negative **tú** commands and **usted/ustedes** commands.
- Here are the present subjunctive forms of **llegar** and **hacer:**

llegar		hacer	
lle**gue**	lle**guemos**	ha**ga**	ha**gamos**
lle**gues**	lle**guéis**	ha**gas**	ha**gáis**
lle**gue**	lle**guen**	ha**ga**	ha**gan**

D. Circle the correct verb to complete each sentence. The first one is done for you.

1. La profesora recomienda que Juan (**saque** / **sacar**) más libros de la biblioteca.
2. Yo necesito que ustedes (**pagar** / **paguen**) por los boletos hoy.
3. Se recomienda que los empleados (**busquen** / **buscar**) cosas prohibidas.
4. La mamá desea que el niño (**tenga** / **tener**) más paciencia.

E. Read the questions below, paying attention to the verbs in boldface. Then, complete the answers with the correct form of the subjunctive verb. Follow the model.

Modelo —¿Prefiere el Sr. Rosado que yo **llegue** temprano?

—Sí, el Sr. Rosado prefiere que tú *llegues* temprano.

1. —¿Quieres que yo **haga** la maleta primero?

   —No, no quiero que tú ____________ la maleta primero.
2. —¿Recomiendan ellos que nosotros **hagamos** las reservaciones?

   —Sí, ellos recomiendan que ustedes ____________ las reservaciones.
3. —¿Sugiere papá que tú **llegues** temprano al aeropuerto?

   —Sí, papá sugiere que yo ____________ temprano al aeropuerto.
4. —¿Necesitas que yo **escriba** el número de la puerta de embarque?

   —No, no necesito que tú ____________ el número de la puerta de embarque.

Irregular verbs in the subjunctive (p. 413)

- Verbs with irregular **tú** and **usted/ustedes** commands also have irregular subjunctive forms.

dar		estar		ir		saber		ser	
dé	demos	esté	estemos	vaya	vayamos	sepa	sepamos	sea	seamos
des	deis	estés	estéis	vayas	vayáis	sepas	sepáis	seas	seáis
dé	den	esté	estén	vaya	vayan	sepa	sepan	sea	sean

A. Look at the infinitive verb in parentheses. Then, read the sentence and circle the verb in its subjunctive form. Follow the model.

Modelo (**dar**) Recomiendo que Ana te (dé) la tarjeta de embarque.

1. (**estar**) Sugiero que el pasajero esté aquí a las cuatro.
2. (**ir**) Quiero que vayas a la agencia de viajes.
3. (**saber**) Deseo que sepas la hora de llegada.
4. (**ser**) Insisto en que sean responsables.
5. (**ser**) Necesito que el vuelo sea de ida y vuelta.

B. Choose the correct verb from the word bank to complete each sentence. The first one is done for you.

estén	sea	den	vayas	sepa	dé

1. Deseo que ustedes *estén* en el aeropuerto muy temprano.
2. Recomiendo que ustedes ____________ sus maletas a los empleados.
3. Sugiero que tú ____________ a la agencia de viajes.
4. Quiero que ella ____________ dónde está la puerta de embarque.
5. Necesito que la maleta ____________ grande.
6. La empleada de la aerolínea quiere que yo le ____________ mi tarjeta de embarque.

Realidades 2 Nombre ______ Hora ______

Capítulo 8A Fecha ______ Guided Practice Activities 8A-5

Lectura: Ecuador, país de maravillas (pp. 418–419)

A. The reading in your textbook is about the country of Ecuador. Write three things that you would expect to find in your reading about the attractions of this country.

1. ______.
2. ______.
3. ______.

B. You can predict what a reading is about by looking at the title, subheads, and photo captions. Look at the photos and read the captions on pages 418–419 of your textbook. Place an *X* next to the attractions you can find in Ecuador. The first one is done for you.

Las atracciones turísticas del Ecuador

__X__ woven cloth	____ la Mitad del Mundo
____ the island of Puerto Rico	____ snow-covered mountains
____ the Galapagos Islands	____ the church of la Compañía de Jesús

C. Read the excerpt from your reading and circle the answers to the questions that follow.

> *Es un país pequeño, pero tiene paisajes para todos los gustos. Desde playas tropicales hasta montañas nevadas, desde ciudades coloniales hasta parques naturales.*

1. ¿Qué clase de país es Ecuador?
   a. Es un país pequeño.
   b. Es un país grande.

2. ¿Dónde nieva en Ecuador?
   a. Nieva en las playas tropicales.
   b. Nieva en las montañas.

3. ¿Hay ciudades coloniales en Ecuador?
   a. Sí, hay ciudades coloniales en Ecuador.
   b. No, no hay ciudades coloniales en Ecuador.

4. ¿Qué clase de parques hay en Ecuador?
   a. Hay parques artificiales en Ecuador.
   b. Hay parques naturales en Ecuador.

Presentación oral (p. 421)

Task: Imagine that you work at a travel agency. You need to provide travel information to a client who would like to travel to a Spanish-speaking country.

A. Choose one of the following Spanish-speaking countries: México, Ecuador.

B. Read the following travel information about each country. Then, circle one or two recommendations you would offer based on what you read.

1. La ciudad de Quito en Ecuador está en las montañas y hace mucho frío. Hay una iglesia muy importante.
   a. Recomiendo que lleven poca ropa.
   b. Sugiero que vayan a la iglesia de la Compañía de Jesús.
   c. Recomiendo que lleven suéteres o chaquetas.

2. Cancún está en México. En Cancún hay una playa tropical de 14 millas y muchos hoteles elegantes.
   a. Si desean ir a una playa grande, yo recomiendo que vayan a Cancún.
   b. Si buscan un hotel elegante, vayan a Cancún.
   c. Recomiendo que lleven trajes de baño.

C. Use your recommendations in **part B** as a model for your oral presentation. You may use the sentence starters below.

Recomiendo que Uds. viajen a ______________________. *Allí pueden ver* ______________________________. *Deben llevar* ______________________

porque ______________________________.

D. Now, practice your presentation using the information you have gathered. Try to present the information in a logical sequence and speak clearly.

E. Present the trip you have planned to your partner. Your teacher will grade you on the following:

- how much information you communicate
- how easy it is to understand you

Realidades 2

Capítulo 8B

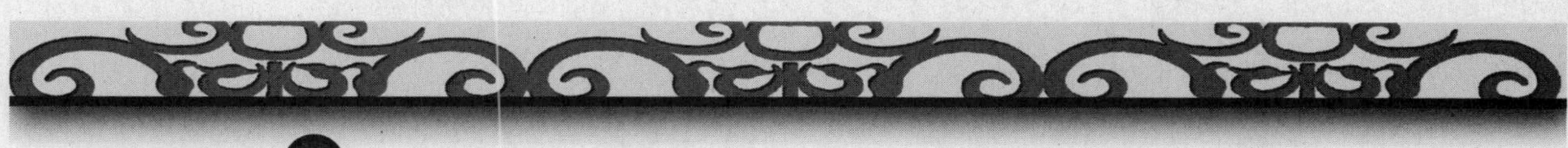

Nombre ______________________ Hora ____________

Fecha ______________________

Vocabulary Flash Cards, Sheet 1

Write the Spanish vocabulary word below each picture. If there is a word or phrase, copy it in the space provided. Be sure to include the article for each noun.

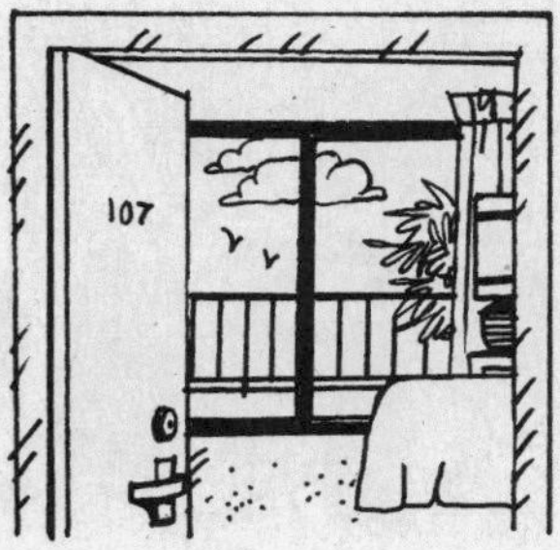

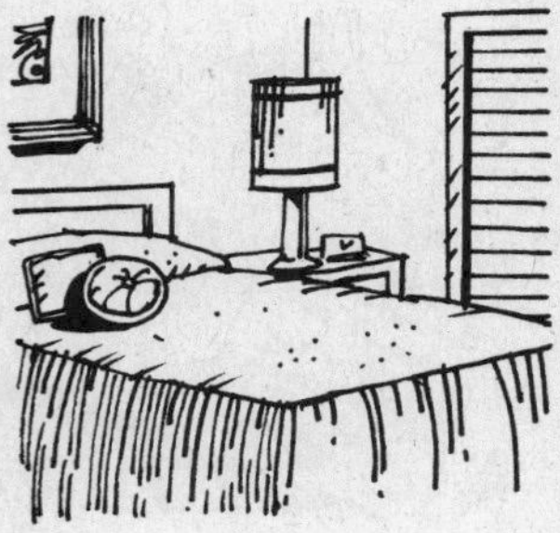

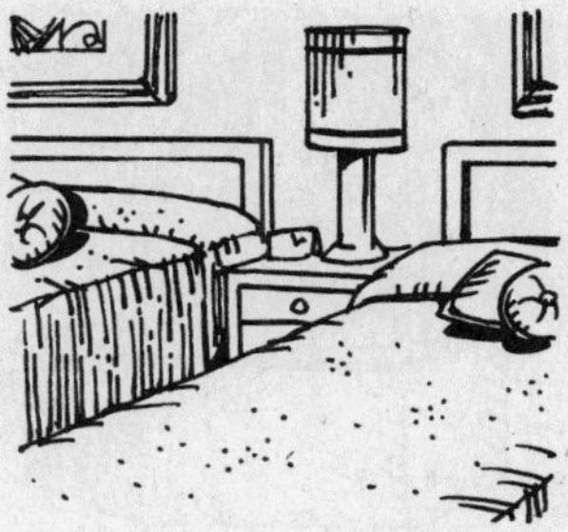

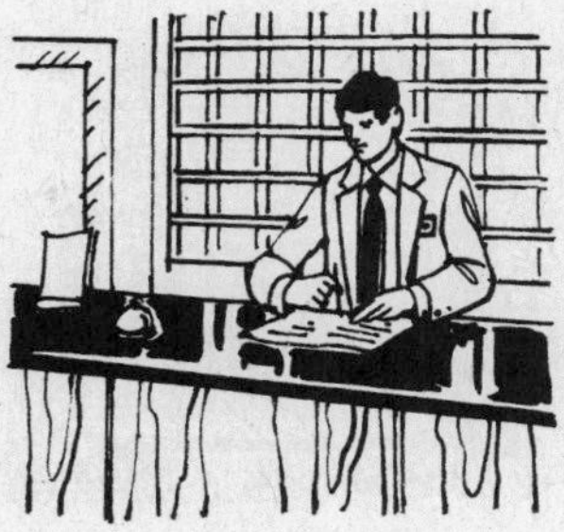

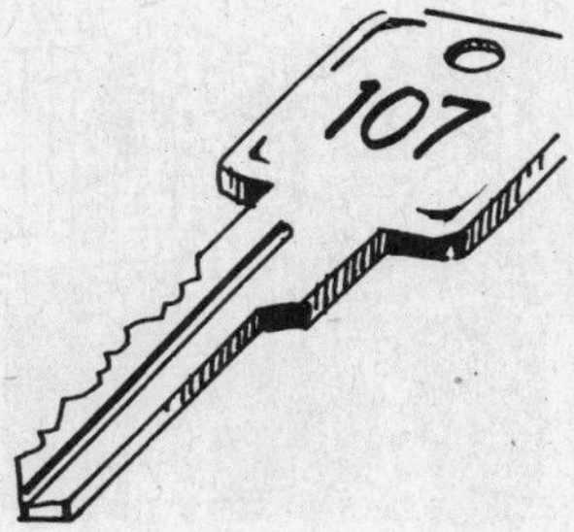

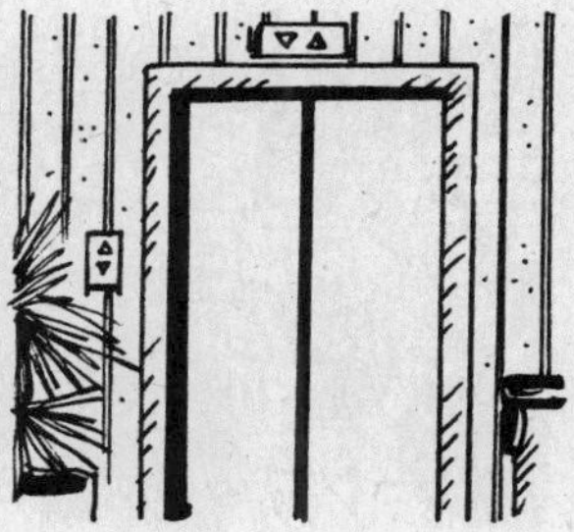

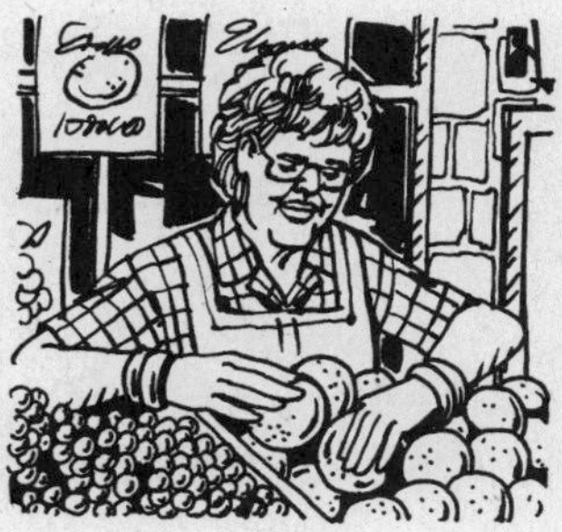

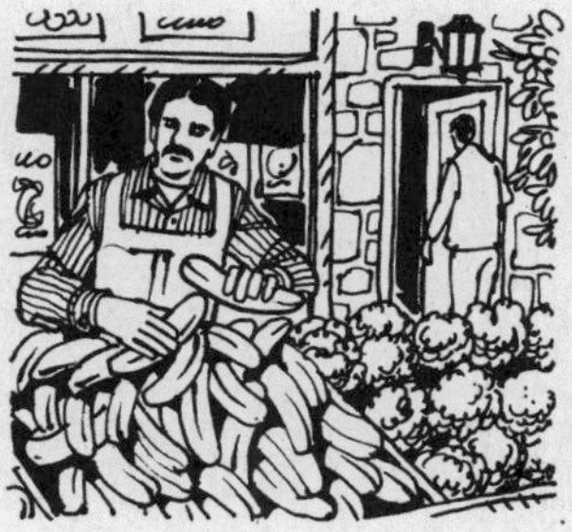

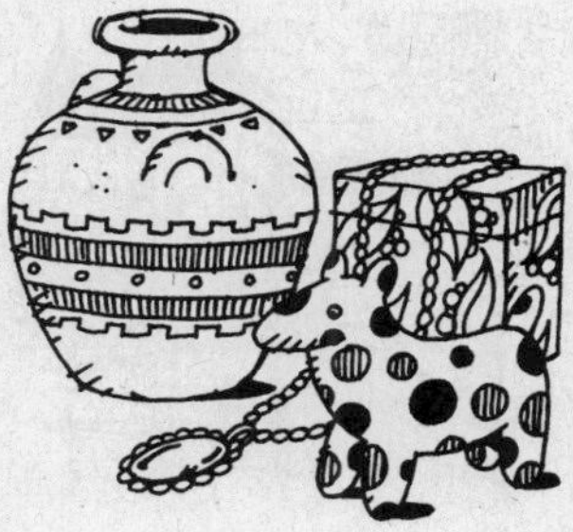

Realidades 2

Capítulo 8B

Nombre _______________ Hora _______________

Fecha _______________

Vocabulary Flash Cards, Sheet 2

Write the Spanish vocabulary word below each picture. If there is a word or phrase, copy it in the space provided. Be sure to include the article for each noun.

Write the Spanish vocabulary word below each picture. If there is a word or phrase, copy it in the space provided. Be sure to include the article for each noun.

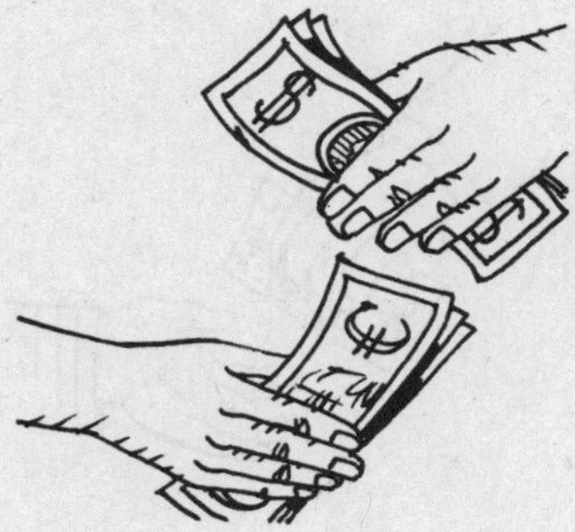 __________	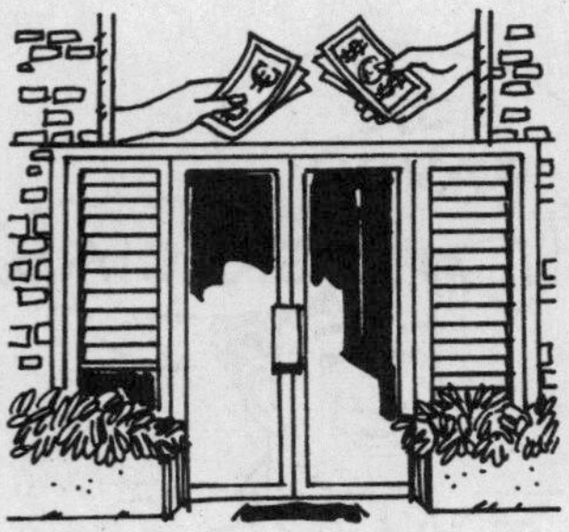 _____ _____	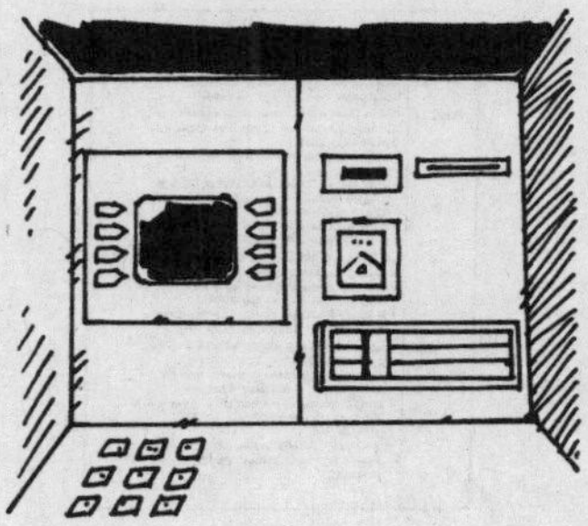 _____ _____
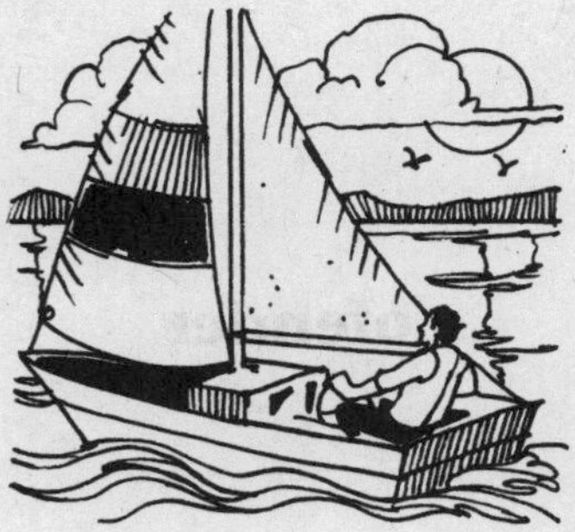 __________	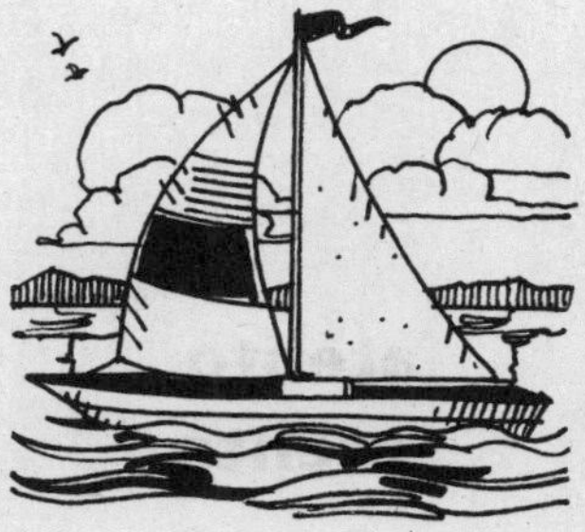 _____ _____	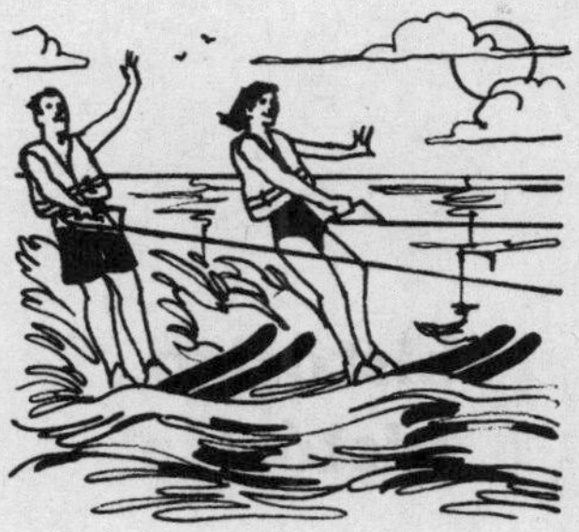 _____ _____
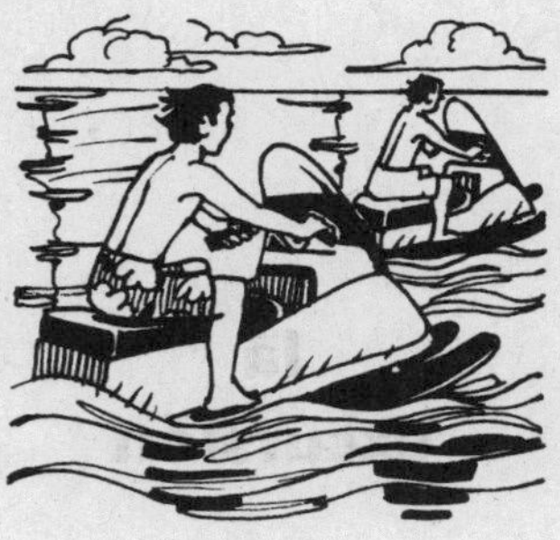 _____ _____	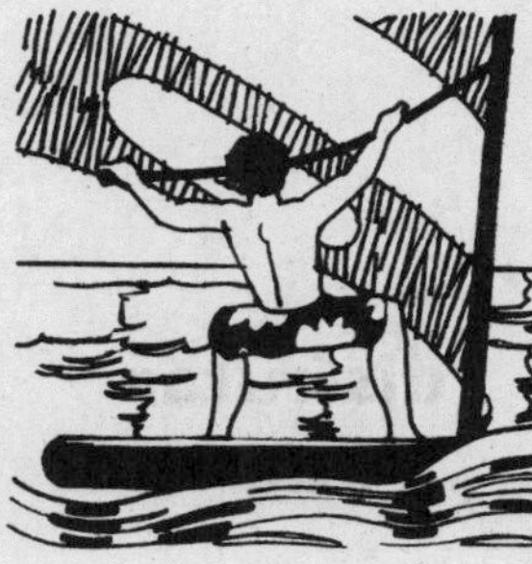 _____ _____	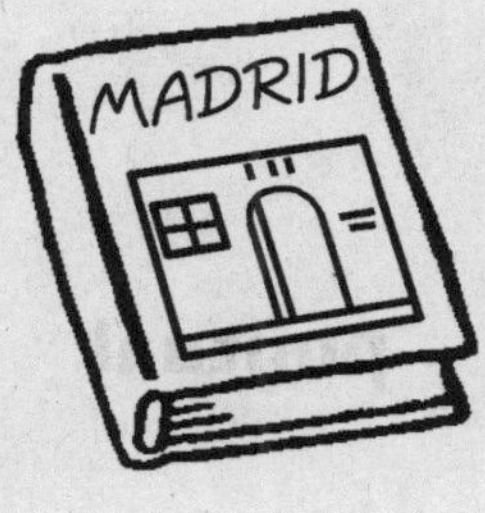 MADRID __________

Realidades 2 Nombre Hora

Capítulo 8B Fecha **Vocabulary Flash Cards, Sheet 4**

Write the Spanish vocabulary word below each picture. If there is a word or phrase, copy it in the space provided. Be sure to include the article for each noun.

histórico, histórica	**atento, atenta**	**ofender**
puntual	**disfrutar de**	**la excursión**

Realidades 2 Nombre Hora

Capítulo 8B Fecha **Vocabulary Flash Cards, Sheet 5**

Write the Spanish vocabulary word below each picture. If there is a word or phrase, copy it in the space provided. Be sure to include the article for each noun.

regatear __________	**bello, bella** __________, __________	**en punto** __________ __________
estupendo, estupenda __________, __________	**famoso, famosa** __________, __________	**siguiente** __________
tal vez ______ ______	**típico, típica** __________, __________	**hacer ruido** __________ __________

Write the Spanish vocabulary word below each picture. If there is a word or phrase, copy it in the space provided. Be sure to include the article for each noun.

conseguir	**observar**	

Nombre ______ Hora ______

Fecha ______

Vocabulary Check, Sheet 1

Tear out this page. Write the English words on the lines. Fold the paper along the dotted line to see the correct answers so you can check your work.

la casa de cambio ______

el palacio ______

el quiosco ______

el ascensor ______

la llave ______

la recepción ______

la artesanía ______

el bote de vela ______

el guía, la guía ______

bello, bella ______

en punto ______

famoso, famosa ______

siguiente ______

tal vez ______

Fold In ←

Vocabulary Check, Sheet 2

Tear out this page. Write the Spanish words on the lines. Fold the paper along the dotted line to see the correct answers so you can check your work.

currency exchange ______

palace ______

newsstand ______

elevator ______

key ______

reception desk ______

handicrafts ______

sailboat ______

guide ______

beautiful ______

exactly (time) ______

famous ______

next, following ______

maybe, perhaps ______

Fold In ←

Tear out this page. Write the English words on the lines. Fold the paper along the dotted line to see the correct answers so you can check your work.

el cajero automático __________

la catedral __________

histórico, histórica __________

conseguir __________

la habitación __________

cortés __________

hacer ruido __________

ofender __________

la propina __________

cambiar __________

disfrutar de __________

navegar __________

el vendedor, la vendedora __________

típico, típica __________

Fold In

Realidades 2 Nombre ______ Hora ______

Capítulo 8B Fecha ______ **Vocabulary Check, Sheet 4**

Tear out this page. Write the Spanish words on the lines. Fold the paper along the dotted line to see the correct answers so you can check your work.

ATM ______

cathedral ______

historical ______

to obtain ______

room ______

polite ______

to make noise ______

to offend ______

tip ______

to change, to exchange ______

to enjoy ______

to sail, to navigate ______

vendor ______

typical ______

Fold In ←

To hear a complete list of the vocabulary for this chapter, go to Disc 2, Track 8 on the Guided Practice Audio CD or go to www.phschool.com and type in the Web Code jdd-0899. Then click on **Repaso del capítulo.**

Present subjunctive with impersonal expressions (p. 434)

- You can use impersonal expressions, such as **es importante, es necesario, es mejor,** and **es bueno,** to tell people what they should do. Sentences with these impersonal expressions are often followed by **que** + subjunctive:

  Es necesario que demos una propina al empleado.
  It's necessary that we give a tip to the employee.

  Es mejor que observes las reglas para el viaje.
  It's better that you observe the rules for the trip.

A. Use the word in parentheses to write an impersonal expression + **que.** Follow the model.

Modelo **(importante)** Es importante que nosotros llevemos la llave.

1. **(mejor)** ______________ nosotros visitemos la catedral.
2. **(necesario)** ______________ ustedes vayan a la recepción.
3. **(bueno)** ______________ tú tomes el ascensor.
4. **(importante)** ______________ yo cambie dinero.

B. Read the sentences below. Circle the verb in parentheses that best completes each sentence.

1. Es importante que ustedes (**visitemos** / **visiten**) el castillo.
2. Es necesario que tú (**llevo** / **lleves**) la guía.
3. Es bueno que nosotros (**navegues** / **naveguemos**) en un bote de vela.
4. Es mejor que yo (**haga** / **hagamos**) una gira.
5. Es necesario que ellas (**sigamos** / **sigan**) el itinerario.
6. Es importante que Mateo (**conozcas** / **conozca**) los lugares históricos.
7. Es necesario que usted (**cambie** / **cambien**) dinero en la casa de cambio.

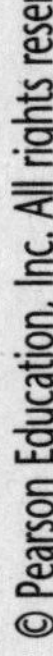

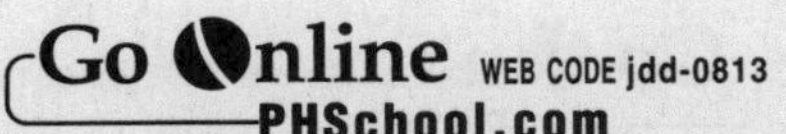

Present subjunctive with impersonal expressions (*continued*)

- If there is no person or persons specified in the second half of the sentence, then the infinitive follows the impersonal expression, and **que** is not used. This is a way to speak generally about things that should be done. Compare these sentences:

  Es importante que tú seas cortés. *It is important that you be polite.* (specific)
  Es importante ser cortés. *It is important to be polite.* (general)

C. Determine whether each of the following sentences is specific or general. Write **specific** if the sentence mentions specific people. Write **general** if it does not mention specific people. Follow the models.

Modelos ___*general*___ Es necesario ser puntual.

___*specific*___ Es necesario que ustedes sean puntuales.

1. ____________ Es necesario estar atento en el bote de vela.

   ____________ Es necesario que ellas estén atentas en el bote de vela.

2. ____________ No es bueno que nosotros hagamos ruido en las habitaciones.

   ____________ No es bueno hacer ruido en las habitaciones.

3. ____________ Es importante observar al guía.

   ____________ Es importante que tú observes al guía.

4. ____________ Es mejor que él no ofenda a los reyes.

   ____________ Es mejor no ofender a los reyes.

5. ____________ Es bueno dar propinas.

   ____________ Es bueno que nosotros demos propinas.

6. ____________ Es importante ser cortés con los vendedores.

   ____________ Es importante que usted sea cortés con los vendedores.

Present subjunctive of stem-changing verbs (p. 437)

- Stem-changing verbs ending in **-ar** and **-er** have the same stem changes in the subjunctive as in the indicative:
  recordar (o → ue) **Es necesario que usted recuerde la dirección.**
  perder (e → ie) **Es importante que tú no pierdas las llaves.**

A. Complete the following sentences with the appropriate verb form from the word bank.

entiendas	despierten	almorcemos	devuelvan	encuentre	recomiende

1. Es mejor que nosotros _almorcemos_ bien antes de ir de excursión.
2. Es importante que tú ________ lo que el guía dice.
3. Rosa no tiene dinero. Es necesario que ella ________ un cajero automático.
4. Es bueno que ustedes se ________ temprano para visitar el castillo.
5. Marta no conoce la ciudad. Es mejor que yo le ________ un buen hotel.
6. Antes de salir del hotel, es importante que ellos ________ la llave.

- Stem-changing verbs ending in **-ir** have changes in all forms of the present subjunctive. Here are some examples:
  pedir (e → i) **Es necesario que tú pidas una habitación doble.**
  divertirse (e → ie), (e → i) **Es importante que ellas se diviertan en la excursión.**
  Es importante que nos divirtamos en la gira.
  dormir (o → ue), (o → u) **Es bueno que ustedes duerman un poco.**
  Es mejor que nosotros durmamos unas horas.

B. Fill in the following charts with the missing verb forms in the present subjunctive.

pedir	
1. (yo)______	pidamos
pidas	pidáis
pida	**2.** (ellos / ellas / ustedes) ______

divertirse	
me divierta	**4.** (nosotros) ____ ________
3. (tú) ____ ________	os divirtáis
se divierta	se diviertan

dormir	
duerma	**6.** (nosotros) ________
duermas	durmáis
5. (él / ella / usted) ________	duerman

Realidades 2 Nombre Hora

Capítulo 8B Fecha **Guided Practice Activities 8B-4**

Present subjunctive of stem-changing verbs (*continued*)

C. Look at the pictures and the sentences. Circle the verb in parentheses that is needed to complete the sentences. Follow the model.

Modelo Es bueno que ustedes (**se diviertan** / **duerman**) en las vacaciones.

1. Es importante que nosotros (**recordemos** / **perdamos**) las tarjetas postales.

2. Tomás sugiere que yo (**me divierta** / **duerma**) hoy.

3. La necesitas. Recomiendo que no la (**pidas** / **pierdas**).

4. Es bueno que Fernando (**duerma** / **se divierta**) muchas horas.

5. Yo quiero que tú (**pidas** / **duermas**) en tu cama.

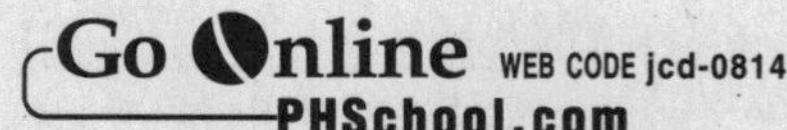

Lectura: Antigua, una ciudad colonial (pp. 442–443)

A. The reading in your textbook is a travel brochure about Antigua, Guatemala. Look at the photos, the heads, and the subheads in this brochure to get an idea of what the reading will be about. What are some of the things this brochure might mention?

_______________, _______________, _______________

B. Read the following excerpt from the reading in your textbook and answer the questions below.

> *¿Qué hay que ver en la ciudad de Antigua?*
>
> *La ciudad de Antigua tiene muchos sitios de interés. Se puede apreciar toda la historia de esta ciudad mirando sus casas y monumentos coloniales. En el centro de la ciudad está la Plaza Mayor. Los edificios principales son el Ayuntamiento (city hall), la Catedral y el Palacio de los Capitanes.*

1. En la ciudad de Antigua, puedes ver _______________.
   a. lugares interesantes **b.** hoteles
2. La Plaza Mayor está en _______________.
   a. el centro de la ciudad **b.** Tikal
3. El Palacio de los Capitanes es _______________.
   a. un bote de vela **b.** uno de los edificios importantes

C. The name "Antigua" means antique, or old. Read this excerpt from the reading. Then, write some of the words or phrases that show that the city is old.

> *Situada a 45 minutos de la Ciudad de Guatemala, Antigua le fascina al turista por sus calles de piedras, su arquitectura colonial y sus ruinas de iglesias y monasterios. El español Francisco de la Cueva fundó la ciudad el 10 de marzo de 1543. La "Ciudad de las Perpetuas Rosas," nombrada así por sus jardines con flores, tiene un clima muy agradable y preserva un sabor colonial único. Caminar por sus calles es como visitar el pasado y descubrir una ciudad típica española del siglo XVII.*

____

____

____

Presentación escrita (p. 445)

Task: Imagine you are going to visit a Spanish-speaking country with a group. Prepare an illustrated brochure so you can share your experience with others.

❶ Prewrite Think about the preparations you must make before you go on your trip. Answer the questions below to help you organize your brochure.

1. ¿Qué país vas a visitar? _______________
2. ¿Cómo vas a viajar? _______________
3. ¿Qué vas a llevar? _______________
4. ¿Qué lugares vas a visitar? _______________
5. ¿Qué actividades vas a hacer? _______________

❷ Draft

A. Use the information from **part 1** to complete the sentences below. You can use the following paragraph as a model.

> *Voy a viajar a México. Voy a viajar por avión. Es importante que yo lleve una guía porque voy a visitar el centro histórico y el famoso castillo. También es bueno que yo haga excursiones y navegue en el océano.*

Voy a viajar a _______________. Voy a viajar por _______________. Es importante que yo lleve _______________ porque voy a visitar _______________ y _______________. También es bueno que yo _______________ y _______________.

B. Include photos in your brochure. You can use photos from home or from magazines, or you can draw pictures to illustrate what you will see and do on your trip.

❸ Revise Reread your draft and check the spelling, vocabulary, and verb usage. Share your draft with a classmate, who will check for clarity, organization, and errors.

❹ Publish Make a new version of the brochure with changes and corrections.

❺ Evaluation Your teacher will grade you on the following:

- how much information you provide
- how clear and attractive the brochure is
- appropriate use of vocabulary and grammar

Realidades 2

Capítulo 9A

Nombre ______________________ Hora ____________

Fecha ______________________ **Vocabulary Flash Cards, Sheet 1**

Write the Spanish vocabulary word below each picture. If there is a word or phrase, copy it in the space provided. Be sure to include the article for each noun.

 ______ ______	 ______ ______	 ______ ______
 ______ ______	 ______ ______	 ______ ______
 ______ ______	 ______ ______	 ______ ______

Realidades 2 Nombre Hora

Capítulo 9A Fecha **Vocabulary Flash Cards, Sheet 2**

Write the Spanish vocabulary word below each picture. If there is a word or phrase, copy it in the space provided. Be sure to include the article for each noun.

Nombre _______________ Hora _______

Fecha _______________

Vocabulary Flash Cards, Sheet 3

Write the Spanish vocabulary word below each picture. If there is a word or phrase, copy it in the space provided. Be sure to include the article for each noun.

Write the Spanish vocabulary word below each picture. If there is a word or phrase, copy it in the space provided. Be sure to include the article for each noun.

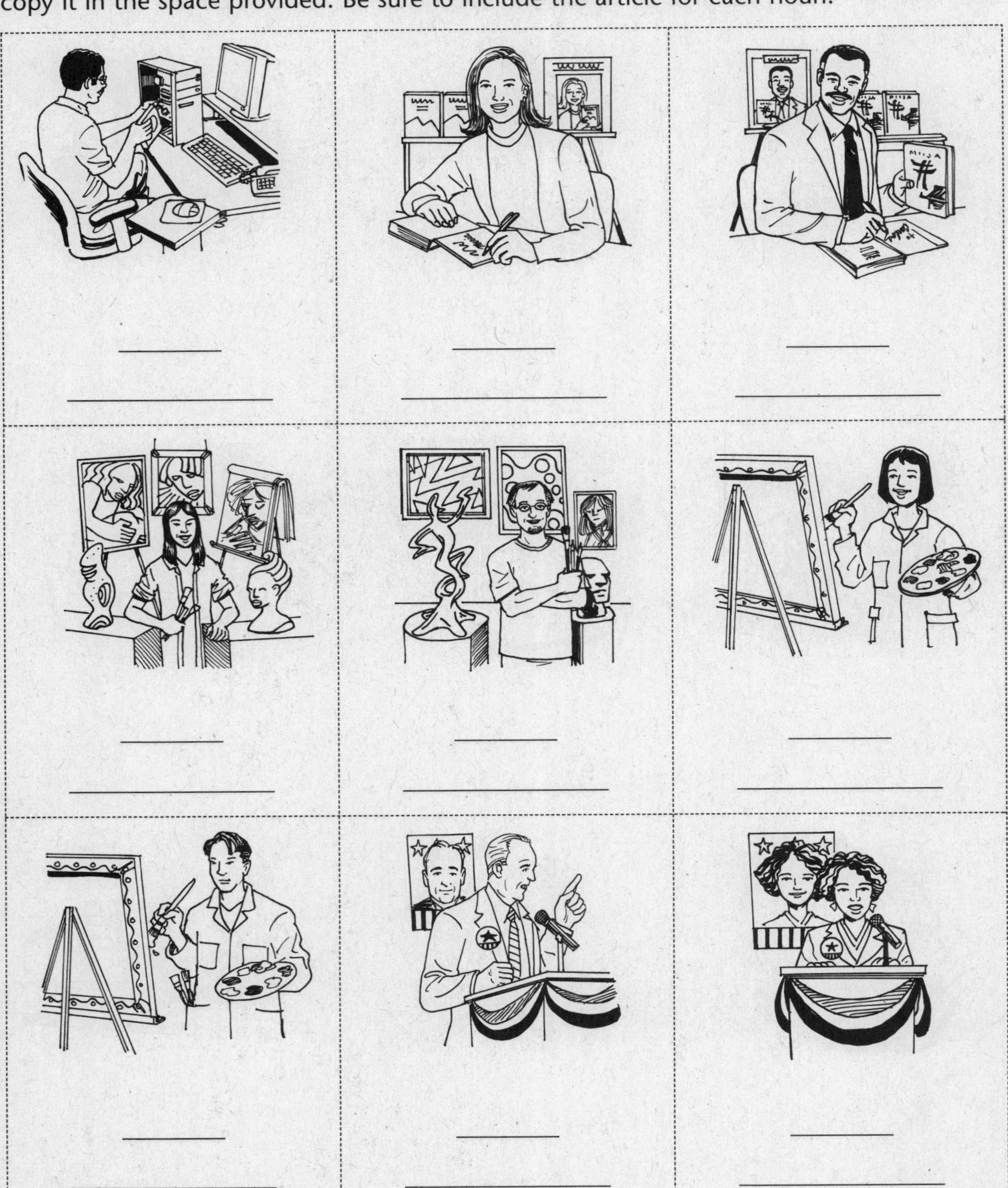

Nombre _______________ Hora _______________

Fecha _______________ **Vocabulary Flash Cards, Sheet 5**

Write the Spanish vocabulary word below each picture. If there is a word or phrase, copy it in the space provided. Be sure to include the article for each noun.

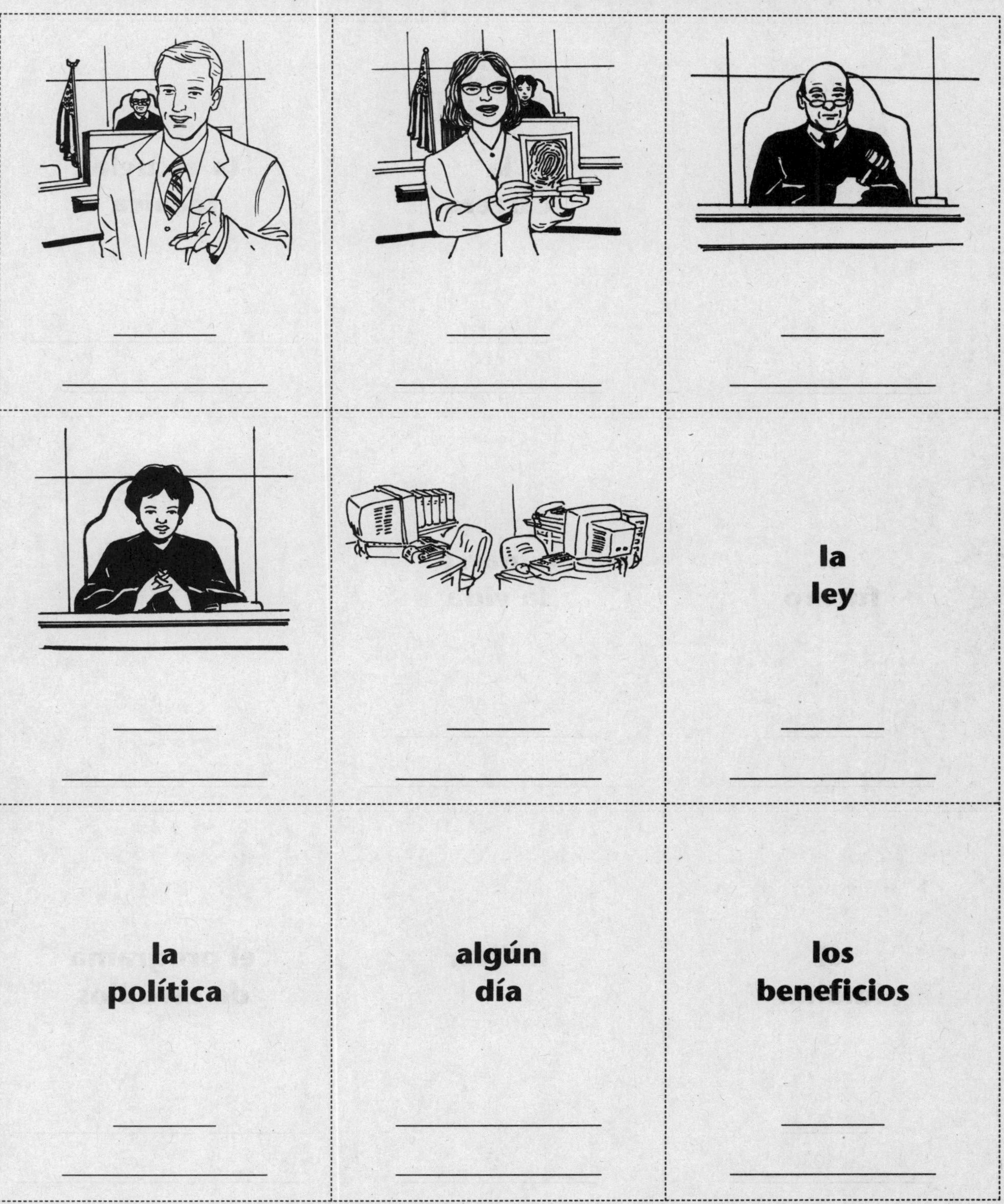

		la ley
la política	**algún día**	**los beneficios**

Write the Spanish vocabulary word below each picture. If there is a word or phrase, copy it in the space provided. Be sure to include the article for each noun.

bilingüe	**la carrera**	**la escuela técnica**
el futuro	**ganarse la vida**	**habrá**
el idioma	**militar**	**el programa de estudios**

Write the Spanish vocabulary word below each picture. If there is a word or phrase, copy it in the space provided. Be sure to include the article for each noun.

el salario	**seguir (una carrera)**	**el dueño, la dueña**
el gerente, la gerente	**las artes**	**el derecho**
la profesión	**los negocios**	

Nombre ______________________ Hora ______________

Fecha ______________________

Vocabulary Flash Cards, Sheet 8

Tear out this page. Write the English words on the lines. Fold the paper along the dotted line to see the correct answers so you can check your work.

el científico, la científica ______

el ingeniero, la ingeniera ______

el veterinario, la veterinaria ______

el contador, la contadora ______

el dueño, la dueña ______

el gerente, la gerente ______

los negocios ______

el hombre de negocios, la mujer de negocios ______

el secretario, la secretaria ______

el artista, la artista ______

el abogado, la abogada ______

el derecho ______

el colegio ______

la universidad ______

Fold In ←

Nombre ______ Hora ______

Fecha ______

Vocabulary Check, Sheet 2

Tear out this page. Write the Spanish words on the lines. Fold the paper along the dotted line to see the correct answers so you can check your work.

scientist ______

engineer ______

veterinarian ______

accountant ______

owner ______

manager ______

business ______

businessman, businesswoman ______

secretary ______

artist ______

lawyer ______

(study of) law ______

high school ______

university ______

Fold In ←

Realidades 2

Nombre ______________________ Hora ______________

Capítulo 9A

Fecha ______________________

Vocabulary Check, Sheet 3

Tear out this page. Write the English words on the lines. Fold the paper along the dotted line to see the correct answers so you can check your work.

el agricultor, la agricultora	______________
el arquitecto, la arquitecta	______________
el diseñador, la diseñadora	______________
el mecánico, la mecánica	______________
el cartero, la cartera	______________
el escritor, la escritora	______________
el pintor, la pintora	______________
la ley	______________
la política	______________
el político, la política	______________
bilingüe	______________
la carrera	______________
el salario	______________
la profesión	______________

Fold In

Vocabulary Check, Sheet 4

Tear out this page. Write the Spanish words on the lines. Fold the paper along the dotted line to see the correct answers so you can check your work.

farmer ______

architect ______

designer ______

mechanic ______

mail carrier ______

writer ______

painter ______

law ______

politics ______

politician ______

bilingual ______

career ______

salary ______

profession ______

Fold In ←

To hear a complete list of the vocabulary for this chapter, go to Disc 2, Track 9 on the Guided Practice Audio CD or go to www.phschool.com and type in the Web Code jdd-0989. Then click on **Repaso del capítulo.**

Realidades 2 | Nombre ______ Hora ______

Capítulo 9A | Fecha ______ **Guided Practice Activities 9A-1**

The future tense (p. 460)

- The future tense tells what will happen. To form the future tense of regular verbs ending in **-ar, -er,** and **-ir,** add these endings to the infinitive: **-é, -ás, -á, -emos, -éis, -án.**

  En unos años seré un abogado.

  In a few years, I will be a lawyer.

- Here are the future forms for **trabajar, ser,** and **vivir:**

yo	trabajar**é** ser**é** vivir**é**	nosotros/nosotras	trabajar**emos** ser**emos** vivir**emos**
tú	trabajar**ás** ser**ás** vivir**ás**	vosotros/vosotras	trabajar**éis** ser**éis** vivir**éis**
usted/él/ella	trabajar**á** ser**á** vivir**á**	ustedes/ellos/ellas	trabajar**án** ser**án** vivir**án**

A. Julieta is talking about what her friends are doing now and what they will do in the future. Read the sentences and write **P** (for **Presente**) if the verb shows an action in the present. Write **F** (for **Futuro**) if it shows an action in the future. Follow the model.

Modelo Mi hermana trabajará en la universidad. F

1. Laura vive en París. ______
2. En septiembre trabajará en Roma. ______
3. Susana y Lucas trabajarán en un laboratorio. ______
4. Tú trabajas de secretario. ______
5. Óscar y Pepe serán ingenieros. ______
6. Ellos estudiarán en una escuela técnica. ______
7. Las hermanas García vivirán en México. ______
8. Yo seré arquitecta. ______

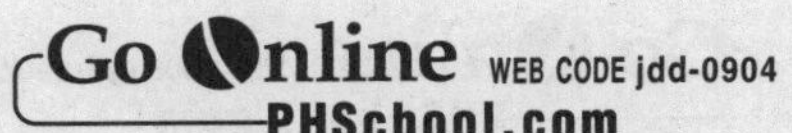
Go Online WEB CODE jdd-0904 PHSchool.com

The future tense (*continued*)

B. Look at the underlined words in the sentences. Complete each sentence by using the future tense to tell what people will do, according to the picture. The first one is done for you.

1. Jaime y Victoria son abogados, pero algún día *serán jueces*.

2. Mario trabaja de cartero, pero el año que viene él ______________________.

3. La familia Pérez vive en un apartamento, pero algún día la familia ______________________.

4. Generalmente Pilar y Mateo no miran videos, pero mañana ellos ______________________.

5. Isabel es estudiante, pero algún día ella ______________________.

6. Yo no escribo muchas cartas, pero más tarde ______________________.

The future tense: irregular verbs (p. 462)

- Some verb stems are irregular in the future tense: **hacer → har-; poder → podr-; saber → sabr-; tener → tendr-; haber → habr-.**

  Algún día tendré un trabajo con un salario muy bueno.
  Some day I will have a job with a very good salary.

A. Look at the infinitive in each item. Then, circle the correct form of the verb in the future tense. Follow the model.

Modelo hacer **a.** hago (**b.**) haré

1. poder **a.** puedo **b.** podré
2. tener **a.** tendrá **b.** tiene
3. saber **a.** sabrás **b.** sabes
4. haber **a.** habrá **b.** hay

B. Read some exchanges between Ramiro and Elisa. Then, underline the verbs in the future tense. Follow the model.

Modelo RAMIRO: ¿Podrás venir a mi fiesta?
ELISA: No, no podré ir a tu fiesta.

1. RAMIRO: ¿Qué harán ustedes este fin de semana?
   ELISA: Haremos ejercicio este fin de semana.
2. RAMIRO: ¿Podrás ayudarme con la tarea?
   ELISA: Sí, podré ayudarte con la tarea.
3. RAMIRO: ¿Sabrá Juan llegar a tu casa?
   ELISA: Sí, Juan sabrá llegar a mi casa.
4. RAMIRO: ¿Tendré yo tiempo de estudiar para el examen?
   ELISA: Sí, tú tendrás tiempo el viernes por la tarde.
5. RAMIRO: ¿Habrá una graduación en la escuela el fin de semana?
   ELISA: No, no habrá graduación el fin de semana.
6. RAMIRO: ¿A cuál escuela tendremos que ir para ser ingenieros?
   ELISA: Ustedes tendrán que ir a una escuela técnica.

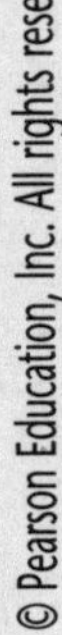

Realidades 2 Nombre ____ Hora ____

Capítulo 9A Fecha ____ **Guided Practice Activities 9A-4**

The future tense: irregular verbs (*continued*)

C. Complete each sentence in the future tense with words from the word bank, according to the picture. Use the correct form of the verb. The first one is done for you.

hacer un examen a mi perro	poder ser una contadora	haber una graduación
tener clases en la universidad	saber de ciencias	poder usar la computadora

1. Francisco *podrá usar la computadora*.

2. Tú ____________________.

3. La veterinaria le ____________________.

4. Marta ____________________.

5. Mis amigos y yo ____________________.

6. En junio ____________________.

Go Online WEB CODE jcd-0905
PHSchool.com

Lectura: ¡Bienvenidos al Centro de Carreras! (pp. 468–469)

A. The reading in your textbook is about a career center in a Spanish-speaking country. Read the heads and subheads to find out some basic information. Then, place an *X* next to the information you may find in this reading.

________ an aptitude test ________ career choices

________ movie listings ________ a personal information record

B. Read the following selection from the reading and the questions below. Circle the correct answer.

> *En nuestro centro, pueden...*
> * *buscar carreras*
> * *buscar y conectar con más de 100 universidades*
> * *crear y asegurar un expediente (record) privado para mantenerse informado(a) de las notas y actividades*

1. What can a student do at the Career Center?
   a. Find out about careers and universities
   b. Find out about restaurants

2. How many universities can students find information about?
   a. Less than 100 universities
   b. More than 100 universities

3. What is the purpose of an **expediente privado?**
   a. To keep information on grades and activities up-to-date
   b. To keep information on your daily routine

C. Fill out the following **expediente personal** by using either your own information or made-up information.

Nombre: ____________________

Dirección: ____________________

Grado: ____________ Intereses extracurriculares: ____________

Universidades que me interesan: ____________________

Presentación oral (p. 471)

Task: Prepare a presentation about a job you might expect to have in the future. Explain why you would choose that job.

A. Charts can help you organize information. Think about classes you like and, in the first column, fill in the two subjects you prefer. In the second column, list two activities that you enjoy doing. The first line is done for you as an example.

Cursos favoritos	Diversiones
literatura	*leer libros*

B. Complete the following statements about what you may do in the future. Use your answers from **part A** and the list of professions below, or choose another profession you have learned about in this chapter. Follow the model.

Modelo Estudiaré para ser *arquitecto* porque me gusta *dibujar y diseñar*.

contador, -a	veterinario, -a	abogado, -a	gerente
arquitecto, -a	ingeniero, -a	profesor, -a	pintor, -a

Mis clases favoritas son ______________ y ______________.

Las actividades que más me gustan son ______________ y ______________.

Estudiaré para ser ______________ porque me gusta ______________.

C. Read your statements from **part B** to practice for the oral presentation. Practice your presentation several times. Try to:

- provide as much information as you can
- use complete sentences
- speak clearly

D. Tell your partner about your interests and what you will do in the future.

E. Your teacher may grade you on the following:

- how complete your preparation was
- how much information you communicated
- how easy it was to understand you

Realidades 2 Nombre Hora

Capítulo 9B Fecha **Vocabulary Flash Cards, Sheet 1**

Write the Spanish vocabulary word below each picture. If there is a word or phrase, copy it in the space provided. Be sure to include the article for each noun.

Vocabulary Flash Cards, Sheet 2

Write the Spanish vocabulary word below each picture. If there is a word or phrase, copy it in the space provided. Be sure to include the article for each noun.

la calefacción	**económico, económica**	**eficiente**

Realidades 2 | Nombre ______ | Hora ______

Capítulo 9B | Fecha ______ | **Vocabulary Flash Cards, Sheet 3**

Write the Spanish vocabulary word below each picture. If there is a word or phrase, copy it in the space provided. Be sure to include the article for each noun.

la electricidad	**la energía**	**conservar**
contra	**la destrucción**	**ecológico, ecológica**
eliminar	**en peligro de extinción**	**la fuente**

Write the Spanish vocabulary word below each picture. If there is a word or phrase, copy it in the space provided. Be sure to include the article for each noun.

funcionar	**grave**	**juntarse**
luchar	**la manera**	**el medio ambiente**
mejorar	**proteger**	**puro, pura**

Realidades 2 Nombre ______ Hora ______

Capítulo 9B Fecha ______ **Vocabulary Flash Cards, Sheet 5**

Write the Spanish vocabulary word below each picture. If there is a word or phrase, copy it in the space provided. Be sure to include the article for each noun.

reducir ______	**resolver** ______	**además (de)** ______ ______
dudar ______	**es cierto** ______ ______	**haya** ______
ahorrar ______	**la naturaleza** ______ ______	**contaminado, contaminada** ______, ______

Nombre ______________________ Hora ______________

Fecha ______________________

Vocabulary Flash Cards, Sheet 6

Realidades 2

Capítulo 9B

Nombre ____________________ Hora ____________

Fecha ____________________

Vocabulary Check, Sheet 1

Tear out this page. Write the English words on the lines. Fold the paper along the dotted line to see the correct answers so you can check your work.

la naturaleza ____________________

el bosque ____________________

el desierto ____________________

la selva tropical ____________________

el aire acondicionado ____________________

la calefacción ____________________

la electricidad ____________________

la energía ____________________

conservar ____________________

la contaminación ____________________

contaminado, contaminada ____________________

la destrucción ____________________

ecológico, ecológica ____________________

el medio ambiente ____________________

Fold In ←

Nombre ______________________ Hora ____________

Fecha ______________________

Vocabulary Check, Sheet 2

Tear out this page. Write the Spanish words on the lines. Fold the paper along the dotted line to see the correct answers so you can check your work.

nature ______________________

forest ______________________

desert ______________________

rain forest ______________________

air conditioning ______________________

heat ______________________

electricity ______________________

energy ______________________

to conserve ______________________

pollution ______________________

polluted ______________________

destruction ______________________

ecological ______________________

environment ______________________

Fold In ←

Nombre ____ Hora ____

Fecha ____

Vocabulary Check, Sheet 3

Tear out this page. Write the English words on the lines. Fold the paper along the dotted line to see the correct answers so you can check your work.

el espacio	____
la Luna	____
la Tierra	____
económico, económica	____
eficiente	____
contra	____
en peligro de extinción	____
funcionar	____
luchar	____
mejorar	____
reducir	____
además (de)	____
dudar	____
proteger	____

Fold In ←

Realidades 2

Capítulo 9B

Nombre ______ Hora ______

Fecha ______

Vocabulary Check, Sheet 4

Tear out this page. Write the Spanish words on the lines. Fold the paper along the dotted line to see the correct answers so you can check your work.

(outer) space ______

the moon ______

Earth ______

economical ______

efficient ______

against ______

endangered, in danger of extinction ______

to function, to work ______

to fight ______

to improve ______

to reduce ______

in addition (to), besides ______

to doubt ______

to protect ______

Fold In ←

To hear a complete list of the vocabulary for this chapter, go to Disc 2, Track 10 on the Guided Practice Audio CD or go to www.phschool.com and type in the Web Code jdd-0999. Then click on **Repaso del capítulo.**

The future tense: other irregular verbs (p. 484)

- Other verbs that have irregular stems in the future tense are:

decir → dir- **salir → saldr-**
poner → pondr- **venir → vendr-**
querer → querr-

Querremos luchar por la paz.
We will want to fight for peace.

A. Look at each sentence and write the infinitive form of the underlined verb.

Modelo Ellos dirán que nuestro valle es bonito. *Infinitive:* decir

1. Nosotros pondremos plantas en las salas de clases. *Infinitive:* ______
2. Yo querré conservar la naturaleza. *Infinitive:* ______
3. Los turistas no vendrán a nuestro pueblo. *Infinitive:* ______
4. Tú saldrás a luchar contra la contaminación. *Infinitive:* ______
5. Ustedes dirán que el agua está contaminada. *Infinitive:* ______

B. Complete the following exchanges by writing the correct form of the verb in parentheses. Follow the model.

Modelo PEDRO: ¿Qué dirán **(decir)** ustedes del medio ambiente?

ILIANA: Nosotros diremos **(decir)** que está muy contaminado.

1. PEDRO: ¿Cuándo ______ **(salir)** ustedes al bosque?

   ILIANA: Nosotros ______ **(salir)** por la mañana.

2. PEDRO: ¿Tú qué ______ **(querer)** hacer para proteger el medio ambiente?

   ILIANA: Yo ______ **(querer)** usar la energía solar.

3. PEDRO: ¿Tu hermana ______ **(poner)** más plantas en la casa?

   ILIANA: Sí, y ella también ______ **(poner)** flores.

4. PEDRO: ¿Ella ______ **(venir)** con nosotros a proteger la selva tropical?

   ILIANA: Sí, ella y mis hermanos ______ **(venir)**.

5. PEDRO: ¿Tu les ______ **(decir)** a tus amigas todo esto?

   ILIANA: Sí, yo les ______ **(decir)** y ellas nos ayudarán.

Realidades 2

Capítulo 9B

Nombre ______________________ Hora ______

Fecha ______________________ Guided Practice Activities **9B-2**

The future tense: other irregular verbs (*continued*)

C. Look at the pictures and read the sentences. Then, look at the expressions in the word bank and complete each sentence with the appropriate expression and the future form of the verb. Follow the model.

decir que debemos	poner energía solar	querer destruir
querer reducir	salir al espacio	venir en bicicleta

Modelo Tú ___*querrás reducir*___ la contaminación.

1. Ellos no ______________________ el bosque.

2. Nosotros ______________________ conservar energía en nuestra casa.

3. Todos los estudiantes ______________________ para reducir la contaminación del aire.

4. Nosotros ______________________ en nuestras casas.

5. Si hay demasiada contaminación en la Tierra, Federico ______________________.

The present subjunctive with expressions of doubt (p. 487)

- The subjunctive is also used after verbs and expressions of doubt or uncertainty. Some expressions of doubt or uncertainty are:

dudar que	*to doubt that*
no es cierto que	*it is not certain that*
no creer que	*to not believe that*
no estar seguro, -a de que	*to be unsure that*
es imposible que	*it is impossible that*
es posible que	*it is possible that*

No es cierto que puedan proteger el medio ambiente.
It is not certain that they can protect the environment.

A. Read the exchanges below. Circle the subjunctive form of the verb in parentheses to indicate uncertainty or doubt in the sentences.

1. —¿Crees que nosotros podemos cuidar la Tierra?

   —Es imposible que nosotros no (**cuidemos** / **cuidamos**) la Tierra.

2. —¿Crees que vamos a luchar contra la contaminación de nuestro valle?

   —Dudo que nosotros no (**luchamos** / **luchemos**) contra la contaminación.

3. —¿Hay muchos animales que están en peligro de extinción?

   —Es posible que muchos animales (**estén** / **están**) en peligro de extinción.

4. —¿Es cierto que en su casa ustedes usan mucha energía?

   —No es cierto que en nuestra casa (**usamos** / **usemos**) mucha energía.

5. —¿Creen ustedes que ellos van a cuidar la colina?

   —Nosotros no creemos que ellos no (**cuiden** / **cuidan**) la colina.

6. —¿Estás seguro de que los bosques se conservan bien?

   —No estoy seguro de que los bosques se (**conservan** / **conserven**) bien.

7. —¿Crees que podemos proteger la naturaleza?

   —Es imposible que nosotros no (**protejemos** / **protejamos**) la naturaleza.

The present subjunctive with expressions of doubt (*continued*)

- While the subjunctive is used to show uncertainty, the indicative is used to show certainty. Compare these sentences:

  No es cierto que ellas ahorren energía. *It is not certain that they will save energy.*
  Es cierto que ellos ahorran energía. *It is certain that they are saving energy.*

B. Read the following expressions. If the expression indicates certainty, write **C.** If it indicates doubt or uncertainty, write **D.** Follow the models.

Modelos Es verdad que tenemos que reducir la contaminación. C

No es verdad que tengamos que reciclar. D

1. No creemos que el aire esté contaminado. ______
2. Estamos seguros de que muchos animales están en peligro de extinción. ______
3. Creo que la energía solar es muy eficiente. ______
4. No estoy seguro de que sea económico usar la calefacción. ______
5. Es cierto que los problemas ecológicos se resuelven. ______
6. Creo que debemos conservar energía. ______

- The subjunctive form of **hay** is **haya,** from the verb **haber:**

  Es posible que haya suficiente electricidad.
  It is possible that there is enough electricity.

C. Complete the sentences by writing either the indicative form **hay** or the subjunctive form **haya.** Follow the model.

Modelo ¿No crees que haya un problema grave?

1. Dudamos que ____________ una fuente de energía nueva.
2. Es cierto que ____________ mucha destrucción en las selvas tropicales.
3. Él está seguro de que ____________ una manera de reducir la contaminación.
4. Es imposible que ____________ vida en el espacio.
5. Es posible que ____________ desiertos en la Luna.

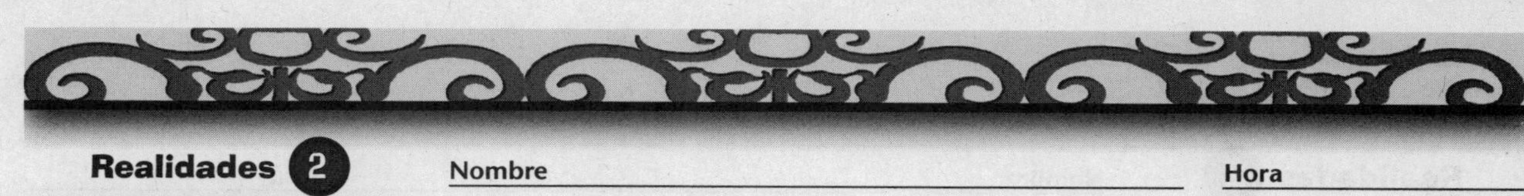

Lectura: Protegemos la Antártida (pp. 492–493)

A. When you read an article, you should be aware that the writer may have strong opinions about the issues. Identify and circle the words below that indicate an opinion.

Dudo...	Hay...	Sabemos...
Es peligroso...	Es importante...	Se llama...

B. Read the following paragraph from the reading in your textbook. Then for each of the words or phrases below, circle the appropriate English word or words based on the paragraph.

> *¡Estamos en peligro!*
> *Las regiones polares son muy importantes para la supervivencia de la Tierra entera. Los casquetes de hielo en las zonas polares reflejan luz solar y así regularizan la temperatura de la Tierra. Cuando se destruyen estos casquetes, hay menos luz solar que se refleja y la Tierra se convierte en un receptor termal. Esto se llama el efecto de invernadero. Es en la Antártida que en 1985 se reportaron por primera vez los hoyos en la capa del ozono y aquí es donde hoy día se trata de encontrar una solución.*

1. casquetes de hielo	**a.** holes	**b.** ice caps
2. efecto de invernadero	**a.** greenhouse effect	**b.** point of departure
3. supervivencia	**a.** abundance	**b.** survival
4. hoyos	**a.** holes	**b.** scientific teams
5. capa del ozono	**a.** rules	**b.** ozone layer

C. Determine the author's point of view in the paragraph in **part B** by circling the letter of the correct ending for each sentence.

1. Según el título, el autor cree que
a. todo va bien.
b. estamos en peligro.

2. El autor cree que las regiones polares
a. son importantes para la Tierra.
b. no sirven para nada.

3. Es posible que el autor piense que
a. es necesario resolver el problema do los hoyos en la capa del ozono.
b. los hoyos en la capa del ozono son buenos para la Tierra.

Presentación escrita (p. 495)

Task: You are organizing a volunteer project to improve your community and have been asked to write an article for the daily paper explaining your project.

A. Choose a volunteer project from the box or write one that you would like to do in your community.

- recoger basura en un parque
- comenzar un programa para reciclar periódicos viejos
- ahorrar dinero para proteger a los animales en peligro de extinción
- ______________________________

B. Based on the project you chose in **part A**, complete the following sentences by circling one of the options listed.

1. Para este proyecto trabajaré **a.** todos los días. **b.** los fines de semana.
2. Pueden participar **a.** personas mayores. **b.** todas las personas.
3. Es importante porque **a.** protegemos el medio ambiente. **b.** ayudamos a las personas.

C. Use your answers from **part B** to answer the following questions about your volunteer project. You may use the model to help you.

Modelo

¿Qué ...?	*Me gustaría recoger basura en un parque.*
¿Quién(es)...?	*Mis amigos y yo vamos a trabajar juntos.*
¿Por qué...?	*Queremos tener un medio ambiente limpio y sano.*
¿Dónde...?	*Vamos a trabajar en el parque del centro de la cuidad.*
¿Cuándo...?	*Trabajaremos todos los fines de semana durante el verano.*

1. ¿Qué...? ______________________________
2. ¿Quién(es)...? ______________________________
3. ¿Por qué...? ______________________________
4. ¿Dónde...? ______________________________
5. ¿Cuándo...? ______________________________

D. Use your answers in **part C** to write your article. Check for correct spelling, verb forms, and vocabulary.

Notes

Notes

Notes

Notes